Joel Shatzky

OPTION THREE

A Novel about the University

Blue Thread Communications

An Imprint of Jewish Currents Magazine

Blue Thread Communications

Option Three. Copyright © 2012 by Joel Shatzky. All rights reserved.
Printed in the United States of America. No part of this book may be used or reproduced
in any manner whatsoever without written permission from the publisher except in the case of brief quotations
embodied in critical articles or reviews. For information, write to
Jewish Currents, PO Box 111, Accord, NY 12404.

Cover design by Lawrence Bush

ISBN 978-0-9851138-7-2

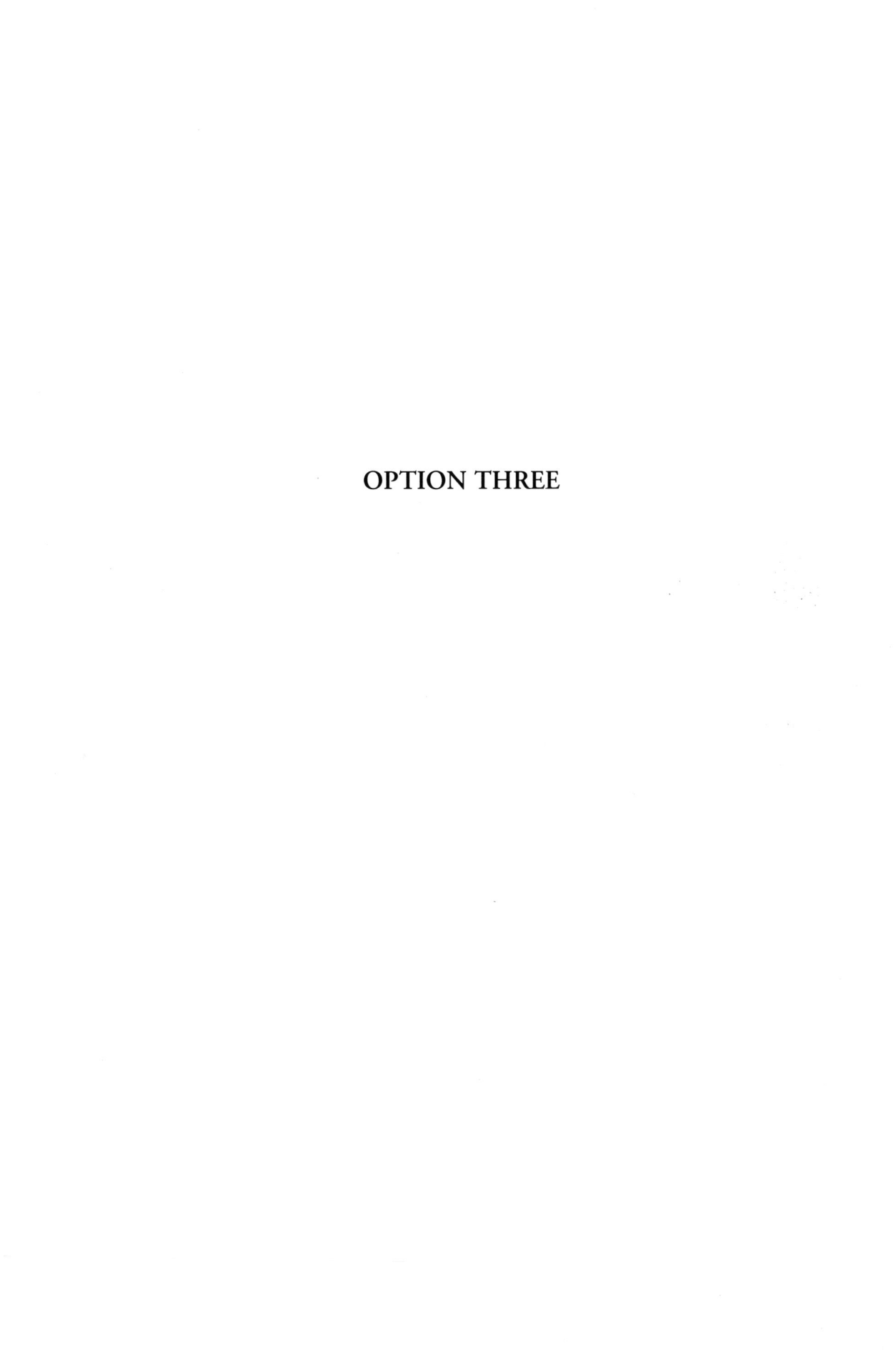

OPTION THREE

Part I: One

When Circassian got the second letter, he reread the first one because he was certain he had missed something.

Date: December 15
To: Acting Visiting Assistant Professor L. Circassian
From: Provost Donald Pickle
Re: Your Employment Situation Next Year
Dear Acting Visiting Assistant Professor Circassian:

As an invaluable member of the faculty whom we cannot do without I have the unfortunate task of informing you that your services as an Acting Visiting Assistant Professor will no longer be needed next semester. Your position has been absorbed into another department. I wish to thank you for your loyal and outstanding services these last five years.

All the best
D. Pickle

Date: December 18
To: Adjunct Acting Visiting Assistant Professor Circassian
From: Provost Donald Pickle
Re: Your Employment Situation Next Year
Dear Adjunct Acting Visiting Assistant Professor Circassian:

It is with great pleasure that we offer you the position of Adjunct Acting Visiting Assistant Professor for the spring semester. Your contributions to the University have been invaluable and we cannot afford to lose you, so we have decided to exercise Option Three. There will be, unfortunately, a thirty-five per cent reduction in your previous salary, since as an adjunct you will be paid the standard amount for a four-course load: $2200 per course. If you have any further questions on this matter see Dean Lean.

All the best,
D. Pickle

It was very clear they couldn't do without him. But for some reason, Circassian was not happy with this development. In fact, he wanted to do something to Pickle but he wasn't sure what would be appropriate. When he passed the chairman, Branch Stark, in the corridor, he barely nodded.

"What the bleep is eating you, Circassian?" Stark always said what was exactly on his mind. That's why he had been re-elected chairman of the English department for the fourth time.

"Did you get a copy of the letters?" Circassian asked.

"Which letters? I get so many bleepin' letters I can't read them anymore," Stark answered.

"Well, these were the letters from Pickle."

"I stopped reading anything he sent me two years ago. What the bleep does he want?"

"The first letter fired me; the second rehired he, but as an adjunct."

"Holy bleepin' shit!" Stark looked angry, but Circassian wasn't sure at the moment whether Stark was angry at him or angry at Pickle. Stark was often angry at everyone. This was due to his being re-elected chairman since no one else wanted to be chairman and he had gotten used to it, but it still made him angry.

"He suggested I see Dean Lean."

"Holy shittin' bleep!"

"He said something about 'Option Three.'"

"Never heard of it," said Stark, a little more calmly. "Oh yes, that's right. It was in a memo I think I saw a few weeks ago."

"Well, what is 'Option Three?'"

"Hell if I know. Listen, Circassian, I can't keep any of this crap in my head for more than a couple of minutes before it turns into nose goo. I guess you'd better ask the dean." Stark walked away muttering about "nose goo," and slammed the door behind him when he got into his office. Circassian promptly made an appointment with Dean Lean.

Two

Dean Dean Lean had been an excellent instructor in the Linguistics department for fifteen years before he was made Dean. His predecessor, Dean Dean, had made a reputation for being very direct with the faculty and very indirect with the Administration and as a result had been wildly successful as a dean. He was presently the president of an institution in need of an overhaul and everyone who knew him thought he wouldn't have one chance in hell of making it work.

Dean Lean was often puzzled by the procedures in the Administration Building, which is why he seldom went there, since he would come back confused and near tears. This was strange because he had always considered himself a very logical person. But now he knew what naked fear meant, something he had never before experienced: the forty-eight grid scan matrix. This was a very complicated mathematical formula devised by someone in Central Administration, which Assoc. VP "Stats" Bendminder would bring out during the budget meetings. The forty-eight grid scan matrix quantified everything in the University, including the allowable floor space for each faculty member and the number of ounces of hamburger meat fed each student, and it determined the allocation of funds to each department based on an even more complex formula that no one had ever understood.

Dean Lean was certain that if God had created the forty-eight grid scan matrix or FEGSM instead of the Ten Commandments, the world would be an entirely different place. People would see each other in a different way, and children and their parents would act differently toward each other. Dean Lean didn't want to imagine what this difference was because, as it was, until recently he'd been getting bad dreams from the memos he'd receive from Pickle, and he was beginning to make strange noises, as his secretary couldn't help notice, any time anyone came into his office.

He also had begun to do shadow play on the wall with his desk lamp against the background of "Bacchus in Flight," an abstract by one of the art faculty which consisted of a canvas about fifteen feet long and eight feet high painted a light gray with two small dots of blue on the upper right hand corner. It made an excellent backdrop for some of Dean Lean's more elaborate shadows like "The Clown" or "Two Coeds and a Jock" and other japes of his imagination. He had just come from a meeting in which Assoc. VP Bendminder had proven to him that the Arts and Science division would lose half of its present faculty in about three years according to the FEGSM when Circassian was announced by Secretary Drew. Dean Lean stifled a yawp as Circassian entered.

Three

"What are you doing here? Why aren't you somewhere teaching?" asked Dean Lean.

"It's intersession, Dean," he answered. Everyone called Dean Dean Lean "Dean" to be on the safe side, since that way they could be both formal and informal at the same time, but this time Dean Lean was uncertain from Circassian's tone which he meant. He would have felt better being informal with Circassian, whom he secretly liked as a man of his own heart, but since he had lost his own heart several years before, he was outwardly cold and guarded with him.

"Now, are you calling me 'Dean,' or 'Dean?'" he asked. "I just want to know the nature of your visit. Is it going to be formal or informal? I'm not in the mood right now for a formal visit."

"I'm just calling you 'Dean' Dean Lean," said Circassian.

"Well, that's the way it should be, I suppose. What can I do for you, Circassian?"

This mollified Circassian somewhat, since he hated his first name and always felt more comfortable with his last. He presented the two letters to Dean Lean and then crossed his legs.

"Why are you giving me these?" asked Dean Lean. "I don't like to read letters that aren't addressed to me."

"But Provost Pickle suggested I contact you," said Circassian.

"Did he send me a memo?" asked Dean Lean. "I don't think he did, although I stopped reading his memos months ago." Dean Lean felt in a confessional mood. He particularly hated Provost Pickle's memos because they never made any sense. But he bent over the letters, as if he were reading the directions to make a stink bomb to be set off in the New York City subway on Christmas Eve, and finally looked up.

"Well, this should be clear enough," he said, clearing his throat for the fifth time.

"But what is Option Three?" asked Circassian.

"Ah, that I can explain," said Dean Lean with relief, because he believed that this administrative procedure was one of the few things he could explain to his own satisfaction.

"What, for instance, are Option One and Two?" asked Circassian.

"Option One is that you are an invaluable member of the faculty that has to be let go; Option Two is that you are a superfluous member of the faculty that can't be let go. Is that clear so far?"

"No, but go on anyway, Dean," said Circassian.

"Option Three was devised several months ago by Central Administration and what it means is that we don't have the funds to keep you but we can't let you go because you are too valuable."

"But I can't survive on this salary cut. I'm just surviving on the miserable salary I've been getting as an Acting Visiting. . . ." said Circassian, but Dean Lean cut him off.

"Of course, we understand that. That's why this is called 'Option Three': it's a combination of two unacceptable solutions to a problem." Dean Lean was about to offer Circassian a cigar but then remembered that neither of them smoked.

"Let me understand this, Dean," said Circassian, interrupting the Dean's rendition of

"The Dying Crane," which he was now absently shadowing on "Bacchus in Flight." "You can't do without me, is that correct?"

"You're invaluable. Pickle got right to the point there."

"But you can't afford to keep me, is that right?"

"Bendminder proved that just last week."

"So you've exercised 'Option Three,' where I can't afford to stay."

"But since we know you can't afford to leave either, we feel that we've given you the most sensible offer."

"I'd like to see Pickle about this," said Circassian.

"He went to a conference in Tonga just yesterday. He'll be back the first day of classes. You can see him then."

"But how am I going to live on that salary?"

"Now, that is no longer the Institution's problem, Circassian. We solved ours in offering you this position; it's up to you to solve yours. This is called 'employee empowerment,' and although I'm not entirely for it, Pickle and President Fred are completely behind it. This is where the institution is going, Circassian. It's what's coming down the shoot. Don't fight it; just let it wash over you and you'll be fine."

As Circassian walked out of the office, Dean Lean realized he had mixed metaphors that made no sense. He decided to leave early and go to one of the local bowling alleys although he had never bowled in his life. It might bring some clarity to his mind. Or if not that, and he hated the experience, at least it might cleanse his soul.

Four

As he was returning from Dean Lean's office, Circassian spied the someone he least wanted to see at that moment: Ron Burble. Burble was aptly named because due to some oddity in his ear drums, he would speak in a loud voice that seemed perfectly clear to him but was often incomprehensible to almost anyone else. This made his lectures rather difficult to understand and was, in great part, the reason most of his students failed his course. His grading profile, however, was invaluable to the History department, which always sent them to the Dean when matters of grade inflation were being discussed. He managed, single-handedly, to bring the grade-point average for the entire department down one full grade.

"Hobble ben lably, Circassian?" he asked in passing.

"I've been fired," Circassian answered. "And then rehired," he added.

"Wobble woo?" Burble asked. (In the interest of readabilty, the rest of Burble's remarks will be translated into comprehensible speech.)

"Pickle sent the letter. He thinks I'm invaluable to the institution but can't afford to keep me so he offered me a salary that I can't accept."

"Sounds like Pickle," said Burble. "But that reminds me of the time my old friend Pete Canard told me what happened to him during the Spanish Civil War. There was some ass-hole commissar that was supposed to give the troops spending money for the cantinas and that kind of stuff, putanas and all that, and he only had scrip. . . ."

Circassian knew this could go on for a long while, and that had to find some excuse to leave Burble, who would otherwise launch into his favorite subject: the Communist menace. Sometime in the middle of the '70's, Burble had decided that being a flat-headed liberal college professor didn't offer the panache he needed to impress the ladies. He had thus become the Village Defamer, and although the USSR had ceased to exist for over a decade, he still loved to twit Circassian and anyone else he thought of as a True Believer — which included liberals and anarchists, of which there were many at the University — of the failures and betrayals of communists, foreign and domestic.

Circassian was about to tell Burble that he was going to lunch (he was almost certain Burble wouldn't join him since it was nine A.M.), when Burble added: "Whibbento gobble. . . ." (Oops!) "Why don't you go to see that witch, Lee Ann Fitz-Proust? She's always moaning and whining and protesting about everybody getting mistreated around here. You're not Black, are you, Circassian? I mean somebody with your background . . . ?"

"Thanks for the advice, Ron. I've got to go to lunch now."

Circassian walked back up the corridor for a few seconds until he noticed that Burble had stopped talking. When he turned around, the Village Defamer had Burbled around the corner. Circassian decided that he'd better get home and see if Tina, his Predominant Other, could give him the kind of advice that would be actually helpful, although at the moment he could think of nothing that would help.

Five

In order to make himself feel able to face the remainder of the day, which included grading a tough final exam from his weakest class and grading another set in which he gave a fairly easy exam to his strongest class — he had gotten the two sets confused since they were both for the same course — Circassian decided to write a draft of a letter to Pickle. He knew it would be useless to send a letter to Dean Lean, who might get very upset and start crying in public again, but since Pickle was rarely seen in public any more, especially since the Big Cut of the previous year, Circassian didn't really care how he reacted.

To: Provost Donald Pickle
From: Acting Visiting Assistant Professor L. Circassian
Re: My New Job Offer
Dear Provost Pickle:

Having thought over your offer for the coming semester, I realize that any interest that you or any other members of the Administration have for this faculty is a sham. There is only one possible reason why you cut my salary by 35% when you knew I was already being grossly underpaid. It was to save money because you anticipate another budget cut. Instead of wracking your brain trying ways to save money, wouldn't it be better if you put some effort in going up to the Capitol and wringing the necks of the people at Central Administration for kissing the ass of the Board of Trustees? After all, isn't one of your jobs to protect the interests of the faculty? How can you claim that you've done that?

I work very hard for my pay little as it is. With morale continuing to decline, I would hope that you could have come up with a more creative way of dealing with the budget than taking more away from those who have the least. You really are superfluous yourself in this University. No one has seen you for the last six months and there are rumors that you are actually dead and that your special assistant, Marigold Markham, is writing all your memos. You are an embarrassment to this institution, Pickle. You'd better retire soon since you can afford to and nobody needs you. You've managed to live up to the nickname the faculty gave you, "Stinky," because you've never been able to do anything around here that was useful except make a stink.

I thank you for your kind consideration of my situation, your cordial letter, your generous offer, and I will tell you what you can do with it, Shithead: Go fuck yourself and then jump off a bridge.

Very truly
Acting Visiting Assistant Professor L. Circassian

P.S. If you think I'm just writing this way because I'm angry, think again: I have never been so glear-headed in my whole life!

Circassian read over the letter, changed the "g" in "glear-headed" to "c," and then pressed the Delete button. He had spoken his mind and he was now sure he would feel better. He called up Tina, who been writing another grant proposal for her Cornfield Sculpture project, and told her that he had some good and bad news. He decided to let her stew over it for a few hours. She had been testy lately and he knew that stewing had a calming effect on her since once she had stewed long enough she became mellow. But Circassian was defintely not looking forward to the rest of the day.

Six

"If I was to choose a character I would trust the most it would probably be Lena Younger from *A Raisin in the Sun*. First of all, Lena Younger is an elderly, woman."

Circassian was grading the first set of final exams, and, as he expected, most of the students in the weak class opted for the easiest question: "If you could choose a character from the plays we've studied that you would trust the most/the least . . ." Having that question available made it almost impossible for most students to fail the exam. But some managed to, even then. This essay came close. He wondered what had possessed the student to write that he trusted Lena Younger because she was elderly, and why he had put the comma between "elderly" and "woman." Then he'd gone on: "I feel when people trust someone else it is easier to trust them," the logic of which seemed to him slightly confusing since he had known some perfectly trustworthy people who didn't trust anyone else, and the reverse. Maybe the student had never met anyone like that. Maybe he had been thinking about his mother and father or his girlfriend. Circassian was fairly certain that he hadn't been thinking about anything. These words just came to him.

Then there was an essay based on another easy question: "If you were having a party, whom, among the following, would you invite, and why?" The student had chosen Colonel Pickering from *Pygmalion*:

"I throw a pretty good party and there would be no time for ignorance or rudeness there, only, nice, respectful, easy to talk to, fun people! I would invite Col Pickering because he would probably pay me and my guests many compliments." Circassian read a lot more about the party, but there was very little in it about Col. Pickering. He often got discouraged reading these essays because so many of them had so little to do with what he had taught, and they had less to do with anything else. At least there were a number of students in the strong class that really could write something that was almost interesting. And the student who had written about the "grand skeptical" struck him as clever. At least he hoped she was being clever.

There were three groups of students at the University. The first group, the smallest, were very bright and really belonged somewhere else that would be more challenging to them, that is, a place with a lot of better students. The second, and largest group didn't belong in any University or college at all and were wasting their time, but having a lot of fun doing it. And the middle-sized third group were perfectly suited to the University. The only problem was their numbers kept on falling, while the bottom numbers kept on rising. Circassian was a fairly liberal grader, but even he was giving out more failing grades than ever, and this was despite the fact that he was making everything easier. But he had a feeling at this point that what he really wanted to do was dump all of the papers into his wastebasket and write in either failing grades or "A" at random. He would feel free and wild and rebellious, but like the impulse he had felt in writing the letter to Pickle, he discovered that, as he had long anticipated, he didn't really have it in him to do that. It would be unfair and unethical and against all of the other things that the academic world had been teaching students for hundreds of years and violating regularly in its treatment of them.

Seven

When he walked into his apartment with the two letters in his briefcase to show Tina, Circassian no longer felt angry or even annoyed. He felt as if he would like to do something else with his life besides teaching. Not that he was bored with teaching; he was just convinced that he could never get any satisfaction from it worth the penury that he saw was to be his academic fate.

He showed the letters to Tina, who shrugged. "What's Option Three?" she asked. "Is that the good news?"

"Yes, I haven't lost my job; no, I think it'd be better if I did." He then explained Option Three.

Tina had long black hair but always wore it up. It was unmangeable, she said, like Medusa's. "Don't worry," she said, "I'll get a job."

"You have a job," Circassian said.

"I mean a paying job." Tina ran a small art gallery in town and had few customers since the students generally didn't have the money to buy anything or the interest even to visit, except for the art majors who wanted her to sell their work. As for the townspeople, they were rarely interested in anything besides the crops and the weather and the cows.

"I don't want you to change your life because a dumb shit like Pickle doesn't know how to manage the budget."

"But he does know how to manage the budget, Circassian. He just doesn't manage it the way you want it managed."

"What kind of job can you get around here, Tina?" Circassian asked when they had finished dinner. The apartment suddenly seemed tiny to him, as if gnomes were supposed to live there.

"It doesn't have to be around here. I mean, I can be around here and the job doesn't have to be."

For a moment Circassian thought that she was leaving him. Then he would really get into Pickle's face!

"What kind of job is that?" he asked.

"With some actuary company in New York City. Remember, I used to do that kind of thing before I met you. Before I became an artist. It's easy enough; I still have connections."

Circassian wondered what that meant. He was becoming suspicious of everyone, now that he knew he was being given Option Three.

Tina explained it had something to do with the Internet, but Circassian looked confused.

"How much do you think it would pay you, anyway?"

She told him. It was more money than he had made since he'd known her, five years before. He thought she was exaggerating, but the next day, as Circassian stayed home to finish grading the exams, he found out that she wasn't. Still, he wasn't relieved. In a way, he felt that a vital connection between the two of them was being severed. He was frightened.

He felt as if Option Three were some kind of diabolical plot invented by the Board of Trustees to make sure that the University would continue to decline and eventually be closed. And he wasn't certain that even Tina might not be part of this plot. Because by now Circassian began to feel there was a plan to get him to leave the University.

Eight

That evening, Circassian went to the grocery to buy some food for the weekend. Tina told him she was in an adventurous mood, which meant something made out of tofu that wasn't supposed to taste or look like tofu. But since Circassian had never tasted tofu plain, it was a pretty safe bet that he wouldn't recognize the taste as tofu, whatever she made.

As he was reaching for some ginger, he heard a voice behind him. "Hiya, neighbor."

He recognized the slightly nasal tone of Dean Steen, Dean Lean's counterpart in the School of Professional Studies. Dean Dina Steen was just the opposite of Dean Lean in temperament and philosophy. While Dean Lean was often jumpy and tearful each time another budget cut was announced, Dean Steen was positively gleeful. She liked power, even the negative kind; Dean Lean hated it.

The School of Professional Studies, which included the Education and Physical Education departments, was notorious for having more students than the faculty could possibly serve. In the past ten years, the number of students had doubled while the number of faculty remained the same — due, in part, to Dean Steen's view that the only way to assure the survival of her school was to make sure there were too many students in it to ever consider closing it down. She would welcome new batches of students with the news that Professional Studies was "growing." This gave her the nickname of "Crank'emsteen," since having more students cranked out each year at graduation gave her particular pride. The fact that many of these students were unsuited for doing much of anything, certainly not for going into a classroom to teach, did not seem to bother her. The School of Professional Studies had the highest graduation rate at the University, and the most students with the highest averages — in their majors — of any in the state. Bendminder would turn out reams of statistics that Dean Steen could show to the Administration to prove anything she wanted to prove, mostly that her school was more than carrying its own weight — and when would Arts and Science do the same, which, certainly in terms of numbers, it didn't?

This discrepancy was one of the many causes of the various wars waged between the two schools, which made cooperation between them difficult, often impossible. Hank Schecht, one of the gurus in the Sociology department, who was noted for his long e-mail messages and even longer memos, once tried to get a Faculty Senate resolution passed abolishing the School of Professional Studies, but the motion was defeated by two votes, and everyone knew that it had no weight with the Administration anyway, although President Fred and Provost Pickle dutifully attended all meetings.

"Hi," Circassian answered, putting a particularly gnarled ginger root into his basket.

"Well, see you around, and Merry Christmas," said Deen Steen.

Circassian was relieved. There was absolutely nothing he could have thought of saying to Dean Steen, especially in his state of mind. He watched her walk away searching for the rutabagas, and he quickly turned toward the tofu, which looked pristine in their white and blue containers.

Nine

The next morning, Circassian went back to the University to check his mail and hand in his grades. There was the usual junk mail from publishers, a free book on a subject he had never heard of, mistakenly sent to him by someone who had mistakenly gotten his address from someplace that had mistakenly given it to them, and a note from Lee Ann Fitz-Proust:

Dear Circassian:

I have heard that you were fired and then hired again at one-third of your original salary. (As usual, the rumor mill had gotten things mixed up.) I am outraged and feel certain that some kind of discrimination suit can be lodged against the Administration. Please see me soon.

Right on,
Lee Ann

Circassian knew that there was almost nothing in hell that Fitz-Proust could do for him; as it was, she was worried about her own job, since she taught almost exclusively courses in intolerance from a multi-cultural perspective, which most of the students referred to as "Hate I." A colleague of hers, Trent Butler, who was known to bed several of his co-ed disciples each semester, taught the advanced course, "Hate II."

There was also a second memo from ULP (United Labor Professions) President Dabs Budweiser, the feisty — this was the term she preferred — head of the local Union. Circassian was pretty certain he knew what it would say.

Dear Circassian:

It's come to my attention that you have been royally screwed by the Administration by asking you to take a 75% pay cut for the privilege of slaving here on what was already an outrageously low salary. Your fight is our fight, so please feel free to see me at your earliest convenience. I am certain that we will be able to do something to address this gross misuse of administrative power.

Yours in Solidarity,
Dabs

Circassian was also fairly certain that the Union couldn't do anything for him, especially since there was nothing in the contract that he knew about concerning Option Three, but Dabs was always good for a few laughs, and Circassian felt that there should at least be some way to make all of this seem funny. He'd once had a very ribald sense of humor, but five years at the University had curbed it into occasional ironies and bad puns that he would resolved to stop making while he was making them.

He decided that instead of going back home for lunch, which meant telling Tina about the memos and getting her into her "go fight" mode, he would eat at the faculty lunchroom, which really wasn't a faculty lunchroom but a space on the second floor of Main to which faculty preferred to go. In the interests of egalitarianism, no public areas were closed to the students, but most of them weren't interested in coming upstairs since the really heavily fried foods were all served in the basement dining area. As Circassian walked in, he noticed that the usual crowd was sitting at the largest table, where most of the important non-Administrative decisions regarding the faculty were made.

Ten

There were many little wars at the University, as well as the big ones between the University and Central Administration, the Administration and the Faculty, the Administation and the local Union, and the School of Arts and Sciences and School of Professional Studies. There were several smaller wars among the faculty, the most prominent of which was the Writing Wars.

Sitting at the table were most of the leaders in this war, the ones against writing, and they were very good at their jobs. Circassian knew them all and admired their vision in a perverse way, for even if everything around them was changing rapidly, they Stayed Where They Were. This enabled them to do pretty much in their classes what they had been doing for twenty years with the added virtue that they were Maintaining Standards. And this was in opposition to the people who had been rapidly changing and didn't seem to know where they were, because often, as far as the SWTW's were concerned, they weren't anywhere.

Gladys DeFoe was one of the central figures in the Writing Wars, along with Burble and Ralph Null, who had a rather lofty view of everything since he and Burble could look down on almost everyone: the two were about thirteen feet tall combined. Or, as one of the less reverent members of the pro-Writing faction would say: "You can lay them end to end anywhere and you can count on a major obstruction."

As Circassian walked in, he hesitated to sit with them since he didn't want to be told once more why he was wrong about most everything he believed in, especially the Writing Requirement that wasn't really about writing or actually a requirement. As he went over to stand on line for a sandwich, he could hear Ralph's voice booming: "If God had wanted these students to know how to write, He would have made them writers." This was Ralph's version of ironic humor, and everyone laughed. That is, everyone except Josh Gutsky, who had been sitting at the table with Seth Shotman before anyone else had joined them.

"Well, you weren't born with a silver pen in your mouth, Ralph," said Josh.

"I was too. Nobody ever taught me how to write, except God."

Ralph was, naturally, the Chair of the Writing Committee, and Gladys was the Vice-Chair. This was so they would be able to prevent anything significant from happening among the other committee members. Almost everyone at the table, except for Gutsky and Shotman, were chairs of committees for the same purpose. This was one of the big advantages of the Committee System: if you were against something happening, it was much easier to get it not done if you were on a committee. Getting things not done was one of the strongest points of the system, especially if you could get things not done slowly.

"Look, Seth," said Gladys, pointing a plastic fork at him like a laser, "you get these freshmen and when they finish with those two semesters of comp. they're supposed to be decent writers; we get them in their junior and senior years, and they can't write again."

"But the ones who could write before they were freshmen, I'll bet they never had trouble writing," boomed Ralph.

"Then why don't you teach at a school where everyone knows how to write before they become freshman?" said Josh.

"Anyway, it's a waste of time making everyone require writing since, except for you folks in English, nobody is supposed to know how to teach it," added Gladys to Circassian.

This argument was the same one that had been pushed around since Circassian had come to the University and been pulled around for years before he'd gotten there. What he knew, what they all knew since everyone told everyone else everything about it, was that the writing requirement had been on the books for five years and anybody who didn't want to do it ignored it. That was the secret of the University's success in maintaining high standards: nobody bothered to make sure they were being maintained. Actually, once Dean Lean had tried to make everyone bother, but he'd been overruled by Provost Pickle when the Chairs complained that Lean was "endangering academic freedom." So everybody agreed that the writing requirement in all courses needn't be enforced but should remain in the University catalogue since to take it out might invoke the wrath of the Board of Trustees, who always read the School catalogues.

"Anyway, most students learn to write in Grad school," added Burble, who always spoke clearly when he was around Ralph for fear of being looked down upon; Ralph was one of the few who could do so.

"But most of them don't go to Grad school," said Seth.

"So they don't need to know how to write. You only need to know how to write when you go to Grad school. No one else is expected to."

"What study did you get that from?" asked Josh.

"Grad school," said Ralph. The rest of the table laughed. Josh shrugged and began pointedly talking to Seth about something else.

Circassian hadn't said a word; whenever he listened to The Table, he would be struck speechless. This, he realized, was a sign that he was Learning.

He decided to ask Seth and Josh for advice: they seemed to have their head in the clouds most of the time, where it belonged. Josh and Seth were known as the "Eternal Jews" because they always seemed to be trying to figure out who was Jewish and who wasn't Jewish. Seth taught a course on the Holocaust in the History department, and Josh taught one in the English department: the students referred to the courses as "Hell I" and "Hell II"; and although they didn't think they looked alike, students always got them confused, and confused them by calling Josh Prof. Shotman and Seth Prof. Gutsky. They had a remote resemblance to each other, both having greying beards, glasses and the world-weary look of people who have Seen Everything and know that they Know Nothing, which was somewhat in contrast to The Table which consisted of people who had Seen Nothing and knew that they Knew Everything. But even sometimes faculty who had known them both for a long time got them mixed up.

"Hey Circassian," said Josh, with a world-weary look. "Did you know that Winona Ryder is Jewish?"

This wasn't exactly the opening gambit that Circassian had expected from Josh, but he nodded and briefly explained his situation.

"Lee Ann thinks that you might have a discrimination case?" asked Seth.

Circassian nodded.

"At least you aren't Jewish, are you Circassian? No chance if you are," said Josh. "In Lee Ann's book Jews aren't a 'protected class.'"

Eleven

That evening, Circassian asked Tina, "What is a 'protected class?'"

"Huh?" Tina was at the computer, coming up with some actuarial data for her new bosses who lived somewhere in the Cayman Islands.

"A 'protected class.' Josh Gutsky said that if I was Jewish I wasn't in a 'protected class.'"

"I didn't know you were Jewish, Circassian," said Tina, a little absently as she stared at the numbers on the fatally tinged screen.

"I'm not Jewish. At least, my parents never told me I was. I might be, who knows these days about these things for sure, but even if I was, that wouldn't make me a member of a 'protected class.'"

"So, then, what's the point of finding out if you're Jewish or not? Some people even say that Hitler's real father was Jewish but that didn't put him in a 'protected class' did it?" Tina had a habit that when she was concentrating on something and didn't want to be disturbed she would begin to deal with all sorts of possibilities that were totally irrelevant to the subject being discussed. This would confuse Circassian generally into silence, but this evening he persisted.

"Tina, I'm not asking you if I'm Jewish; I just want to know what a 'protected class' means."

"Something about the groups of people who are considered most discriminated against and aren't part of the Establishment," Tina answered, shutting off the computer and giving Circassian the Stare. The Stare meant: "I'm not going to pursue this subject right now." Circassian didn't. He decided to call up Lee Ann and find out if he was eligible for what she thought he was eligible for: being discriminated against.

"Lee Ann: this is Circassian. Thanks for writing that note to me. It gave me some hope," Circassian said, loudly over the phone. He had to talk loudly because it sounded like a lot of people were talking at Lee Ann's.

"Hey, Circassian. I can't talk too long now. I've got a meeting going on and it just started," Lee Ann answered. "It's something you might be interested in: bandicoots."

"What's a bandicoot?" asked Circassian. He didn't really care what it was but he felt he might as well be polite.

"It's a marsupial that is native to India and Sri Lanka. It's in danger of extinction," said Lee Ann. She began to giggle. Someone might have been tickling her to get her off the phone.

"You mean it's a rat of some kind?" asked Circassian. He wasn't certain, but he wanted to keep up his end of the conversation.

"Look, I'll talk to you tomorrow. Can you meet me in my office? I have all the stuff there."

"Do you think it will help?" asked Circassian, doubtfully. He didn't feel he could rely on Lee Ann now any more than he had in the past, which was not at all.

"I'll do what I can — ha! ha! — stop it!"

Since Circassian hadn't said or done anything that would have prompted that remark, he decided he'd better get off the phone.

Lee Ann beat him to it. "Bye, Circassian. And. . . keep the Faith!"

Circassian sighed as he hung up the phone; he was an atheist.

Twelve

That night, Circassian had a dream. He was in a large office with a lot of other people, all naked and wearing little pointed hats on their heads. There was a clock directly in front of them and it had only one hand, a second hand. Behind him he heard a voice that called out, "Line up!" Everyone began shoving and pushing to line up, and Circassian, who hadn't heard clearly what the voice had said, at first found himself pushing near the back of the line; he seemed to want to get in front, but every time he tried to get ahead of someone, he was pushed back. He was being pushed further and further back when he awoke suddenly.

It was mid-morning, and he thought he was going to be late for class when he realized that it was the Holiday Break and he could stay in bed if he wanted to. Then he remembered that he was supposed to see Lee Ann that morning. At breakfast, Tina asked him what he had been mumbling that night. Obviously, he had been talking in his sleep.

"It sounded like 'I'm first,' something like that." She looked concerned and poured some coffee.

"I don't remember," Circassian said. He knew if he told Tina what his dream had been, she would give him some kind of psychoanalytical explanation for it, and he didn't want to worry any more than he was now.

"Hey, Lover, you're not cracking up, are you?" she asked. She really seemed concerned, even if she was trying to pass it off as a joke.

"I'm fine. I'm seeing Lee Ann today. She's going to tell me if I'm a protected class or not," he said.

"What makes you think you're a protected class?" asked Tina.

"Well, my father's family comes from what was Armenia, and my mother's family, it's hard to say since she doesn't talk about the past very much, but I think they came from Birobijan."

"You never told me any of this, Circassian," she said.

"I never thought it was important because you never asked me," he said.

"I never asked you because you never brought it up," she answered, a little curtly.

"Something really terrible must have happened to my mother's family since whenever I'd ask her, she'd tell me it wasn't important. My grandparents died when I was very little so there's no one else I could ask. Mom's an only child."

"All right. I just thought that if there's any chance you might know who you were, it would straighten things out a little."

Tina went into the study to get back to her computer. She'd just started, but already he could tell that something was happening to her. He was certain it had something to do with his new situation, but he didn't want to say anything that might set her off. This was obviously getting to be a bad time for her, too. She loved the art gallery.

When Circassian got to his office, the building was almost empty. Finals were over and most everyone had turned in grades. Before seeing Lee Ann, Circassian decided to look to see if he had any e-mail that might be important. He hadn't looked at his e-mail since he'd gotten the first memo from Pickle and when he opened it, there were one hundred and twenty-six messages, only two of which were of any relevance to him. This was the accumulation of less than a week.

Part II-A

Provost Donald Pickle was in a jam. He looked at the figures on his desk that had just been given to him by Bendminder. It was clear that the Board of Trustees and Governor Putski were on a personal mission to drive him bonkers. He didn't know how he could keep President Fred happy, considering that Pickle was notoriously inefficient, and keep the faculty happy, considering that he was not so inefficient that he was unable to do something terrible to them almost every day.

Pickle had been raised in Iowa in a small Mennonite community and had himself been a reasonable, rather passive man when he first became an academic. Twenty years in Administration had changed him considerably. It was the kind of experience a Christian Scientist might have undergone if he had become chief surgeon in a large urban hospital: either cut or quit. The only way he could do his job at the University was to make sure that few people saw him and then only briefly.

He had become terrified of the faculty whom he was convinced, as was Governor Putski of people in general, that if they saw him in person in an unguarded situation, such as in the bathroom or alone walking down a corridor, they would do cruel things to him and if not that, certainly say cruel things. The only person whom he could rely on was Marigold Markham and that only because Marigold's ironic sense of humor kept her from letting Pickle screw himself up in administrative details. Pickle had convinced himself that he was such an incompetent at red tape because he was a "Big Picture Man," but as the Big Picture at the University was becoming smaller every month, it was difficult for him to delude himself much longer.

The possibility that he might leave the Administration and return to the classroom left him with a pang of desire, dim as it was by now, but also dread. He truly loved the classroom and hated the endless meetings, memos and minutiae of his job, but he also dreaded going back to a much smaller salary and missing the leisure time he had each day to go off to play golf in the spring and fall with Vice President of Students T. P. Sealey, and work on his scrimshaw in the winter. Pickle's children were grown and married, and his wife, Alicia, was an artist who had occasionally exhibited her glasswork at Tina's art gallery, so it was with some trepidation that Pickle had sent the first memo to Circassian.

But then Alicia had announced that Tina was closing the gallery — and when she found out why, life at home would become almost unbearable.

When Bendminder had come into the office that morning, Pickle was busily carving "The Ghost Ship," a piece of driftwood Alicia had found for him in Hawaii that he was turning into a three-master. The wood was shaped in such a way that it had an uncanny resemblance to the Administration Building, and perhaps that was why Pickle had decided to call it "The Ghost Ship," but nobody dared to point out the resemblance for fear that he hadn't noticed the resemblance at all and had no intention of being ironic. Lack of a sense of irony was not only the habit of mind of most of the Administration and some of the faculty; it was a necessity for someone like Pickle; lack of a sense of irony was what kept him going.

Bendminder had been holding onto the sheaf of figures in his hand for about twenty minutes as if it were a new-born infant , trying to explain what they all meant in summary, since Pickle did not have a head for numbers.

"It's another .5% of the GS budget, which comes down to $88,550. That's a bit of a squeeze but I've got a few bottom-line figures that might work out without really changing the configuration, Don," said Bendminder. "Of course, if you'd like to open up the possibilities, we can factor it so it doesn't even hurt any of the programs." Bendminder was also a Big Picture Man but his Big Picture was a series of numbers that added up to two converging lines: an increasing number of students and a decreasing number of faculty that would merge at some point in the future in what he called "optimal symbiosis."

Actually, Bendminder hated the faculty with a passion that he could never reveal. He was convinced that the only thing wrong with the University was that there were any faculty at all; they always messed things up, they were more expensive than they were worth, and they always prevented him from showing a clear profit for the year. The fact that the University was state-run and was not supposed to show a profit never bothered Bendminder in his calculations. He had gotten his degree from a small business school in Ohio, where he was taught that any enterprise that did not make a profit had no right to exist. He thought it should be made constitutionally illegal but hadn't thought the time was quite right to launch a national campaign with some of his friends in Operation Change. This was an organization that Governor Putski had set up with private money after his inauguration. It had a shadowy relationship with Central Administration and a not-so-shadowy relationship with the Board of Trustees, a number of members of whom were on the governing board of Operation Change.

"Does this mean that I have to send out more memos? I hate sending out memos; people always read them the wrong way!" whined Pickle. He had never been a whiner, but these last few years had taken a great deal out of him, of what little there had been in him before.

"I never send out memos for that reason," said Bendminder. "The faculty never seem to get anything we send out right, and I think they do it deliberately. After all, most of them have Ph.D.'s. They've been taught to read memos the wrong way. And you have to be carefully taught." Bendminder had just reminded himself of a show tune of his childhood but he thought it might be inappropriate to point it out to Pickle, appropriate as the subject seemed to him.

Bendminder had a passion for show tunes, which explains why he had recommended the abolition of the Theater department. This left the University in a bind, considering that one of the few ways it had proven to the general populace of the town that it existed was through public performances. But Bendminder saw this as an opportunity to suggest a Musical Theater program at the University, although the music faculty and the two theater faculty left knew very little about musicals. "Don't worry," he'd assured Pickle, who assured Dean Lean, who assured the Music department, which assured the two remaining faculty in what was the theater department: "Musical Theater will be a fun thing."

"I know you're a Big Picture Man, Don," said Bendminder. "And I have something here that you should look at. It's a logical extension of Option Three."

"Option Three? Well, let's at least be thankful for Option Three," said Pickle. Option Three had enabled him to send out the memos that Circassian and about half of the faculty at the University, those who were either Adjunct or "Acting-Visiting," had received just a few days before. Now Pickle would have to send out another memo, which, according to Bendminder, would mean just an additional 10% reduction in salaries. "Compared to that first 35%, this should be easy enough for them to take," he pointed out. "Besides, most of them wouldn't know what to do with the money anyway. The adjuncts are used to living on very little and this way they can concentrate more on their real love of teaching."

Pickle didn't entirely agree with this line of reasoning, but he was convinced that Option Three had cleared him of any culpability as far as the University was concerned. He had made sure that the memo had indicated that each of the recipients was invaluable to the University and that what was happening to them was no one's responsibility, at least no one's on the campus level. Besides, as Bendminder had by now convinced Pickle, the faculty were a spoiled bunch and needed something to give them a "reality check." The fact that they were going to be retained despite the financial difficulties of the budget should be enough to make them realize how valuable they were.

"Here's my 'Option Three' plan. I can assure you, Don, that I've looked at the Union contract and there's nothing they can do about it. What I've suggested was ratified as part of the last agreement. They'd have to break their own contract in order to do anything about it. It's foolproof, and I'm sure you'll be able to appreciate it," said Bendminder, presenting his report to Pickle and giving him a large wink as if the two were now engaged in a conspiracy, which wasn't far from the truth. The report was entitled, "Option Three:

The Big Picture," and across the page, in large, printed letters, were the initials: FYEO. Bendminder had spent several years in the auditing department of the CIA and had never abandoned the idea that good Administration was a form of conspiracy.

After Bendminder left, Pickle stared at the Report for several minutes as if it were some kind of hate letter that he knew he had to read, painful as it might be. He opened the manuscript and skimmed the first page. "Holy God!" he said, but there was a smile on Pickle's face for the first time in many months.

When Marigold Markham was called into Pickle's office a few minutes later, she already knew what he intended to have her write, since Bendminder had spoken to her about the .5% cut. Bendminder always repeated to Marigold what he had said to Pickle, since he wasn't sure that Pickle would get it right on his own. He hadn't however, given her a copy of his FYEO report, since he knew that Marigold was capable of putting her own spin on what was happening at the University. Not that she had any official power whatsoever, but she had a power that was lacking in most of the Administration Building: intelligent analysis.

Marigold knew what President Fred thought of Pickle and what Pickle thought of Fred, and if the two knew what the other one really thought, they would not have been able to work together or even speak to each other. Marigold had heard Fred admit that if he thought he could get someone who was less incompetent than Pickle to fill in as Provost, he'd do it in half a heartbeat; she also knew that Pickle knew that President Fred was a secret member of a paramilitary organization of corporate executives and other John Wayne wannabes of means that would go out into the woods not more than five miles from the University every Friday evening to play war games and end up giggling with each other at one of their homes over hot toddies.

"What can I do for you to make your day?" asked Marigold Markham as she entered Pickle's office. Her own office was filled with some of the better work of members of the Art department, including "Venus in Flight" which consisted of a canvas ten feet long and six feet high painted a light blue with three dots of grey in the upper left-hand corner. There were also some excellent sculptures and a few etchings by emeritus and departed faculty. Marigold had been a graduate of the University and gotten her doctorate elsewhere but returned to find herself recruited for a job that she thought she could never want: Assistant to the President and Provost. After a few years of being able to pull strings in one direction or another, she realized it was the perfect job for her.

"I want you to send out another memo to all those faculty that we'd sent out the other memos to," said Pickle. "This time it's only a 10% salary cut. I'm sure they'll be reasonable; times are bad," he added. "Governor Putski's planning another austerity budget for the University."

"I know, Provost Pickle," said Marigold, pretending to make the note to herself that she had already made about the memo.

"You know?" asked Pickle, nervously. "How could you possibly know? I just got it on my e-mail this morning." Pickle was deathly afraid of two things concerning information in the Administration building: that the faculty might actually know more about why he was doing things than he did,; and that they would know it before he did. That's one of the reasons why he was always trying to prevent leaks, even of the most trivial things like the shut-down of the fourth-floor bathroom. Of course, he never understood that the secretaries read everything before anyone else, and they talked to each other from one department to another constantly.

"I read about it in today's *Times*, Provost Pickle. It was a front-page item," said Marigold.

"Oh, yes, of course. Only how did they find out before I did?" asked Pickle, still defensively. "After all, if we're going to carry out a policy, we should be the first to know."

"It's called 'Freedom of the Press' or something like that," said Marigold, somewhat ironically.

"Well, that's no damn excuse," blustered Pickle. "Just get those new memos back to me by this afternoon. . . . Please." As much as he was afraid of what the faculty would do to him if he let down his guard, Pickle was even more afraid of what would happen to him if Marigold decided that she had had enough of his confusions and occasional tantrums and left. Then Fred would blame him and he might have to go back into the classroom.

After Marigold left, Pickle had to deal with a dilemma: whether to read further the "Option Three" report left him by Bendminder or continue carving "The Ghost Ship." He decided on a third option and told Marigold that he wasn't going to be in for a few hours. He needed to take an extended lunch at the Alpine Inn which served excellent veal sandwiches.

After leaving Provost Pickle's office, Marigold sat down to draft the memo. She knew it wouldn't sit well with the faculty that were going to be getting a 10% cut over the 35% cut they had already been given, but on the other hand, she knew that if Pickle had pressure put on him, he might actually decide to go to the State capitol and see some of the people who might do something about it. But where would the pressure come from?

The State capitol had the most convoluted legislative system Marigold had ever studied, which she had tried to master as a political science major in college. She finally gave up in baffled disgust. The University had only two elected representatives that had a direct interest, since it was in their legislative district and was the largest employer in the area. Senator Seymour Kutz was of the Party in Power in the Senate, and he was noted as someone who was out in front on most issues when he saw that everyone else was already on his side. He had tried, in a lukewarm way, to make sure that budget cuts were no more severe than those of any of the other units of the University system, but he had to be on

Governor Putski's side most of the time because he was a team player.

Assemblyman Jake Golden was quite different. First of all, he was smart and had a definite idea of why he was in politics. Second of all, he was in the Party in Power in the Assembly, which was not the same party as Kutz but since the two houses pretty much neutralized each other, there wasn't very much anyone could do without the consent of the Governor and the head of the one house, Senator B. Brutus, and of the other, Assemblyman T. Rend. How anything got done with that part of the budget that involved the University was a mystery known to only two or three people in the entire system, one of whom, Marigold was beginning to suspect, was none other than V. P. Phineas "Stats" Bendminder. She knew of his connection to Operation Change and had reason to believe that he was their chief budget advisor. Just how Operation Change was able to determine the University budget, considering that none of their members were elected to any office, was a mystery that Marigold had hoped to unravel before long.

She was sympathetic to the faculty, but she was even more sympathetic to President Fred who, weak and ineffectual as he was in most cases, she still believed had a good heart and was trying to deal with a lot of people who would have liked nothing better than to close down the University, especially the Board of Trustees, most of whom had been appointed by Governor Putski for just that purpose. Of course, the Governor, who often boasted about the "strong University system," could not afford to make his plans obvious to the public, but he had been raised in a similar school to Bendminder's — "if it's private, thrive with it; if it's public, fuck it"— known among insiders as the "iptwit-ipfit" or further abbreviated as the "twitfit" agenda. This was the agenda of Operation Change, as Marigold had been able to ferret out from overheard conversations and various memos that passed across her desk from Bendminder's office, and she saw these additional cuts as a next step in that direction. But she knew that most of the faculty were just hunkering down, hoping the axe wouldn't fall on them. Besides, she'd already seen what happened when the Union wanted people to get together: bedlam and lots of finger pointing. And Marigold was on the other side of the street from her union days now.

B

Frank Short was one of the few faculty who actually bothered with the Big Picture, but his was considerably bigger than Pickle's or even that of Operation Change. Frank had once been friends with an academic who was subsequently hounded out of his job during the McCarthy Era, and though no one could call him a leftist, Frank was extremely suspicious of what had been going on in the country over the past forty-five years. He called it "Tolerant Totalitarianism," and he and Burble had had a strangely amiable relationship, considering they were about as opposite on issues as any two people could be in the same department. Frank was also able to understand what Burble was saying on a first hearing, which made their conversations much more coherent than when people had to guess at Burble's words.

Although the History department did not have the stability of leadership that the English department had, since no one was willing to be chairman for more than one term of office, most of the people in it worked pretty well together, a rarity at the University. In fact, a number of departments were being chaired by people in other departments since no one trusted anyone else enough to elect him or sometimes her to a position of power. Thus, John Strunz, a physicist, was chair of the Biology department and Dan Collingsworth of the Art department headed Geology, where he felt comfortable. The disharmony among colleagues had even gone so far that Peter Ochello, an astronomer, was now a member of the Math department where he managed to get along with his new colleagues although no one there got along with anyone else; thus it was likely that Peter would soon be made chair of the Math department. But at present, none of that concerned Frank.

"It's all in the numbers, friend Circassian," said Frank when Circassian came over to visit him a few days before classes were set to resume. In the interval, Circassian had decided that it would be useless to refuse to accept the contract, especially since he still wanted to teach and didn't think he would be employable doing much of anything else. Besides, Delilah Cotton's plan to get the Adjuncts and the Visiting Acting faculty together failed miserably since they had never been able to get together about anything before. The Adjuncts disliked the Visiting Acting because, until now, they had been paid considerably more for doing the same amount of teaching; and the Visiting Acting resented the Adjuncts for agreeing to the pitiful remuneration they'd been receiving which they felt was devaluing the profession. Now that they were all being paid the same amount, they blamed each other for what happened. This is what Fred and Pickle had counted on, since what they were even more afraid of than the Board of Trustees or Governor Putski was a united Adjunct and Visiting Acting staff that could very easily stop the operations of the University almost completely. Since they could not be punished by having tenure taken away from them — they had none — there would be no way to force them to return to the classroom.

Frank Short pointed out some of these things to Circassian, who had really come to find out if there was some way he could get back at Pickle directly for what he'd already done. Circassian knew that feelings of revenge were petty and demeaning, but since he had been demeaned already, he felt it wouldn't make much of a difference if he demeaned someone else, especially someone who had been the original source of the demeaning.

"I want to get back at Pickle in some way, since I can't do anything now about this salary cut," said Circassian.

"Has Dabs told you anything about what the Union can do?" asked Frank. He was dubious, but he felt there might be some possibility that hadn't been tried yet. Dabs would be back in several days to tell him.

"By the way, I heard the story about you almost getting Provost Pickle to swallow one of his own memos," said Circassian.

"Actually, we were at a dinner party. This was when he still showed up at dinner parties," said Frank. He crossed his legs and leaned back in his swivel chair, something that he had mastered although when Circassian had tried it himself when he first came to the University, he had fallen backwards and done a complete tumbleset. This was particularly unfortunate, since it was in front of several students who had come into his office for guidance about a paper they were writing. But it had created quite a stir among the student wits who gave Circassian the nickname "The Tumbler," which had only recently begun to wear off. Frank, however, was a master of balance when it came to the swivel chair. "And Old Don had had a few. This was before he was on his guard about every damned thing. And he and I made a silly bet that if a certain football team won, I think it was the Giants or the Bills, against his favorite team, the Cowboys or Dolphins or Rams, I can't remember, well, I would eat one of my memos to him if I lost and he would eat one of his memos to me if he lost. And he did lose but he cheated on the memo; he got Marigold to bake him one out of ginger bread. Still it was in the form of a memo."

"My God, that's an incredibly stupid story!" said Circassian, unafraid to speak his mind to Frank. "Why would that be going around all this time?"

"Because people are hungry around here for telling any story that will make Pickle look stupid. Now it's not that I have anything personally against Pickle. He's about as typical an administrator as you'd find, Circassian. It's just that under 'Tolerant Totalitarianism' the function of administrators is to nail on the lid and keep it as tight as they can until it finally blows. Then you get out the police and the army and start over with a new crew. But I think we're a long way from anything blowing up around here."

"Even with 'Option Three?'" asked Circassian. He was gazing absently at Frank's collection of presidential campaign buttons, which hung in a glass case over his desk. Circassian particularly liked the ones from the Hoover-FDR era.

"'Option Three' is a perfect example of what I've been talking about, Circassian. It takes the responsibility out of the hands of the Administration for what the Governor wants to do, and turns it all into a series of abstractions: numbers, charts, graphs. It's not people that are doing things any more, it's forces. And 'Option Three' is a force. It's been around in different forms since Frederick Taylor pioneered the 'time-and-motion' system. It wasn't a person any more telling you to work harder; it was a 'system' and numbers that could always prove whatever they wanted to."

"Like what Bendminder does?" said Circassian.'

"Precisely, old boy," said Frank. Frank was still prone to archaic expressions from a more genteel era, but Circassian was never bothered by them. At least he remembered to always address him by his last name.

"If you look closely at the memo, you'll see that 'Option Three' is supposed to be an explanation for your salary cut; not Pickle's decision, or Fred's, or those bastards on the Board of Trustees, or Central Administration, or the Governor. It's a number!"

Frank was getting almost vehement, which was unusual, since he was generally very soft-spoken. But this was one subject on which the cockles of his heart would almost burst. He had had a serious heart operation several years before, and for the most part was not an excitable person. He was one of those fortunate people who had made a happy second marriage after an unhappy first, and this is what often consoled him as he witnessed what he saw was the unsystematic but persistent dismantling of the University.

"We live in interesting times, Circassian. The national government is playing around with a few social issues and getting people to line up on one side or another: abortion, gay marriage, civil liberties. But what most people don't notice or don't want to notice is that the rich are getting more and the rest are getting what's left, and that includes me as well as you, friend." Frank took out his mirschaum, which he no longer smoked but which felt good sucking on occasionally when he got tense.

"Do you think there's some kind of organized conspiracy?" asked Circassian. Frank was quite a specialist in conspiracy theories and his courses on the 1950s were called "Paranoia I" and Paranoia II."

"That 'Operation Change' is probably a conspiracy, but the really big social and political movements in this country aren't a product of conspiracies, just a commonality of interests. I can see that by the middle of the next century about ten per cent of the eligible voters will participate in elections, because the rest will realize that it doesn't make a damn bit of difference whom they vote for," he said.

"I didn't realize you were that cynical, Frank," said Circassian. He felt that his original purpose, to find a way of getting back at Pickle, had been lost. And by now he no longer felt that there was any reason for trying to get back at Pickle. Pastor Castor, the college chaplain, had once explained to him in a distraught moment for both of them: Pickle was just an instrument, and one day Circassian himself would understand what it felt like to be one.

"Oh, by the way, Circassian, if you really want to get back at Pickle, just ask Tina to explain to Alicia Pickle why she had to close up the art gallery the next time she sees her. I'll bet that would light a fire under Pickle's pickle," said Frank, half in jest, as Circassian was about to leave.

"I can't do that, Frank. It would be getting Tina involved in my own pettiness, and that wouldn't be fair to her," he answered.

"So you do have some principles after all — as if I didn't know that already, Circassian," Frank said, taking the pipe out of his mouth and giving Circassian a warm, friendly smile. Circassian gave Frank a double take: it was the first warm, friendly smile he remembered seeing from someone on campus since the memos had first gone out.

After Circassian left the room, Frank Short wrote a note in his memo book: "Watch out for Circassian; candidate for cracking up." Frank did not mean that he should beware of Circassian, but that he should keep a helpful eye on him.

There were about fifty people Frank knew on campus who were candidates for cracking up, Circassian being only the latest. Others included Lee Ann Fitz-Proust and Josh Gutsky. He knew that Burble and Schecht and Dabs Budweiser would never crack up; they were too confident in their own view of things to ever doubt themselves. Besides, they were often too self-absorbed to really understand how fragile everything really was.

Frank Short had gone through a difficult divorce and, after making a happy second marriage, he had almost died from a series of heart attacks. He valued life a lot more than he had ever imagined, and this is what gave him some perspective on what everyone else was doing. But it also gave him a dark vision of what was to come. Option Three was only the beginning; he saw a world that would be completely controlled by the bottom line. Faith in mankind's goodness would be turned into faith in good business, and the only social contract that would be taught to students in the future would be one that you would need a lawyer to draw up in triplicate. Some of his colleagues thought he was being paranoid and absurd, but he had seen some of these shadows on the face of democracy for many years. With Option Three, he was certain that the darkness had finally arrived, only it would take a long while before enough people recognized it to do anything about it — and by then, he was certain, it would be too late. He pretended to puff on his mirschaum for a few more minutes, then shut his door to read Schopenauer.

C

President Dick Fred was one of those people you look up to until he opens his mouth, and then you realize that he's really a strange person. Fred had managed to move up the academic pole by being tall enough to make people look up to him, and he had learned to keep his mouth shut for the most part, until, as President of the University, he couldn't afford to do so any longer. Fred had never been very good at sports, being a gawky, scrawny, clumsy type, but he had a vast admiration for athletics, especially at the University, which was still turning out superb athletes, some of whom were even well-educated in the face of Dean Steen's program of increasing enrollments with decreasing staffing.

The one annoyance that Fred had to deal with was Provost Pickle, because every once in a while Pickle would ask him for a meeting to discuss such unpleasant subjects as the budget cuts and the decline in the morale of the Arts and Science faculty. (Steen had already taken care of the morale of the Professional Studies staff; they didn't have any that they could call their own.)

Like Pickle, Fred was supported by an ambitious, intelligent, and very personable wife who was a wonder at damage control of her husband's faux pas. Fred, who was fluent in Swabian, thought of himself as a world traveler and had actually gone to several African countries that began disastrous civil wars a few months after his visit; whether there was any direct connection between his tours and the vast disharmony that arose in the countries he visited was the subject of endless speculation by the faculty. Burble had once hoped that Fred would visit Russia soon, since Burble still hated Russia, but he relented when he finally realized that Russia couldn't be more of a mess whether or not Fred visited it.

When the names of the people whose contracts had to be renegotiated came up, Fred clucked with annoyance. This should never have happened, and someone should be responsible for it. But he was a little afraid of Bendminder, who, he was convinced, could prove through his maddening mastery of figures that Fred himself wasn't cost-effective; he knew he couldn't do without Marigold Markham since she did his daily thinking; and he didn't want to tangle with Pickle, who could be a pretty slippery character, even if not as slippery as VP T.P. Sealey — so Fred was in the sulks when he decided to call a meeting to set out the agenda for the new semester.

He always began the spring semester with a number of agenda items, all of which he regarded as vital, and none of which were addressed by him after the second week of the new term. And since no one else thought much of his agendas, they were left to be recycled each subsequent spring. One of his pet agenda items at one time had been the Writing Program, but he lost interest after the faculty began to balk, and so, as one senator had proposed about Vietnam, he pulled out and declared victory. At any conference he went to, Fred would proudly point out that the University had had a Writing Program in place for years and wasn't it a pity how difficult it seemed for some of the other units to get with the program?

The President's Council consisted of the Provost, the two VP's, T.P. Sealey and the VP for Finance and Management, Leon Leone (who was more frightened of Bendminder than even Pickle or Fred), Marigold Markham, Bendminder, and a few middle-level management types who were permitted to attend as long as they kept their mouths shut no matter how absurd the conversation.

Fred began by reading off the Major Agenda items for the spring semester:

1. Collegiality — get the faculty to be nice to each other more often;

2. Cultural diversity — get the Black 3% of the student population and the Hispanic 2% and the Asian 1% and the Other .5% together to do fun things with the rest of the students;

3. Better advisement — get the faculty in Professional Studies to do a better job advising their 75-per students with a more personal approach;

4. Sharpen the University's Profile (A.) — find ways to make us known as THE University in something besides sports;

5. Sharpen the University's Profile (B.) — find ways to merchandize the new Sports Complex to enhance the sports program;

6. Make the Budget Cuts an Opportunity — encourage the faculty to innovate as a positive way of responding to the decline in financial resources.

"Well, what do you want to talk about first?" asked Fred. He really wanted to talk about the Sports Complex and he didn't want to talk at all about the Budget Cuts, even as an Opportunity, but he had to pretend to some form of democratic procedure because he didn't want to antagonize Marigold Markham who would always tell him after a meeting that he'd forgotten his own democratic procedures. This was when he would begin to sulk.

"I think number two, 'Cultural Diversity,' would be a good place to start," said T.P. Sealey, who was Fred's very own golf partner and could do no wrong in his eyes, and no right in anyone else's.

"Fine, fine," said Fred, a bit miffed. This might actually be a long meeting.

"Let's appoint a committee to study the issue," said Marigold Markham, reading distress in Fred's body language: he had his hands folded, his legs crossed, and was looking down at the floor.

"That's an excellent idea," said Sealey, realizing that he had almost made a faux pas, something that Fred, not he, had mastered.

"Get Deans Lean and Steen to appoint a group; make sure the Fitz-Proust woman is involved," said Pickle. Pickle was in a good mood considering that this meeting was coming at a time he had planned to work on "The Ghost Ship," but he had just finished reading the "Option Three" report from Bendminder and had given his approval to have it discussed when the subject came to the budget. Even if the subject of the budget didn't come up, he was planning to distribute the report, FYEO, of course. The fact that Marigold had leaked most of it to Dabs and Hank Schecht two weeks before, even if it meant risking an e-mail to Dabs in Curaçao, was something that none of the other members of the committee could know, or, actually, care about, as the Report made clear.

"What about the new Sports Complex? The alumni are really anxious to find out what role they will have in the naming of the various gyms and the hockey rink," interjected Fred, as there was the inevitable lull in the conversation once a committee was being appointed.

"I think we should get Dave Coven on that right away. There are a whole group of alumni that would love to have their names anywhere in the Sports Complex," said Leon Leone, tentatively. He was never sure what side of Fred he was on since he had to give him the bad news about the budget after Bendminder had spun it as good news.

Several of those at the meeting began making suggestions about places that plaques could be put to commemorate alumni contributions and for the next half hour, it seemed, the subject was discussed in exhaustive detail until everyone was exhausted about discussing the subject. Then the conversation picked up as Marigold Markham added: "You forgot the toilets. That's one place where alumni can be remembered that's right in front of their noses." She was a tad dismayed when the secretary wrote it down and no one laughed; she wondered how the alumni would take the suggestion that they would be warmly remembered in one of the urinals and celebrated for their generosity roundly at the crappers.

The only question, as someone delicately put it, was whether or not the plaque should be on the lip of the seat where it might prove uncomfortable to the sitter, or inside the bowl where the donor might feel a bit put upon. The Council was evenly divided between the outsies and the insies, and it was decided that all of them would sleep on it and see what they would come up with at the next meeting. Marigold wrote a memo to herself never again to try to lighten things up at a Council meeting.

Finally, the matter of the budget cuts came up. Bendminder launched on an exposition of the merits of the forty-eight grid scan matrix in proving to the faculty that less was better in some cases and not bad in most other cases. VP T.P. Sealey pointed out that since faculty members were already often overindulged — he had heard a few more of the student horror stories about Burble and a number of other of the faculty on the Option Two list — he felt the best approach would be to point out how much of an opportunity it was to teach at the University. Pickle advised to "tough it out," and besides, he had a "plan." (This was Bendminder's idea, of course, but Bendminder knew when he gave it to him that Pickle would take the credit. This would put Pickle in Bendminder's debt, something he might need in the future.)

Fred actually perked up a little when Pickle mentioned a "plan," since Fred had no plans whatsoever, just agenda items that would be ignored as soon as they were launched. He wondered how Pickle could have possibly come up with his own plan, since he rarely worked on anything except his scrimshaw and golf, but he assumed that Marigold would explain it to him.

"As you know," said Pickle, "our budget has been cut again, by another .5%, which means that I had to send out another set of memos to the Adjunct and Acting Visiting. Since they are invaluable to the institution and we cannot do without them, we must begin to think of other ways to deal with these cuts. I think that this is an opportunity that we cannot afford to miss, and this report will show you why."

He distributed the "Option Three" Report and asked the Council just to read the first page. As each finished, there was the beginning of a collective sigh among the Council members; they all saw the same thing and they were passing glad.

()

Circassian remembered the day several years before that President Fred had decided to "go it alone" and improvise a speech to a group of potential students and their parents; Circassian had been asked to talk about "opportunities in English." He had been asked to speak since none of the tenured faculty were in the mood to, considering that there had been another budget cut. Since Circassian had very little faith in "opportunities in English" — he was in English and had no real opportunities — Branch Stark had decided that he would be an appropriate speaker. "Be honest," Branch said, "but not too bleepin' honest."

But before Circassian's talk, President Fred had tried to explain to the assembled the "opportunities in World Culture" that the University afforded him. Fred's first impulse was to address the group entirely in Swabian, but his wife had managed to convince him that as good as his Swabian was, it was likely that not too many people would understand a word he was saying. He told her sulkily that he was really at a loss without Marigold, who had gone on a cruise to Tobago with her husband, and whom Fred had forgotten to ask for a speech to potential freshmen. He tried to remember parts of other speeches, but they became confused, and he was a little wary of beginning a speech when he would have no way of knowing how it would end. So Livonne Fred suggested that he tell about his recent trip to Swabia; that would give them an idea of some of the opportunities for cultural exchange at the University.

"Parents, students and friends of the University (that was from another speech but Fred liked the cadence):

"University College has many opportunities for students who are bold and daring enough to find a challenge in International Studies. We pride ourselves here on our International Studies program, which is second to none in the University system. And to give you an example of how broadening the experience can be, I would like to share with you one of mine."

Fred had then launched into a rambling description of his recent visit to Swabia with the University football team which was challenged to play an exhibition game with a local Swabian team. The President chortled that the score against their hosts was astronomical, but that may have in part been due to the fact that the average Swabian football player on the team weighed 155 pounds, about a hundred less than the boys from the University. But then Fred told the story of the great robbery he and about twenty-five members of the team had helped foil when two misguided Swabian "*gonifs*" (Swabian for "thieves") thought they would make off with some of the football equipment. Why they would try to steal something so useless in Swabia might explain why they were so easily caught. Fred glowed with glee in thinking how the players had made a circle around the two stupid thieves, as if daring them to try to break through. When the gendarmes arrived, Fred and the whole team, it seems, handed them over.

While this story was going on, Circassian was looking around to see where Marigold was to try to stop Fred or pass him something to read and save the situation. Only later did he find out that she was about as far away from him as transportation would take her.

Circassian had then gotten up to speak, hoping that the assembled crowd would go away now that they realized that the place that they had intended to send their children for higher education was run by a very silly man. But they stayed, perhaps hopeful that the next speaker would somehow explain what the President really meant. Circassian knew that would not be a good idea, since he didn't know what the President really meant and he was certain that President Fred didn't know what he meant.

Circassian spoke for about fifteen minutes on the subject of "change," and how important it was for young students to adapt since their world was going to be one of very rapid changes. "Some of you may have to learn three or more entirely different jobs in your lifetimes," he said and now, thinking back to that talk as he walked across the quad to the parking lot with Frank Short's sober, balanced voice in his mind, Circassian was wondering how many different jobs he himself would have in his lifetime.

〇

Before he had a chance to get a good look at the "Option Three" report, President Fred stared at his Option Two list. These were the names of the superfluous faculty whom he could not let go. He could not let them go because there was no way he could find to fire them, since they had all achieved tenure many years before, and they all refused to retire. Travis Blitz, a terrible physics teacher, was on the list, as well as several younger members of the faculty who had proved to be terrible teachers, irresponsible colleagues, and not very nice human beings, but there was nothing that could be done about them. Even Bendminder, who was able to prove that the twenty-seven names on the list factored out to a minus ten in terms of student enrollment, could not figure out a way of getting rid of them. In the past, a few who had a history of indiscretions, the attempted rape of a freshman, racially disgusting remarks in front of a class, flashing in one of the women's wings of a dorm, were asked to retire immediately as a "deal." But Blitz, who managed to get students to transfer to other institutions in order to avoid taking another course with him, was not guilty of anything but horrible teaching. And even though most members of the Music department wanted him to retire, or resign, or die, he was still valuable to them in balancing out their grade point averages so they would look lower — and therefore more highly esteemed — than those of any other department.

Fred imagined a conversation with Blitz, pretending that he could actually have a conversation with him. "*Travis, I was wondering if you've considered retiring?*" was the way Fred — and only in his imagination — would have approached Blitz.

"*Why should I retire, Dick? I like teaching,*" he would answer.

"*But you're a terrible teacher, most of the students hate you, and the few who admire you are often later diagnosed as psychotic and have to be removed from campus,*" Fred would boldly say.

"*You're not so hot as an administrator yourself, Dick. You send out confusing memos, you never stick to any plan for very long, and people laugh at you behind your back a good deal.*" (This isn't the way Blitz would have expressed it, but it's how Fred imagined he would express it if he were Blitz.)

"*But don't you think after all these years of what the University gave to you, it would be neat if you gave something back to the University? Your retirement would mean we could save three jobs of junior faculty that we have to cut,*" Fred imagined he would say.

"*Well, that's too fuckin' bad.*" (This is what Fred imagined Blitz would really say.) "*I don't see why I have to do any sacrificing around here. When was the last time you did any sacrificing around here?*"

Fred was tempted to point out that he had stayed at his present salary for the past three years, but since he was making about twice as much as even Blitz, he decided not to say it.

No, the list would have to remain as it was. That is, unless . . . and at that point Fred decided to look at the "Option Three" report. He read it through quickly, occasionally chortling to himself and saying "Yes! Yes! Yes!" like a lover in heat. He then asked Marigold Markham if she would get him through to Central Administration to see if he could get an opinion on the plan from the Chancellor's Office, if not the Chancellor himself, Thaddeus Thwart. In fact, Marigold was able to get him through to the Chancellor's office very quickly since it was about the "Option Three" report. It seems that Chancellor Thwart, who was really a cipher put in the position he held by the Board of Trustees since they couldn't trust anyone in it who deserved trust, knew a great deal about "Option Three" already, which was rather strange since the document was supposed to be FYEO and that "Y" didn't include him. But after a brief discussion with Chancellor Thwart,

President Fred knew what he had to do. He had to act. He first called in Bendminder.

"This is really your work, isn't it, Stats?" said Fred, using Bendminder's nickname for the first time in five years.

"Well, I got a little help from some friends but, yes, it's really mine," he said.

"I didn't think Pickle was sharp enough to do this himself. It's brilliant, and according to Central Administration, it's perfectly legal. It's even in the contract. This will really get us out of a very ticklish situation."

"And we can even have a budget surplus," said Bendminder, almost salivating all over himself.

"The only question is, what would be the best way of doing this, that is, without too much fuss?" Fred asked, for him, calculatingly.

"I've thought of that already, Dick. Pickle gave me the go-ahead on a list and we can begin as soon as we have the right people in place," he said.

"The 'right people?'" said Fred, who was not quite as sharp on these matters as he thought he was.

"There are all sorts of wrong people for this kind of project, but I think that the right people have to be carefully screened. We don't want to screw this up. Then Budweiser and her crew would come at us with everything the Union has."

"Which isn't very much, when you come down to it," chuckled Fred. He hadn't enjoyed himself so much since the first year he was President and everyone seemed to love him for what he was.

D

Dabs Budweiser was at a loss for words. This in itself was a very strange state for her to be in, since she was known to have conversations, vehement ones, in her sleep. But she had just come back from Curaçao after visiting one of her successful sons, had enjoyed a tan, and now was subjected to the wintry blasts of Upstate which was one of the sources of pride of the local residents: "Jeb, it went down to fifteen below last night on the barn thermometer!" "Well, if that don't beat all," and so on.

Dabs had been certain that when she got back from her vacation she would get something going for Circassian. After all, he had been a loyal union man, signing the membership form and check off for the dues payment the first day he was on campus, and he actually represented the "Acting Visiting" faculty on the Union Executive Board. She remembered the day he made a motion that would have requested the tenured faculty not to sneer when they walked by one of the "Acting Visiting." It passed almost unanimously, with the lone dissenting vote coming from Hank Schecht, who felt it would be an abridgement of freedom of expression.

But now Dabs felt that she had let Circassian down. She had looked through the contract and thought there was a glimmer of hope, but then she got the gist of the Option Three report. This almost astonished her, and being the veteran of many wars with the Administration, it was not easy for Babs to be almost astonished. So when Circassian came into her room, which was adorned with every possible variation or version of the Mona Lisa that one could ever imagine, she felt that there was really nothing positive she could tell him.

"You mean the contract doesn't cover this?" asked Circassian, more in sadness than anger. He had been in sadness a great deal lately.

"It would have covered you if you were still a Visiting Acting, but once you became an Adjunct Visiting Acting you were in another category which means you serve at the pleasure of the President," Babs explained.

"But I wasn't an Adjunct when this contract was given to me," he said, trying his best to be logical.

"Technically you weren't, but what Option Three does is give the President or his appointed representative the power to define your position according to the interests of the University," Dabs answered, trying to appear to be logical.

"Where in the contract does it say he or his appointed representative have this power?"

"It doesn't, unless there is something called 'economic exigency,' which is when the University will not be able to function if something isn't done to meet their budget."

"But the only reason they can't meet their budget is that Governor Putski decided that we have to have another budget cut," said Circassian, remembering that when Putski had been first elected, although no one expected him to be, Tina had voted for him "as a joke." He wondered now how many jokers were still laughing at Putski.

"What the Governor does and what Central Administration does are two separate things. They could have sliced the pie any way they wanted; we got the cut we did so they could call it an 'economic exigency' and fuck up the contract any way they wanted."

"So if I had been offered the contract as an Acting Visiting I would have been able to appeal?"

"That's what you've got a contract for, Circassian," said Dabs.

"But because Pickle had designated me an Adjunct Acting Visiting, the contract doesn't cover me?"

"Not exactly," Dabs said, inadvertently giving Circassian a moment of hope.

"Then what exactly?" asked Circassian, beginning to feel, if not act, testy.

"We can appeal the timing of the designation and see if it violates due process. If we win at Step One, then we have a chance at Steps Two and Three, and then we'll be able to get Central Administration to make a ruling. I know it's a long shot. . . ."

"Since when has Central Administration ever made a ruling against management in your memory?" asked Circassian, expecting Dabs to remember something so remote in the history of the Union.

"There was the Jeckel case; it was a long time ago, but there's always the chance that yours might get some favorable treatment."

"Why would my case get favorable treatment? "asked Circassian. "What would make me so special?"

"We can make it a test case," said Dabs, for the moment improvising. She had no idea if the Union would want to make a test case out of the rights of an Acting Visiting since they were less than 5% of the membership, but she just didn't want Circassian to walk out of the office feeling that he had been let down. Dabs' function had always been to give hope to her membership, even if it was totally unfounded.

"How long would all of this take? The three steps and the appeal? A month?"

Dabs stifled a guffaw. (She didn't chortle because she knew that President Fred chortled and the two hadn't gotten along ever since he vetoed a commendation she would have received in lieu of extra compensation. Dabs always rubbed Fred in the wrong direction.) She knew that the appeals process sometimes lasted the lifetime of the plaintiff, but it was just possible Circassian might live to see the results of his appeal.

"It's going to take some time, Circassian. A lot longer than a month, but maybe I can find some way to keep your original status while the appeals process goes through," said Dabs.

"That wouldn't be bad," said Circassian. "Even if it took a long time, I would at least have my original salary back and Tina would be able to quit her computer job and return to the art gallery. She's beginning to get 'The Look,' you know. You've seen it around here."

"The Look" was when an employee began to stare without blinking at some distant object for no apparent reason. Someone would have to throw cold water on them, or do something equally annoying in order to snap him out of it. But Tina had been taking "The Look" into the kitchen and had almost caused several small fires.

"Uh, Circassian: one little thing. We can make them keep your title but your salary cut couldn't be renegotiated until the appeals process was over."

"But if I have the status of an Acting Assistant, I am included in the contract," said Circassian, trying to see where his logic would send him this time.

"Technically, you are," said Dabs.

"But according to you, even if I am included in the contract, my salary isn't?" He was hoping she'd say no, but she nodded her head.

"That's the way the contract runs. An 'economic exigency' takes precedence."

"But that sounds like 'Option Three.'" '

"You've got that right, Circassian."

"So because they can't afford to do without me but can't pay me the salary I'm entitled to, they can do whatever they want to my salary? Is that the deal?" Circassian felt like foaming at the mouth but decided that Dabs might take him literally.

"I wouldn't exactly put it that way," said Dabs, knowing that that is exactly the way she would put it. "Look, there's an Exec. Board meeting coming up next week. I'm putting this on the agenda. I'm sure they'll be passing a resolution. Remember, you're only one of about fifteen Acting Visiting Adjuncts affected. But you're the only one with the balls to try to do something about it."

"And you can see how far I've gotten doing something," said Circassian, getting up. He had just noticed the Henry Wallace photo Dabs had hung over her desk. It seemed a new addition to him.

"Don't give up hope, Circassian. We're all behind you," said Dabs, and Circassian walked out of the office and into the cold corridor. He wondered what fresh labyrinths of logic awaited him to wade through.

()

Dabs hadn't even been tempted to be feisty with Circassian, since she knew that he was right; the Union really could do nothing to protect him, or any of his fellow newly appointed Adjuncts. She could be feisty with President Fred or Pickle; she was even feisty with T.P. Sealey, but these were the enemy. They deserved her feistiness; Circassian deserved a better answer. But she couldn't give him one, and felt stymied and balked. She rarely had felt both at the same time because when she was stymied she could always find some way out, and when she was balked, at least she wasn't stymied. It was all the results, she was convinced, of the Option Three report.

In the last contract, the Union had made what Dabs now considered a fatal mistake. It had allowed the Governor's office to put a clause into the contract that would allow it to take "all necessary measures" when the budget needed to be cut in order to make up for the short-fall. The measures had been written out in language so obscure and convoluted that no one was absolutely certain what it meant; no one, that is, except Bendminder. He had managed to figure out a way the contract could be used to establish not only Option Three but the other Options that Option Three opened up.

Dabs decided that she had to call an emergency session of the Exec. Board as soon as possible. This could be a disaster if Bendminder decided to implement it, and she began to suspect that he might have had a hand in the original wording of the contract itself. She'd prided herself on being able to see through all of the elaborate dances management had mastered over the last six contracts, but she had to confess to herself — certainly not to anyone else — that they had pulled a fast one on her and the rest of the membership, especially Chief Negotiator Shep Sharman, who had "guaranteed" that the Union would be no worse off in signing this contract than they had been in signing the last one, as wretched as it was.

She stared at the newly found picture of Henry Wallace that she had taken as a teenager when she had marched in a parade supporting his candidacy for President back in '48. Dabs was not the nostalgic type, but she couldn't resist recalling the time in which Labor counted for something in this country besides a nuisance that the politicians could shit on any time they wanted. She'd had hopes that it was making more than a feeble comeback in recent elections, but Option Three almost convinced her that when it came down to that bottom line Bendminder was always talking about, the Union wasn't a factor at all.

That brave picture of Henry Wallace, a big grin on his face, his hands in the air in a gesture of imminent victory, reminded her that Wallace had lost that election by thirty million votes to the runner-up, Dewey. Then she decided that this was no time to forget how feisty she really was and she began to call up the members of the Exec. Board for an emergency meeting as soon as possible. But something inside her told her that it was probably already too late.

()

Circassian decided that he would eat at school instead of going home for lunch. He dreaded seeing Tina blurring into the computer screen and he was afraid to tell her that he was stuck with the salary he was getting for the foreseeable future.

As he approached The Table, he noticed Seth Shotman motioning to him to take a seat at his table. Circassian nodded and got a sandwich. While he was waiting on line to pay, he heard Ralph Null say: "Did you hear about this Option Three report? It sounds like something Bendminder would think of." Branch Stark had decided that for the hell of it he would sit at The Table for a few minutes even though he couldn't stand Ralph or Gladys, and Burble he hadn't spoken to in ten years. But Frank Short had sat down at the end of the table, and Branch was kind of fond of Frank.

"I don't think it was just Bendminder. I think this came from Central Administration. Bendminder probably put the numbers in somewhere," Branch said. Bendminder was someone else that he rarely talked to, but once in a while he was handy in giving numbers on student enrollment that helped Branch prove that enrollment in the English department had really levelled off when it actually had gone down.

"Branch," said Gladys, "I've heard some rumors that Governor Putski's actually behind this and that it might be the work of Operation Change."

"I don't think Putski's behind anything. I think Operation Change is behind Putski, and I'm just a little curious to know how Bendminder got to be so influential," said Frank

Short, sipping a diet drink. He seemed relaxed, leaning back ever so slightly in the plastic chair that was the commissary's idea of comfort for the faculty.

"Ah, a conspiracy theory!" said Ralph. "Or do you think that Bendminder is the secret playmaker behind Operation Change?"

"Then if we could ever figure who or what was behind Bendminder we'd be in good shape, eh, Frank?" said Gladys.

Circassian drew up a chair beside Seth. Seth was playing with his food, which was probably better than eating it. He was upset about the argument that Josh, he had heard, had had with Circassian.

"I want you to know, Circassian," said Seth, "that whether you're Jewish or not, I respect you."

This was not what Circassian had expected to hear. In fact, Circassian had decided that the best way to handle the situation with Josh and Seth was to tell them that he felt Jewish sometimes and that that might be enough to satisfy them.

"Seth, I hope you don't get the wrong impression. I'm not really interested in whether or not I'm Jewish right now. It's not the kind of thing that keeps me up nights. What keeps me up nights is not to be able to do anything about my pay cut," Circassian explained.

"Well, Jewish or not, it wouldn't help you as far as the pay cut is concerned; Jews aren't a 'protected class.'"

"I think that Acting Visiting Assistant Professors should be a protected class because nobody seems to be able to protect us worth a warm piss," said Circassian, forgetting himself for once in the presence of The Table.

"Did you talk to Dabs about it?" asked Seth.

"That's why I'm sure that people who are stuck with my rank need to be a protected class," said Circassian, looking on absently while Seth played with his food.

"I have a sense that something really terrible is going to happen soon to all of us here, only I'm not sure what it is," said Seth. "But being Jewish can be a real comfort, believe me. We've been through so much."

E

Camille Faux, member of the Board of Trustees, B.A., M.A., D. Litt., had just received an e-mail from Chancellor Thwart. It simply read:

"Option Three is underway,

"T. Thwart"

She smiled slightly, finished her toddy, and pressed the "Delete" button. She then called several other members of the Board to give them the news.

At the State Capitol, Ambler Slaughter, managing director of the Operation Change Institute, was doing lunch with Train Johnson, an elderly umbrella manufacturer and an important supporter of Slaughter's program, when his cellphone told him that Camille Faux was calling.

He knew what the message would be and as he clicked on the phone, he smiled slightly.

In his office in another part of the State Capitol, State Senator Seymour Kutz had just come from an emergency meeting of the Higher Education Appropriations Committee. He seemed relieved by the news that they'd just gotten from the Board of Trustees. His smile was slight but his heart was full; he knew that many of the problems he had faced in the past would now be solved. He wondered how his colleague from the other party, Jake Golden, would react to the news. He was certain it would be negative. He felt a little badly for Jake, but he felt even better for himself. This was a good thing.

At Central Administration, Thaddeus Thwart, the nonetity Chancellor of the University system, was preparing to take an indefinite leave of absence before the shit really hit the fan. He hated confrontation, almost as much as Fred, only he believed that he might suffer irreparable bodily harm if he stayed until this whole matter blew over. He had always wanted to travel to the Seychelles, even if he wasn't sure where they were.

When Dabs Budweiser found out that afternoon, she immediately called up Chief Negotiator Shep Sharpman to see whether it didn't violate the contract. Shep was unavailable because he was at a meeting with those members of the Union leadership that were immediately available. That told Dabs that whatever the Administration was beginning to do, there was nothing in the contract that could stop them.

Marigold Markham had deleted for the fifth time the letter of resignation she was planning to put on President Fred's desk as soon as she got the news. But whenever she was about to press "Print," she hesitated. She knew that anyone else brought into the position she held would probably be even more under Fred's and Pickle's thumb than she was. And the faculty would need her to leak information now more than ever. No, she decided that it would be best if she stayed on, at least for a little while longer. But there was no smile on her face as she began writing the President's speech to the faculty. It was probably the most difficult she'd ever been asked to ghost.

()

When Branch Stark got the news, the secretaries heard what seemed like a great outrush of wind from his office and then a shout that was so loud and sudden that no one could tell what it meant. It was Branch's version of a Primal Scream. He then stormed out of the office and before anyone could ask him what happened, he was half-way down the hall to Dean Lean's.

()

When Seth Shotman found out, he automatically began considering whether this was "bad for the Jews or good for the Jews." Then he realized that it really had nothing to do with the Jews and remembered that Circassian had talked with him the day before about just this problem. He suddenly felt prophetic, but it was something he really didn't want to be prophetic about.

()

Hank Schecht began writing an e-mail to the faculty which he felt was the most important of his many e-mail messages. He had checked it out with Dabs and was sure that the faculty would be behind him and the Union on this. The only problem, he suddenly realized, was that the Union could do nothing and so any appeal to action would be ill-advised. Still, perhaps an unofficial act of protest might be in order.

()

Just moments before Branch Stark stormed into his office Dean Lean had finally mastered one of his most difficult shadow plays. He had just gotten the memo from Pickle that he knew he had to read and as Branch's size twelve shoes came stomping into the room, Dean Lean was casting "The Dying Swan" across the room onto the "Flight of Bacchus." Somehow, he felt, the two of them fit.

()

That evening, Student Council President Tilly Owlglass and Vice President Todd Zarathustra, who was also the President of the Greek Council, decided to make a joint declaration applauding the actions of the Administration. They were voted down, noisily, by Mona Pilgrim, one of Circassian's most admiring students, and a contingent of, in Tilly's words, "stick in the muds." But Tilly could not surpress a slight smile.

()

Although it did not affect her School as yet, Dean Steen called Bendminder to see if the figures for Professional Studies were still unconscionably high. She sighed in relief when he told her that her faculty were still teaching about twice as many students as they were supposed to, even by the Board of Trustees' standards. She felt a little sorry for Dean Lean, but not too; she'd never really trusted him: he was too pro-faculty.

In his office, Ron Burble got the news from Gladys DeFoe. At first he was delighted that the English department was the first, but when she told him that History was the second, he began to feel emotions that he had banished from his mind many years before: fear and trembling. He knew this was what he wanted, had wanted for years, but it wasn't quite the way he wanted it. And for one of the rare times in recent memory, Ron Burble began to feel a sense of doubt.

Lee Ann Fitz-Proust stared at the e-mail message that Hank Schecht had finally brought himself to write. It was, as usual, extremely long for what it had to say, but the first paragraph told her everything she needed to know. And she was certain that something could be done, if only the students and the rest of the faculty could finally be mobilized to do it. She started writing her own call to action.

After Delilah Cotton had read through Hank Schecht's memo, she glanced at Lee Ann's. Neither of them did very much of anything for her, but she found the situation strangely laughable. It was as if the wish of every Adjunct who had been exploited by the faculty as well as the Administration had finally been granted. But it was in such a terrible way, that, laughable as it was, she did not laugh.

In his suite in the Executive Office Building, Governor Putski was putting the finishing touches on a letter of support to the Board of Trustees for their courageous action. Actually, the Board of Trustees had not done anything except to approve what Bendminder had already put into motion. He smiled broadly until he remembered that he would have to hire several extra body guards for a while.

Walking across the quad, Frank Short puffed for real on his mirschaum. He had almost anticipated that this was going to happen as soon as he had heard of "Option Three." Now it was happening faster than even he could imagine in his wildest dreams, and he was prepared to be having wild dreams for the foreseeable future.

In the Administration Building, Bendminder was factoring in the numbers that would be necessary for the final draft of the contracts. The deal had been completed much too quickly for him to get all the data he needed. What surprised him was how they had snapped up his first offer. That's why he hadn't really been prepared with all the figures on the contracts. It was this first bold step that forced, out of those rarely untightened lips, a small smile.

In his office in the Administration Building, VP T.P. Sealey was very satisfied with the developments of the last day. He had not much use for the faculty, and this would considerably relieve the pressure on his office, especially since now he would be able to concentrate on protecting himself from any rear-guard action Pickle might consider, a fear unfounded since Pickle was not about to launch any more actions on anyone. But at least T. P. was certain of one thing: this would get the faculty in line.

()

When Circassian got the news, he went directly home and took a bath. When he got out, he still didn't feel cleansed but he was sure of one thing: His life in academe might be soon coming to an abrupt end. That might not solve any of the many problems that were plaguing him, but it would certain eliminate any uncertainty. Now this was a whole new ballgame. And he wasn't sure of the shape of the ball, let alone the rules.

()

Next morning, the daily paper of the town, *The Daily Paper,* put the story on the front page, slightly below the lead article on a treed cat that had been pulled down from some high-voltage wires by two courageous firemen.

UNIVERSITY COLLEGE SELLS TWO DEPARTMENTS

University College has just announced the sale of two of its departments to Intell-Ex. Corporation, a manufacturer of computer discs and educational materials. The sale, the details of which are not as yet available, will go into effect immediately. The two departments involved, English and History, will still function at the school, but their budgets will now be determined by the management of Intell-Ex.

Provost Donald Pickle said in a brief memo: "The quality of the University was increasingly at risk because of continued budget cuts. This sale of the two departments puts us on a firmer financial footing." Asked to comment on the sale was Dabs Budweiser, President of the ULP local at the University. "We are studying the situation but at this time we have no public statement." Assoc. VP President "Stats" Bendminder, in a prepared statement, declared, "This is a necessary arrangement that will put the entire institution on a much firmer footing. It is part of a long-range plan that has developed from 'Option Three,' a new method of dealing with staffing and other financial problems. Before long, we may even see a profit at this institution for the first time in memory."

Several meetings of the faculty and students have been called to address the impact of the sale on the rest of the University. President Dick Fred in a telephone call to his office, said that "everything is under control" and "I'm in charge."

Part III

(A large room, dimly lit except for a spotlight on the dias where George Putski stands to address the annual convention of NNUT (No New [Unconditionally] Taxes). The Governor speaks.)

Dear Friends and Adversaries:

I want to share with you my vision of a future of Jobs, Competitiveness and Prosperity for our state. In my State of the State Address, I told you that I wanted to put us back to work again. That is why I am planning to eliminate 14,000 state jobs in the next fiscal year and another 10,000 the year after. I also want you to know that I plan to make the state more competitive in terms of the quality of our work force. That is why we are planning to raise tuition and lower enrollment in the University. Remember, not everyone needs a job to go to college — I mean, needs college to get a job. I am sure that, statistics aside, there are plenty of good-paying, high-benefit jobs in the private sector that do not require a college degree, and if any of you hear of one, let me know.

I realize that I did not mention the University once in my State of the State address. After all, it goes without saying that I have had the University on my mind constantly for years. And the sooner the University is off my mind, the better. But I would like to share with you a vision of the University in the year 2012; a vision that will reflect the Restructuring, Reconfiguring and Retrenching plans that I am sure will be in the offing as we continue to Readjust the size, shape and quality of the University for the future.

(Lights off Putski and on an unfamiliar figure for the Putski Administration: an Acting Visiting Professor. He is dressed in a shabby suit, a white shirt with frayed cuffs, with a look of emaciation and despair on his face.)

Welcome, consumer students of PUS (Privatized University of the State) to English 433. I am about to tell you the content of the course, but first, a few words from our sponsors. English 433 is sponsored, in part, by the makers of No-Doz. Remember, if you find yourself nodding in class, take a No-Doz: it'll keep you awake no matter how boring the lecture. No-Doz is available at a 25% discount at your local drugstore with this coupon, which I am now handing out. It also can be obtained in bulk quantity by calling the following number, which I am now writing on the board. If you should have any questions about No-Doz, detailed information will be available on request after class — or, if the impulse to buy moves you — even during class. Remember, every sale of No-Doz and the other twenty-six fine products which sponsor English 433 help contribute to continued offering of this course, which is partially funded through a 10% commission for each order of over $10 on any of the sponsoring products. Don't forget our motto: "To Learn, To Serve, To Buy."

And now, a brief overview of the content of this fine course, sponsored by No-Doz and, after the first twenty-five minutes, by Trojenz Brand condoms, the most reliable contraceptive for men. Trojenz are available in bulk quantity through the Book Store or can be obtained at a 25% discount at any local drugstore with this coupon, which I am now handing out. Remember, as you look around the room, you will see at least five people who will have AIDS in the next ten years. Please try not to be one of them: the economic loss to our society in earnings and consumption of goods and services would be approximately $450,000. This alone should give all of you pause when you think about sex.

Next week, in the interest of equal commercial time, the sponsor for this segment of English 433 will be a spermatoidal gel whose name I am not at liberty to divulge right now. For those of you eager to know the brand, I will be able to tell you at the beginning of next week if you make an appointment with me in my "Student-Consumer Guidance Program Listing." At that time I will be able to provide you with detailed information about this amazing product.

I would also like to remind you that there will be a $5 user fee which I must collect from each of you in cash at the beginning of every future class. This fee is to pay for the rental of the room, which is the property of OPCHANGE Enterprises with offices in New York, Tokyo and Brussels. In addition, there will also be a $2.^{50} desk rental fee for each hour's use of a desk during class time. Taking notes standing, or sitting on the floor is free. I would like to point out to you, however, that we have lowered our rates by 50¢ an hour on this fee for any of you who are considering switching to the History of Commodities or Economics of Consumerism majors. We do so at considerable personal sacrifice, but in the interest of increasing volume and becoming more competitive in our field, we have decided to lower our rates. If any of you wish further details on other money-saving plans the Department of English and Advertising has in the offing, please make an appointment with me in my Consumer Guidance Listing directly after class.

And now, the product at hand: William Shakespeare. As you may know, Shakespeare was one of the greatest early entrepreneurs of Elizabethan drama. It is estimated that he earned, in 2012 adjusted dollars, approximately $90,000 a year net once he became a regular shareholder in the Lord Chamberlain's Men. When he retired from the stage in 1613, he had amassed a sufficient fortune to become an upscale member of Stratford Society, although he had left his home base in his youth with a father in debt and three dependents of his own.

The three plays we will be studying to introduce you to "Shakespeare: Man of Business" are T*he Merchant of Venice, King Lear,* and *Julius Caesar.* In the first of these, we will see how an unwise businessman, Shylock, puts personal feelings ahead of making an honest profit and comes to a bad end. In *King Lear,* we will analyze the results of a catastrophic land distribution scheme concocted by a senile old radical; and in *Julius Caesar* we will follow the downfall of a CEO who is too trusting of his board of directors, who stab him in the back when they get the chance.

But I see that time has run out on the first half of the class. I would now like to introduce you to the sponsor Trojenz, the safe way to safe sex. Remember Trojenz' motto: "Buy us now or its bye, bye later."

(Slow fade out.)
THE END?

Circassian was tempted to delete this too, as he had the letter to Pickle, but he decided it would look good on the faculty bulletin board, that is, until one of the assistant supervisors from Intell-Ex. saw it and tore it down. Some of the faculty in the English department might get a laugh out of it. Some of them were already laughing a lot for no apparent reason: in the hallways, in class, in the dining area: they had found something else funny about the situation but were afraid to share it with anyone. There were rumors that several of the adjuncts had been hired as "supervisory assistants," that is, spies, by the Company to make sure that the esprit de corps in the department would not suffer.

The Company had even insisted that Branch Stark take down his favorite sign from over his desk: "The beatings will continue until morale improves." This was regarded as poor taste and when Branch objected rather strenuously, he was removed from his position as Chair and it was given, reluctantly on his part, to Phil Frasier, a well-meaning Assistant Professor of the old school who had been known only for his wonderful calligraphy. Branch was demoted to Associate Professor and was relegated to teaching Freshman comp. along with the Adjuncts. This, the Company said, was simply to serve as an example of the need for everyone to "get with the program" and become "team players." This is also why Circassian decided to present his little jape anonymously.

As the morning classes were beginning in the English department, Circassian took the Intell-Ex. coupon book that had been put on his desk the day before by one of the Supervisory Assistants while he was out of his office. There was no longer any real privacy in the English department. To even have a department meeting that would not be reported verbatim to the Intell-Ex. Chief Supervisor, the faculty had to meet in clandestine places like the hall closets and bathrooms — which presented a problem to one or the other gender — in order to get any business done that they thought could still be their own.

The first thing that Intell-Ex. had done to make sure that their special "entry fees" to classes would not have a negative impact on attendance was develop a coupon book system. Each time class met, students would be given a coupon entitling them to some free gift or discount on CD's or weekends in the Bahamas that the corporation was able to get gratis through their connections with the tourist industry. In this way, although they were paying several hundred dollars more a semester than the students in Economics or Geography, they would get their money's worth in freebees that made the extra costs seem reasonable. Intell-Ex.'s motto, "Give them what they want and it'll be what they need," seemed to work well. By the middle of the semester, the English department was turning a profit of 14% on a volume of 2,200 students. Even their long-time rival, History, was only turning a profit of 11% but they were thinking of starting a new designer line of courses in Corporate and Consumer History, complete with a logo and animated computer graphics, which would be put on-line for all the students in each course.

This week's specials, Cicassian noted, as he walked into one of the classrooms that had been bought for the use of the department, were a Club Med weekend in St. Kitts and a special four-for-one deal on CDs at all of the branches of Sounds Fine in the immediate area. Circassian was teaching *King Lear* and feeling very much in the mood of the old King, more sinned against than sinning, when Dean Lean saw him in the hall.

He thought the Dean was trying to avoid him by hiding behind one of the ornamental pillars in the rotunda. "Say, Dean Lean," said Circassian, trying not to shout since he wasn't sure the Dean wanted to hear him, "do you know of any students that would like to sign up for my new 'Lit. of the American Empire' class next semester? I'll give you a 5% finder's fee if you steer some people my way." He heard a tortured gurgle that might have been a giggle coming from the Dean, who then quickly retreated back into his office. But Circassian really wasn't kidding. He was lucky that his Intro. Drama still sold well. He was even able to get a small commission by exceeding his quota for the class. Some people weren't so lucky. They didn't meet their quotas and their salaries were cut accordingly. Although a semblance of seniority had been observed when the corporation took over, most of the full-time faculty, now detenured, had to accept the same 35% pay cut that Circassian had been given. But instead of promoting a sense of unity among the faculty, it seemed that the back-biting continued, even increased, even though the stakes were now no longer petty.

There was a chart on the bulletin board in the office which listed the performance rates of each member of the English faculty, and although Circassian had managed to hold his own, some of the senior staff were lagging badly. There were even rumors that several would be cut and replaced with the up-and-coming Adjuncts who had handily exceeded their quotas and were continuing to come up with innovative ideas for courses to attract a larger portion of students: "Sex, Love and Death in Shelley"; "Pederasty, Perversion and Poe"; and one of Bendminder's favorite — it was he who was managing supervisor now for Intell-Ex. —"Shakespeare for the Masses: The Bard Made Easy." This was proposed as a new approach to Shakespeare using the most up-to-date versions of the plays in colloquial English with rap lyrics added. Bendminder saw this as cutting-edge and was anxious to market the texts once they were completed.

As he entered class, Circassian saw the faces of eager students — eager to know what deals Intell-Ex. was providing for this week's marketing. Circassian had initially tried to distribute the coupons at the end of class because they had been a distraction, but the students' anticipation of the buys they might have put a damper on the class period until the end, so he now decided to work on getting their attention after he had handed out the deals. Unfortunately, he had found them just as distracted about how they would take advantage of the offers as they had been waiting to know what they were in the first place.

As soon as he had handed out the coupons, the questions began:

"Hey, doc, where's St. Kitts?"

"Would it be warm enough there for spring Break?"

"Is food included in the deal?"

"What's the drinking age? I lost my fake I.D. last week."

"What are the women like?"

"What are the men like?"

He was tempted to tell them what the children were like. He filled them in on St. Kitts: mild climate, its location in the Lesser Antilles east of Puerto Rico, and something he had been given in the packet about the customs of the local inhabitants. No, he couldn't tell them anything about the drinking age, but most of the people who went would probably be expected to drink a lot.

He could see the direction of this class, which was the same as it had been for *Oedipus* and "The Second Shepherd's Play" — about fifteen minutes of teaching squeezed in somewhere between the merchandising and the high spirits of the newly invigorated student body, who would arrive in class with the eagerness of the audience at a Grateful Dead Concert in the '60's. Spring Break was only three weeks away and most of them didn't have the money for a sun-fun vacation without the discounts. That's what Intell-Ex. knew before they had purchased the English department at the University: These students would be ripe for the taking. Some were so naive they thought you float a loan by buying a yacht. And most didn't understand that the interest on their credit cards started as soon as they bought something. Like most students, they were under the impression that time stopped until they graduated. That's why a lot of them were doing their best not to.

One of the few students who seemed annoyed about all the merchandising was Mona Pilgrim. Mona, who was referred to derisively by many of her friends as "Seriously" Student, as if it were some kind of local ailment, had taken every class that Circassian had taught over the four years she had been at the University. This made her a "Circassian Major," which was difficult since he only taught four different classes. She once even retook a course with him in which she had gotten a "B⁺," ostensibly to get a higher grade but really because she thought she was in love with him. This had not happened to Circassian often, but he decided to introduce Mona to Tina one afternoon when she had gone by the office, and that seemed to have taken care of the problem. Or so he hoped.

Mona shot up her hand. "I think it's time we got to *King Lear*, Doc," she said, as a chorus of whistles and guffaws of disapproval erupted.

"Just one more question, Doc," asked a frat person who had the uniform baseball cap, brim-back, perched on his shaved head. "Do they have an extradition treaty?" Circassian didn't know, and why the frat person had asked that question he definitely did not want to know. What he now wanted to know is how many of the students wanted to know anything about *King Lear*.

He gave some of the background on Shakespeare's theater, talking in double-time since there were only the usual fifteen minutes left to teach the class. And then he launched into *Lear*, anticipating the usual questions, at least those that had been asked in the past (no, Shakespeare did not intend a pun with the name and King Lear was not a dirty old man). Once upon a time, when he first began teaching as a grad student, those comments would get a few snickers and even a chortle or two. Now the students — with Mona the exception — stared blankly at him. He was certain they hadn't read the first act. But this time he was wrong. Some of them had actually read the whole play, but it took him a few minutes to realize that this was part of a plot, probably concocted by Tilly Owlglass, the Student Council President, as a way of getting back at him for spoiling her plan to give the Student Government advertising space on the English department's bulletin boards. Actually, he had not been the only one to oppose this plan: Branch Stark and a few others of the older faculty had stood firm at the officially sanctioned meeting and put enough of a scare into Bendminder that he relented, for now. But this demanded retribution.

"Hey, Doc. Why does Lear say he's 'more sinned against than sinning?' He made those two daughters put up with a lot." This from a student who had never raised his hand or answered a question in class before. Circassian was immediately suspicious.

He tried to explain that although Lear was "difficult," he had the right to expect some filial loyalty from Regan and Goneril.

"You know what, Doc," said another rarely heard-of student. "I think that anyone who expects to put up with that crap about his fifty knights should have her head examined. My grandad lives with us and he is one big pain in the ass."

For the next ten minutes a half dozen other students, who, it seemed, were burdened with cantankerous elderly relatives, told their stories of woe.

"But they send him out into a storm!"

"He walked out himself, Doc."

"And then they barred the gates against him."

"He was acting nuts. Maybe a little bad weather would have made him get his act together."

"He was eighty years old."

"He probably had Alzheimers. He should have been put in a nursing home."

As the class ended, some of the students were starting a chant: "R and G, you're for me! R and G, you're for me!" and doing some improvised line dancing down the aisles. Circassian was actually flummoxed, something that had never happened to him in class before. But just as the contingent of line dancers was about to leave the room, they all turned toward him as if on a signal and yelled out, "JOKE!"

"What happened?" asked Circassian to the still-agitated air whiffling around the classroom.

"They planned it, Doc," said Mona. "Half of them belong to Theta Beta and Todd Zarathustra worked with them on that line before class. I overheard a couple of them talking about it when they came in. Big woof!"

It occurred to Circassian that Todd Zarathrustra was Tilly Owlglass' right-hand person. And he'd fallen for it, headfirst, without a parachute.

۞

On his way back to the office, Circassian passed Ron Burble, who looked terrible. Great fright lines creased his mouth, and his eyes almost bulged with despair.

"Hey, Ron, how's it going?" Circassian asked with just a touch of malice, since he was fairly certain that it wasn't.

"It's awful! Just awful! They told me that if I didn't get my quota up by next semester. . . . " He left off and walked down the corridor, his hands in his back pockets, as if he were feeling to see if his wallet were still there or had been mysteriously lifted by the minions of Intell-Ex.

Circassian was suddenly in a frisky mood. At least Ron Burble was miserable about something that he had always said he wanted and finally gotten: the end of "a free ride." Now he was seeing the end of his own. But since Circassian knew that gloating wasn't really that comforting, he decided to commiserate with Branch Stark about how he was taking his demotion.

As soon as he approached Branch's office, he realized he had made another mistake, his second big one of the day. But he knocked anyway and heard a soft thudding sound from inside. "Hey, Branch. You okay?"

"Hell, sure. Come the bleep in, Circassian."

Branch was sitting at his desk, the usual pile of old papers, recent brochures, unexamined and unsolicited copies of books covering it. The soft thudding noise was being made by Branch throwing little balls of Stick-em Goo at several blown-up portraits that now hung on his wall, where his favorite posters of Marlon Brando in *The Wild One*, and Paul Newman in *The Hustler* had been. One was a photo of Bendminder, smiling at a student working at a computer. A second was of Provost Pickle addressing the faculty. A third was a full-length shot of an elegantly dressed woman who Circassian realized, after looking at her for a few moments, was none other than Camille Faux, the most outspoken member of the Board of Trustees. She was a good friend of Ambler Slaughter, who was the subject of the fourth picture, on which was daubed dozens of grey pellets of fury.

"Aha!" shouted Branch, after a direct hit on Pickle's right cheek.

"I guess you're not in the mood right now," said Circassian, but the former Chair for Life of the English department motioned him to sit down on what was the only available chair in the room.

"Oho!" yelled Branch, seemingly unmindful that his booming voice was clearly audible across the corridor where several classes in English dept.-rented classrooms were taking place. He had just taken with now practiced aim at what seemed to be, and probably was, Madame Faux' genitalia beneath her colorful tulle dress.

Finally, Branch stopped his bombardment of the photos and turned to Circassian. "Well, this is the bleepin' limit, huh, Circassian? The bleepin' limit!" he snarfled.

"I guess it probably is, Branch, but there could be something worse," he added.

"Okay, you tell me. I can't think any more, anyway," said Branch, resuming his tossing at the rogues' gallery of his spirit.

"We could have been bought by Disney," Circassian said, meaning to make a joke of something he immediately realized was unjokable to Branch.

"What the hell, Circassian. What the hell."

Branch stared for a flurried moment into Circassian's eyes and what Circassian saw there was the red raw truth of hate. He was certain that if any of those photos had come to life before him, Branch Stark would have gone stark raving and torn each one of them into bits. Branch again began to aim his missiles at the photos when there was another knock on the door.

"What the bleep now? I'm busy," he shouted.

There was a timid clearing of the throat on the other side of the door, and at a nod from Branch, Circassian opened it. It was Daphne Friend, the departmental secretary. She had been almost terrified of Branch when he was Chair and now that he had lost whatever composure was expected of him, she was petrified that he might lift her up and heave her out the window. Branch was a large man with large hands.

"Prof. Stark, it's some students. They wonder when you're going to show up for class. It's ten after two. . . ."

"Damn it! Here I was on a roll and you've got to remind me what the hell I'm supposed to be doing!" And without another word, he grabbed a handful of books from his desk, his ancient briefcase with the leather handles, and bolted out the door, muttering, "Bleep it! Bleep it!" into the corridor. Halfway down he stopped, turned around, and came back. He apparently had taken his books for "Kings of Industry and the American Dream" when what he needed was his freshman text. A moment later he had grabbed the right books, dropped the others on the floor, and was walking again down the corridor now muttering, "Shit for brains," and other self-abusive ephithets. When he got to his classroom at the end of the corridor, there was a moment of silence, a clearly audible, "Oh boy!" and then the slam of a door being shut with behemythic force. Both Circassian and Daphne Friend winced at the same time and then looked at each other.

"He's been like this for days," she said. "I don't know where it will end. Mr. Bendminder has been prowling around lately, to check on morale, he says, and he hears the thumping."

"Maybe Professor Stark better take a leave of absence," suggested Circassian, which, he realized as soon as he said it, was with naive grace.

"He can't. They abolished leaves of absence in the new contract for the department. I can't even take a sick day without a note both from the doctor and my minister," Daphne added, almost sobbing. It had not been easy for her either. The only fortunate thing about her situation since the English department's sale was that she was actually given a slight raise since her pay was so laughably low under the old administration that even Intell-Ex. was ashamed to keep her at that salary. It was quite another thing with the faculty which, according to Bendminder's computations, were not at all worth their keep under the old system and barely worth it under the new one.

On his way home, Circassian stopped to get a paper at Bart's and bumped into Clarence Ridge, one of the Town Fathers.

"Well, I see you boys are finally getting someone in there that knows how to run things," Clarence twitted Circassian.

"Who's that?" asked Circassian. He was already tired of the jokes, he was already tired of being on the defensive, and barely a month into the semester, he was already tired.

When he'd gotten home, he found Tina packing a bag.

"Now, you're leaving me!" he whined.

"Stop whining! I've got to go to the City for a couple of days to meet with some of the people from the firm. They want to show me the new programs and it'll be easier if I do it hands on than over the net." She looked at him for a moment with pity, but then went back to packing. It had been a rough month for her too, since Circassian didn't feel like whining to the people in the department who were whining enough to each other, especially the ones who used to have the highest pay, so he had whined to her, and she wasn't the sort of woman to whine back.

Now, on top of feeling lousy about everything except that everyone else in the department was in same boat he was, Circassian would have to spend the next few days alone, abandoned and bereft, reminded of Tina every time he'd go into the kitchen to find something to eat and not know where it was. He felt as helpless as a flounder in a tub of batter but, as he recalled, not as helpless as President Fred when he had delivered the speech to the faculty that had been originally written for him by Marigold Markham the day after the buy-out of English and History.

There were about as many faculty who turned out for that speech in the Main auditorium as Circassian had ever remembered seeing in one place at one time. Ralph Null was there, and Gladys DeFoe, and Frank Short, and Ron Burble, and Gutsky and Shotman, in a sad, "*vey iz mir,*" tandem, and Dabs Budweiser and Hank Schecht, Trent Butler, Lee Ann Fitz-Proust, Pastor Castor, Frank Short, and of course Deans Lean and Steen, VP T.P. Sealey and Provost Pickle. Branch had been conspicuous in his absence, telling Circassian when he'd asked if he was coming that he "wouldn't give that dumb putz-head the satisfaction."

Fred began his speech with the usual genuflections to the faculty, staff, concerned friends and general public, the latter of which none came and most of which wouldn't care if the University levitated into the night and disappeared forever. Unfortunately, he had misplaced his glasses and so most of Marigold's sharpness was dulled through improvisation.

"We have been given a challenge that will test our resolve to continue to offer a high-quality education at a low-quantity cost, but the road is filled with pit holes and wharfs and we have to find our compass where we may.

"I come to you, in the fourteenth year of my Presidency, with confidence that we are up to this challenge as we have been up to a lot of other challenges that have challenged us over the time gone by. And we know whereof we speak; we've been there . . . and we've done that . . . and we can do it again." (Long pause while Fred waited for applause and fumbled to find his glasses, unsuccessfully.)

"We are not easily dismayed by the forces without as much as we are heartened by the forces within that will enable us to maintain ourselves in the style to which we are accustomed. And I am certain that when this debacle is over, we will meet again here, fulfilled and perhaps even overwhelmed by our success. For succeed we will and do our darnedest to make that success something we can tell our grandchildren about when we have them, unless, of course, we have them already in which case we can tell them right away.

"All I can offer you now is my undying support and confidence that whatever the future may hold we will be up to it, and hold aloft as our flag our love of learning, the traditions of this institution, and a faith that the Almighty is somewhere in the wings, waiting to snatch us from the jaws of defeat and put us on the lips of triumph.

"Are there any questions?"

There was first about a full minute of silence in which people around the auditorium looked at each other and shrugged. There was so much shrugging going on that Fred, who could barely see very far with his glasses on and nothing but petulant blobs with them off, thought that the faculty were about to assault him and were flexing their muscles before the attack. He began to flinch and cower when Marigold, almost too embarrassed by the hash he had made of her written speech, came to his rescue by repeating the request for questions.

Josh Gutsky raised his hand first, as he usually did when something was particularly confusing, and simply asked if Fred could repeat the last part because Josh thought he had missed something. Since it was apparent to Marigold that Josh had missed nothing and probably found something that wasn't there, she went onto the next question, which was from Lee Ann Fitz-Proust.

"How will the sale of the English and History departments affect the gender ratio of the faculty in the future?"

"Huh?" said Fred.

"That's an irrelevant question at present," interrupted Marigold. "We don't know yet whether gender is covered under the new contract with Intell-Ex. Next question."

"What the hell are you talking about, President Fred?" This from Trent Butler, who, like Branch, called them like he saw them.

"Can you be more specific?" asked Fred, quickly cutting off Marigold, who he knew would probably get him into trouble with her wit.

Trent Butler decided he had made his point and sat down. Only a few other people ventured questions, such as, would there be more sales of departments, what about seniority, where did anyone get the right to do this, and who was responsible in the first place?

"There will be a detailed memo responding to these questions that President Fred will send out to all of you early next week. As far as concerns about who had the right to do this, I would suggest that you look at Option Three in your contract. The Union approved it, you voted for it, and now we all have to live with it," added Marigold, skillfully deflecting the growing wrath of the assembled from Fred to Dabs Budweiser, who was now bombarded and pummelled and pilloried with questions. That is how the meeting ended, dying off with more shrugs, some head-scratching and a few loud chuckles from several of the local wits that were still functioning among the faculty.

The next day there was a counter-speech by Dabs Budweiser to try to repair what was now left of a shrivelled reputation for being up front in all things concerning management. She led a rally in front of the steps of Main, hoping that some people besides the members of the English and History departments would show up. But the faculty who, as usual, demonstrated their backbone to be something in their tailbone, opted for meeting their classes and being "responsible."

Dabs' counter-speech was barely more coherent than Fred's. She promised that the Union leadership would be coming down soon to demonstrate their solidarity with the still- unsold departments. But when Circassian raised his hand to ask a question, she reacted as if he were about to fling a cow chip in her direction. "Is this legal?" he asked.

Dabs waited until there was maximum noise around her, and then shouted as unintelligibly as possible: "Yes." She paused until the crowd began to disperse, and added, "But it's immoral."

Hank Schecht paused a moment before asking a question that he regretted as soon as it was out of his mouth. "But the faculty who just had their departments bought out from under them can count on the Union support, can't they?" He was trying to buck up the half-dozen dazed Full Professors who were still standing beside Dabs in an academic's form of sticker shock. Dabs had been signing to Hank, "No, no, no" in big letters, but was too late, because it suddenly occurred to Circassian:

"They can't do a damned thing for us because we're no longer members of the Union, right Dabs?"

"Technically, that's correct but we are examining the process by which you were de-unionized. We think it's grievable."

"But not winnable," Circassian said, beginning to walk away with the others who had commenced that buzzing, muttering sound that had since become a common drone in the English department office and in the corridors on their wing of Main. He heard Dabs calling after him as if he were Shane: "Don't worry, Circassian. We're not going to let you down."

That had been almost a month ago. As Circassian expected, nothing had happened since. The head of the Union, Bob Wallet, had come down a week later to say a few words at another rally, which was sparsely if raucously attended. But when Circassian again asked what the Union could do for English and History, the only answer he got was that they were "studying it," as if it were some strange foreign substance that had seeped through the cracks of their well-being. Because until Option Three had been used by Bendminder, the Union had felt that all was going well, despite the loss of about one third of the positions in the University over the previous decade. Now it looked like it would only be a matter of time before other segments of the University would be sold off as well, unless, of course, the plan turned into a fiasco. But with Bendminder in charge of the numbers, Wallet knew, the privatization profits would always end up in the black.

()

Tilly Owlglass was sitting in the Student Government office, going over a column of figures with Todd Zarathustra. They had managed to factor in everything they could imagine going wrong and still came up with a net profit of $100,000. This surplus could then be used the following year for any eventualities, but with the guaranteed revenue from the new $25 annual entertainment fee they had gotten passed by a compliant Student Senate at the beginning of the semester, they could realize another $150,000 in the coming year. Tilly was aware that the fee might be rescinded by her successor, but since she had cultivated Mary Magdalene for the position, and since Mary's main interest was in the Bible study programs, she would be willing to get on board in exchange for a considerable increase in the budgets of her favorite clubs, the ones with a spiritual dimension.

"We can even get Iggy Pop with this kind of money," Tilly said, and Todd smiled assent. He knew that agreeing with everything that Tilly Owlglass said was the surest way to get supporting funds for the activities that the Greeks particularly favored, such as karate, rugby and polo.

"I can see it now: In ten years, the University will have one of the biggest rock concert programs in the state. All we need to do is convince VP T.P. Sealey to support our using the football stadium for the concerts."

"What if it rains?" Todd ventured.

"We've got Mary M. on our side. She'll pray," Tilly said, a slight snicker in her voice.

Tilly was tall and blonde. From the time she'd been seven, she'd had the face of a woman you would not want to mess with and a squeaky voice that she tried to modulate but would break when she became excited. She had planned the takeover of the Student Government from the time she'd been a high school senior class president, bound for the University. By her freshman year, she was already treasurer of the Student Government and was recruiting allies who would run for the Student Senate, always successfully, since rarely was there more than one candidate for each position. Her father had prepared her well; he was a presidential advisor and CEO of his own polling firm.

Some of the students had squawked when the new entertainment fee had been imposed, but except for Mona Pilgrim's rally, which only drew fifteen students, there was no real opposition. This was particularly true when Tilly announced the program for the spring semester, which included a few groups that most of the students recognized, and, in the spirit of multiculturalism, one rap group, a Latin combo, and a Chinese jazz quartet directly from Beijing.

"I only hope it doesn't rain," repeated Todd. He wanted Tilly to reassure him, especially since rain was as common in that climate as mildew in the Amazon basin.

"Well, we can put a dome on the stadium. I've checked with those people over at Intell-Ex. and they said they'd look into it."

"How'd you get them to do that?" asked Todd.

"I promised to let them rename the stadium Intell-Ex. Bowl. They were hot on the idea," Tilly answered.

Todd seemed bowled over, but he had suspected that Tilly would try something like that. Todd wasn't terribly bright, but he was a stickler for tradition. "The Stadium's named after Coach Hank 'Spear-'em' Mattel, Tilly. He's almost a god around here. And I don't think it's a good idea to mess with a god." He really felt that Tilly had overreached this time.

"It'll be hyphenated of course," she said, a slight, sly smile on her slightly cunning face. "The Mattell-Intell-Ex. Bowl. It even rhymes."

"Oh, that's different then," said Todd.

Tilly had other plans, however, that made the dome over the Stadium and the rock programs look like a modest beginning for her Big Picture. She was reluctant to discuss it with Todd, but since he controlled about a third of the votes in the Student Senate, she felt that he'd better be told before he found out from someone else. She was planning to invest some of the Student Government funds into a share of the purchase of the Psych department, and Todd was a psych major.

"They've got over seven hundred majors," she said, "and they've got a guaranteed 60% share of the freshman class since the Ed. department requires Ed. Psych and they can't get Ed. Psych without Psych 100. It's a fuckin' goldmine, Todd!"

Tilly was really getting excited now, and the fiduciary possibilities made her think of sex. She calmed herself with a can of Surge and went on. "I've got Intell-Ex. interested but there's another company that's looking for an investment in the University: Compel-Tex; they make educational technology and video games — one of those interlocking conglomerates. We can have a bidding war, and if you help me bring this off, there's a 5% finder's fee from the company that lands the department. We can split it."

She was getting excited again, but Todd was out of the question; she never felt comfortable having sex with an inferior being.

Tilly had the good luck as well as savvy that whenever she got into trouble with one of her deals, she would always be able to land on somebody else's feet. Todd's size eleven's seemed very comforting to her.

◊

That weekend, while Tina was out of town, Circassian got a phone call from Mona

Pilgrim. She had been in another part of the office doing some clerical work for the Student Government when Tilly and Todd had been making their plans. With her keen sense of hearing and the aid of a special listening device that she'd just happened to have with her, she had been able to overhear everything they said. She somehow thought that Circassian would be interested in the next department take-over. He really wasn't.

"Thanks for the information, Mona, but right now I'm getting ready for my classes next week. Anyway, I expected that something like this would happen. Psych is a much more attractive buy than either English or History. Intell-Ex. was really sold a bill of goods when they bought us." Circassian realized that he was beginning to sound like Them, Them being the Pickles and Bendminders of the world.

"Don't you really care what happens to the people in the Psych department?" She sounded annoyed at him for the first time that he could remember in their frequent chats at his office. But that was literature; this was commerce.

"I guess I'm a little numb about what's happening to the people in the English department, but you're right; I should be concerned. There has to be a way to stop it. I have no idea what that is, but maybe you can come over sometime and we could talk about it some more," he answered. He didn't want her to think that he was being callous, although that's what he was hoping he could be; then it would be easier for him to teach.

What Circassian didn't realize is that when he said "maybe you can come over" Mona would think he meant his house, and when he said "sometime" she thought he meant "tonight." So when he answered the doorbell at nine o'clock after making himself a dyspeptic meal with some freezer-burned frozen dinners, he did not expect to see Mona standing in the doorway, dressed in what she must have imagined was a very sexy outfit.

Mona had a very decent figure and was not at all unattractive, but in the state Circassian was in, it wouldn't have mattered if she were a Greta Garbo look-alike or a Madonna twin. He missed Tina and was thinking about getting to bed early, with no one but himself. But he realized, a little too slowly, that Mona had other plans.

"Well, hell . . . hello," Circassian said, tongue-tied. "What brings you here, Mona?"

"Didn't you just invite me?" she asked, cunningly, which Circassian seemed to miss. He was missing a lot of things in these hellish days, even an obvious move by the student for whom he was the Favorite.

"I thought we could discuss this matter in my office, maybe next week. I didn't mean . . ." He left the sentence, which had begun to hang in the air like an unwanted elbow in the ribs, unfinished.

"May I come in?" Mona asked, coming into the house.

"I guess . . . sure," Circassian babbled. He didn't seem to know what to do. If only Tina were here; but then, he remembered telling Mona after class the day before that Tina was gone for the weekend, and complaining that he'd probably get sick from food poisoning by the time she got back. He hadn't thought of it as an invitation.

Not knowing what else to do, he offered Mona some liquid refreshment: "We've got all sorts of fruit juice . . . that is, I thought we had but there's a whole bottle of prune juice if you'd. . . ." He'd gone into the kitchen, expecting Mona to follow him. It was only a moment he'd been in there when he heard what at first he thought was an imaginary sound: a little girl laugh that could have only come from a big girl. He saw a light down the hall that at first he hoped was the bathroom; it was the bedroom.

When he walked in he really hadn't expected to see Mona, her clothes strewn in various parts of the room, in the chaos of the bedclothes that Circassian had left around, sitting in the middle of the bed under the covers, a red ribbon around her neck and her version of a lustful smile on her face. To Circassian, who hadn't been in this kind of situation since his years in grad school, it appeared more as if she were trying to hide a stomach cramp and was doing a poor job of it.

"Take me, Doc! Do anything you want with me," she chuffled and smarmed in a low foggy voice.

"I don't know what . . ." Again Circassian seemed unable to find a way to complete a sentence because while he was groping for words, Mona had gotten off the bed, decked out only with the ribbon, and was beginning to grope him.

In another moment, Circassian got his first good idea of the night: He bolted for the bathroom and locked himself in. At first he thought that Mona, who was not nearly as sturdy as the formidable Tilly Owlglass, would still manage to break down the door. Then she tried being coy, which didn't work either. Finally, she began to cry. This was not what Circassian had bargained for; he had an inherited weakness for a woman's tears, and so when he peeked out of the bathroom door and saw Mona's face-swollen eyes, he felt he should try to comfort her. This led to the second fundamental misunderstanding of the evening.

When he finally was able to get Mona out of the house, with tender words of affection if not love, he realized that he had made a grave mistake, not the kind that he thought could lead him to lose his job, but the kind that could lead other people to get him fired. And he really hadn't done much of anything; Mona had been busy enough for both of them. He wouldn't call what happened between them sex, but he knew that a lot of other people might not see it that way.

It was with this sticking in his mind like a newly sprung wart on a model's nose that made him self-conscious when he came into the office the following Monday — and there was Mona, waving hello to him with a blissful smile on her face. How long he could keep her smile there without compromising himself was something he didn't want to think about. It was one of a dozen things he had to think about and didn't want to as he began the week.

◊

While Tilly Owlglass was making her plans, Bendminder was making his. He saw the initial sale of the two departments as just the beginning of what would be a Grand Plan. What it would entail was difficult for him to predict, since, although he had always thought of himself as a Big Picture man, like Pickle, he had never had an opportunity to do much with his aspirations.

He was looking forward to the next meeting of the Intell-Ex. English department. The district manager, Jack Swift, would be there to, as he liked to say, "stir the kettle a bit," a metaphor Bendminder, who had almost flunked English in college and loathed the subject as something that spoiled the way people read, particularly enjoyed. Swift was a hot-shot manager who had previously organized Intell-Ex.'s Bangor branch and then had been promoted to Boston. Although the College Campaign was merely another step upward, it was considered a challenge and the English dept. branch was among the most challenging. Its productivity lagged considerably behind other corporate acquisitions in the University system, which included a set of three Computer Science departments, an Economics department and one Philosophy department, which was acquired for a tax break.

When Circassian walked into the conference room, he was surprised to see everyone there. Not that the department was notorious for lack of participation in its deliberations, but several of the adjuncts who lived about sixty miles away had made the time to go to a Friday afternoon meeting on a snowy day. Whether they were there to mourn or gloat would depend on the direction in which the meeting would go.

Phil Frasier made a brief introduction for Bendminder, who, in turn, introduced Jack Swift. Swift was a very tall man, taller than either Burble or Ralph Null, but he gave the appearance of being so tall that it seemed doubtful that anyone would be able to reach him at eye-level talk, even if he was sitting down. He knew that being tall had helped him a great deal in his career, and he took his tallness as a point of particular pride, like an unusually fine achievement. He had also developed his voice so it would sound as if it were coming from a great distance, although it was quite distinct. This gave people the impression that he wasn't really listening to them, because from that distance he wouldn't be able to hear them, no matter how loudly they talked. So when they began to shout, he could always tell them to calm down, which put them at a disadvantage from the start.

"I'm pleased to present to you our District Supervisor, Jack Swift. Jack has a degree in business from the Wharton School and has been with Intell-Ex. for over twenty years. He has managed a number of projects but, and I hope I am not speaking out of turn, regards the English department as his most interesting assignment." Bendminder chuffled. He couldn't resist emphasizing the word "interesting."

Jack Swift, who had, until this point, been sitting with his legs crossed in such a way as to suggest a praying mantis about to strike, suddenly stood up and seemed to be in danger of his head banging against the ceiling as he unfolded himself. (In addition to his actual 6'7" he liked to wear two-inch heels, since once he had been confronted by a 6'8" employee, which had made him feel very uncomfortable.)

"Thank you for that brief introduction, 'Stats.' I want to get down to the gist of this meeting right away. That way you can all get back to what you do best: providing our consumers with the knowledge-product. Now 'Stats,' if you can just show those charts you put together."

Bendminder had made up several charts on Power Point. Before them were the bottom-line figures of the English department for the past five years. The black line, which indicated productivity, calculated by taking the number of credit hours students generated divided by the number of total hours taught, had been going down each year. The red line, which indicated cost per student unit, was going up, much more slowly in the same years, but still rising.

The second graphic was a break-down, in descending order, of the productivity of individual members of the department, with the bottom three names being those of Daphne Dart, Harold Hanes and Toddy Dance. Although the rest of the department had suspected that these three probably had the most well-known reputations as "difficult," the figures on the chart seemed devastating, at least to Bendminder and Jack Swift.

"As you can see, these numbers are not very encouraging right now, but I intend to see them reversed by the beginning of the next season. It's not going to be as difficult as you think, team, if you follow my suggestions to the letter."

He gave every member of the department a single page of suggestions, which seemed to elicit a collective gasp from all assembled. Several laughed; several others seemed to be restraining themselves from weeping, but there was silence after that first reaction for a full sixty seconds. Then Daphne Dart raised her hand.

"What you're trying to do is lower our standards, Mr. Swift. You should realize that all of these suggestions . . ."

"Will get your numbers back up where they belong," Jack Swift interrupted. "This is why we bought into the education industry; to make a profit; not to lollygag around with programs that simply aren't getting the numbers in the right direction."

"I'm not sure what you mean by 'Fun-100' to replace our Freshman comp course," asked Harold Hanes. He had a deep voice which made him sound like a train announcer with a bad cold, and partly due to that the students had nicknamed him "Sleeper Hanes," because he never changed the tone he spoke in.

"One of the first principles of marketing is that first impressions make the sale. If you give a lousy first impression, then you might as well fold up your tent and sneak away. The first impression you give with Freshman comp is of a very difficult, low-grade level product that isn't particularly inviting to the consumers. We've done studies all over the country on this particular product, and if it weren't a requirement everywhere, it would never sell. We tried an experiment at one of our acquisitions in North Dakota and made Freshman comp an elective. It went down to a twenty per cent market share from the ninety-eight per cent among freshman it had before. So we figured we would build back the share with Fun-100, and it's worked so well that we've nearly recovered all of the ground that we had lost. Besides, Fun-100 shouldn't be such a novelty to you. Branch Stark experimented with something like that a few years ago, if I'm not mistaken." He pointed to Branch, who seemed ready to yarp a protest, but considering that he had already been demoted the last time he had opened his mouth, he thought better of it.

What Stark had experimented on, with Josh Gutsky, was a video-based section of Freshman comp. that introduced students to writing by using visual examples. But the point of the course was to stimulate writing with a relatively limited number of videos. What Fun-100 meant was almost exclusive use of videos. Gutsky thought he might try to clarify that point, but by this time Jack Swift had launched on his plan.

"The idea is to make consumers realize how much fun writing can be; so you have to make it fun. Be creative; think of ways to get them to be interested in you, not just the subject. Wear bright colors to class, dress up in costumes at appropriate times, like wearing green and a shamrock hat around St. Patrick's Day; or a beard and stove top hat for President's Weekend. Circassian: you teach drama; I want you to give me a few ideas on how to make the classes more theater by next week. Gutsky, you and Branch come up with a few ideas on a series of videos. We've got the staff to put them together."

"And what if we don't?" asked Branch, finally having raised his big paw in the air against his better judgement.

"Doesn't matter; we have a whole series of Fun-100 videos that we're going to start using next fall if you don't come up with something better. You'll see, by the time word gets around, the kids'll be killing each other to get into Freshman comp."

Swift seemed to soar with enthusiasm as he began to put a DVD into a player. Before any image had appeared on the screen, a howling sound erupted in the room that seemed to come from the depths of hell. It was a wail and a groan and a yelp and the grinding of enormous gears that apparently had been clogged with sand and ball-bearings. A bright green-and-red logo of a clown and two peppy-looking youngsters dressed in shorts and tank tops appeared on the screen. Then a voice that sounded like Dick Clark in his prime announced: "Hey, gang: time to start grooving with Fun-100: it's cool, it's now, it's awesome, it's radical, it's the bomb: it's how to write and have fun, all in one!"

Then the screen was bombarded with a series of images, including Shakespeare, Dickens, Mariah Carey, Blondie, Joe DiMaggio, O.J. Simpson, JFK, LBJ, FDR, Ronald Reagan, Woodstock, Andy Warhol, Frank Sinatra, Bill Clinton on sax, Harry Truman on piano, Charlie Parker, Torie Amos, ABBA, Joe McCarthy, Roy Rodgers, Michael Jordan, Jerry Stiller, the Empire State Building, the Golden Gate Bridge, Mick Jagger, Einstein, Martin Luther King, Fred Astaire and Ginger Rodgers, Richard Nixon, Mark McGwire, Fidel Castro, Death Valley, a Toyota, a dead sheep in a slaughterhouse, George Gershwin, Clint Black, Lefrak City, Beaver Cleaver, Auschwitz, John Belushi, Henry Kissinger, the Statue of Liberty, and Janis Joplin, to name a few.

"The rest of this is interactive," explained Jack Swift, swiftly turning it off. "But you can see how it can grab them."

"How does it teach them to write?" asked Branch. He was on the edge of the pit, but by now he didn't care. Besides, his numbers on the chart were just about in the middle — not too bad, not great, respectable.

"The prompts will ask them questions about what they see, and then they'll have to answer them by writing in the program; it will automatically evaluate how well they did. There's a whole sequence for each unit. By the end of the last unit, these kids will actually like to write, and they'll be begging for more stuff from your department. It can't miss!" Jack Swift was getting caught up in his vision, as was Bendminder. The English department members looked at each other as if to confirm what they saw, but it wasn't a vision.

"What supplementary text do you use for their reading?" asked Toddy Dance. He normally never spoke at meetings, but he had a sudden compulsion.

"There are no supplementary texts," Jack Swift answered. "Everything you need is right in this box," he said, holding up a square black box with the words, "Fun-100; Intell-Ex. Educational Resources" printed in bright gold letters across the top. "There's the master DVD and two other shorter videos on composing the paper and editing. The interactive software will do the rest. All you need to do is go over the drafts with them, once they're finished. The program practically runs itself!"

"But what do they read?" asked Daphne Dart.

"They don't. That's the beauty of the whole system," said Jack Swift. "We've found in our research that what discourages most kids from writing is that they have to read. Reading is really a drag for most of them, and they don't like it very much. Of course, there are the exceptions, but that's the thing: they are exceptions. For most of the knowledge-consumers in our surveys, when asked to choose between reading and interactive learning with our programs, our system won hands down. We've noticed that when we've been observing their reading habits, that most of them begin to get up and do something else, drift off or fall asleep after ten minutes, fifteen at the most. These consumers today are just not meant for reading — that is, from a book. But give them Fun-100 and they can be at it for hours. You'll have to practically kick them out of the room at the end of class!"

"What you're suggesting we do is to end civilization!" Josh Gutsky called out, without even raising his hand.

"You mean *your* idea of civilization," said Jack Swift, a steely sterness creeping into his voice. He hadn't been known among his employees when he was in Boston as Jack "Ripper" Swift for nothing. "It happens that most young people today have a different idea of civilization, and that's the one we're going to market. You guys have been living in the 'Shadowlands' most of your lives, and we're going to take you out into daylight. It might not be too pretty for you to see at first, but it's there and we're not going to let you turn your back on it any more if you want to work for Intell-Ex.!"

"I thought that these were just suggestions," said Harold Hanes.

"The kind of suggestions you can't afford to ignore," said Jack Swift. "In Intell-Ex., we like to think of ourselves as a team; that's why we make suggestions, not give orders. But if you don't want to take our suggestions after they've been reasonably presented to you, they can be orders."

"Well, I, for one, am not going to do it," said Daphne, a slight tremor in her voice.

"Somebody fire that woman!" Jack Swift shot back, and turned to Bendminder.

"Uh, Jack, I don't think you can just do that," said Bendminder in half a whisper.

"Why not? You mean I can't just fire anyone I want to? Who told you that?"

Daphne walked stiffly out of the room, trying to hold back her tears. True to academic form, nobody else moved

"I think there's some kind of precedure we've had for a while; it's called due process," Bendminder tentatively added.

"Well, that's one hell of a note!" said Jack Swift. "We'll see about that! Meeting adjourned." And with those last words, he walked out the door, leaving the black box of "Fun-100" DVDs in the middle of the conference table, like a time bomb. Bendminder left a moment later.

Nobody spoke for over a minute, and then Branch Stark opened up: "This is one fucked-up situation if I've ever seen it! Phil, can they fire Daphne?"

"I don't know, Branch. There's a lot of opinion on what he can do on one side or another, but I'm sure it's not certain," Phil ventured. This was, for him, bold talk, since he didn't like to be speculative and he wasn't really willing to venture a guess.

"Well, we can be sure of one thing: a lot of students would just love to take a course like Fun-100. No reading! It's sure-fire," said Josh Gutsky, giving the rest a quick glance for a reaction.

"Does anyone want to do anything, or do we just sit around and wait for that shark to eat us all?" asked Circassian. He hadn't said anything until then, but he decided that he might as well try to put a little life into the living dead sitting around the conference table.

"Well, I'm not going to stay here with my thumb up my ass," said Branch. "Let's go over to Dean Lean and tell him what happened."

He got up and walked out of the room, expecting the rest to follow, but by the time he had gotten to the Dean's office, it was just he and Circassian. The rest hadn't felt quite as strongly about Daphne, whom most of them secretly disliked anyway since she had now the lowest per capita ratings in the department and was pulling the rest of them down. There was a touch of doom about her, now, which they didn't want to get too near to for fear they, too, might be infected. And Jack Swift had really frightened them. They had never seen anyone fired before, even if it might not stick, but the experience had put most of them, particularly Toddy Dance and Harold Hanes, into a state of well-deserved paranoia.

When Branch Stark and Circassian had gotten over to Dean Lean's office, the dean had by then abandoned his shadow play and was now indulging in obscene crossword puzzles that he had picked up somewhere on the net. Naturally, he was a little frazzled when Branch buzzed in, unannounced, Circassian behind him, just as he had come up with a six-letter French word for whore.

"Why are you here, Branch? Aren't you supposed to be teaching?"

"We were just at a department meeting with that son of a bitch Jack Swift," Branch bellowed, sitting down in front of the Dean.

"Swift? Oh, yes, the District Manager for Intell-Ex. I met him just the other day. Quite a snappy dresser, isn't he? And very tall." The Dean chuffed. He had no idea why Branch had called Swift a son of a bitch except that Branch had been using that term to describe a lot of people lately.

"I don't give a flying bleep how he dresses, Lean! He just fired Daphne Dart or told Bendminder, that other son of a bitch, to fire her. How'd you like them apples?" Branch sat as immovable as a great oak in an apple orchard, directly in front of Dean Lean.

"Did Bendminder say anything?" Dean Lean asked after a moment's pause. He didn't want to pause too long because he didn't want to know what Branch might begin to say about him.

"He told that bastard that there was something called due process, but I don't think Swift knows due process from a warm turd. I just want to know if he can fire her."

"Well, he can and he can't; it depends on how Pickle interprets Swift's jurisdiction, but it's also probably out of our hands," Dean Lean explained, as lucidly as he dared.

"You mean it's Option Three?" asked Circassian, nodding along with the Dean.

"Well, yes, it is. You see, Branch, the English department is still under the jurisdiction of the University because we can't afford to do without you."

"But it really couldn't afford to keep us as part of the University budget," Circassian continued. By now he knew the drill.

"That's right, Circassian. See, he understands," said Dean Lean, a shifting smile on his face which he was prepared to erase instantly if Branch scowled.

"I really don't, Dean Lean. Explain it to me," added Circassian.

"Well, it's a little complicated, but since Swift's company owns the English department, he can make personnel decisions if he wants to, but Daphne Dart can appeal to the Administration to ask him to reconsider because of due process," the Dean explained, floundering somewhere in his explanation for an explanation.

"And what happens if she appeals?" asked Branch, beginning to steam ever so slightly while he sat tightly in the chair.

"I'm sure Pickle will back her. After all, we stand for due process for all the faculty," said Dean Lean. "That's part of academic rights and privileges."

"So Swift can't really fire her," said Circassian.

"Of course he can; he has the final say on any personnel matters in the English department. But if we appealed to him nicely, he just might let Daphne stay. What did she do to make him fire her?"

"She refused to get on board and become a team player," said Branch, looking at the Dean to see if he could catch any sign of levity in those morose features.

"Well, I don't think we can do much about that. But ask her to come in sometime before she has to leave and we'll see what we can do."

"It doesn't seem to me that you're going to do much of anything! Except sit around with your thumb up your ass!" Branch suddenly bellowed. This caused Dean Lean to almost fall backwards off his swivel chair, but he righted himself in time.

"I wouldn't put it that way if I were you, Branch," said Dean Lean in what could almost be seen as a warning. Dean Lean didn't want to warn people because he wasn't supposed to; that was Pickle's job, which he didn't much care to do. That left it to Marigold Markham to write the warning memos.

"How would you put it?" Branch asked, getting up from the chair and staring down at the Dean.

"I would say that there's a question of who has the final say on this kind of matter; I would say it's not completely resolved; that it wasn't something we thought of when we signed the contract with Intell-Ex. But if you want, why not see Pickle? He'll give you an answer."

"See Pickle? Who the bleep sees Pickle any more? When was the last time you saw him?" asked Branch.

"That's neither here nor there," said Dean Lean, who hadn't actually seen Pickle in the flesh for about two months.

"Well, I just hope Pickle is here rather than there," said Branch, strompling out of the room like a herd of wildebeestes or an insulted pride of lions. He strode, Circassian in tow, out the door of Main, only dressed in his jacket, sweater and blue jeans against the chill winter air.

When he and Circassian got to the fourth floor of the Administration Building, the word had obviously gotten out from Dean Lean's office that Branch Stark was on the rampage, because as he passed the doors of each office on the way to Pickle's, the secretaries and some of the administration minions stuck their heads out timidly like spectators at the running of the bulls in Pamplona.

Branch walked into Pickle's office and over to Pickle's personal secretary, Rachel Rue, as if he were about to knock her down, desk and all. "I would like to see Provost Pickle. . . please," he added as a definite afterthought.

"Provost Pickle is at a meeting off campus. He won't be back until tomorrow," lied Rachel Rue. This was one of her most important jobs: lying for Pickle.

"Well, when can I see him tomorrow?" asked Branch, almost ready to compromise.

"He's at meetings all day tomorrow. Come back next week and maybe we can arrange. . . ."

"Bleep next week!" bleared Branch. "I know he's somewhere around here; you just aren't going to tell me."

"You're right: I'm not going to tell you," said Rachel, folding her arms and meeting Branch's gaze with a steely one of her own. She was fairly certain that Branch wouldn't hit a woman. But while they were staring each other up and down, Circassian noticed out of the corner of his eye someone signaling to him. He turned slightly; it was Marigold Markham peeking out of her office.

Circassian nudged Branch, hoping to divert him from his staredown with Rachel. Branch was almost mesmerized now and seemed impervious to Circassian's hints.

"Say Branch, when you finish here you can find me in Marigold's office," Circassian said as casually as possible.

When he walked in Marigold had a sign in front of her reading: "Don't say a word; my office is bugged," and she slipped Circassian a piece of paper with the message: "4-Tony's Lanes." He gave Marigold a quick and grateful smile and walked out of the office, nudging Branch to follow. Branch had finally gotten tired of staring and turned on Circassian: "Who put a bug up your ass?" he asked.

"Don't worry; it's okay," said Circassian, waving to Rachel Rue, who was also tired of staring. Finally, with an "I shall return look," Branch walked out the door.

"Marigold gave me what we were looking for," Circassian explained when they were out of earshot of the many ears on the fourth floor and into the elevator. He showed Branch the paper. Tony's Lanes was a well-known hangout for serious bowlers, and Pickle was known to be a serious bowler with a handicap that didn't interfere at all with his bowling.

"You bowl?" asked Branch.

"I used to bowl when I was in college," said Circassian. "I guess I can still knock over a couple of pins if I try."

"I don't care whether you still can or not; I was just wondering what anyone, even Pickle, sees in such a stupid, bleeped-up game," said Branch. Branch had once bowled when he was seventeen and had gotten his back out, something that happened to him periodically ever since. He hated bowling with a passion he normally held for Republicans. But at four o'clock they were at Tony's Lanes, pretending to be getting themselves ready for bowling.

They wanted to check whether Pickle was a regular or just turned up periodically, so they asked a few of the locals who seemed to be hanging out, getting ready for leagues to start, if they knew anyone named Pickle. After the usual jokes about the name, no one seemed to find it familiar. Then they described him. His florid face was what identified him to a short, severe-looking man with a stiletto smile and a Chicago Cubs baseball cap.

"I think you must mean Moe Grange. Yeah, he comes here about two, three times a week. Not bad either. I'd say he bowls one-eighty, one-ninety pretty steady."

"Moe Grange?" asked Circassian. "Are you sure that's the one we're talking about?"

"Sounds like him. He runs a feed store somewhere around here, although I never heard of it. Probably in one of those little towns on the other side of the valley."

"I guess he doesn't want anyone to know who he is for obvious reasons," said Circassian to Branch.

"You mean if they knew who he was around here they'd hate his guts just as much as we do?" asked Branch.

A few minutes after four, Provost Pickle showed up, alone, carrying his own bowling bowl in a bowling bag. "Yeah, that's him," said stiletto smile. He walked up to Pickle, said something to him, laughed, and clapped him on the back. Pickle got an alley, took out his ball, shined it up, removed his shoes and put on the bowling shoes he had brought with him. He was completely oblivious to the fact that Circassian and Branch were standing behind him when he began to move down the lane.

"Provost Pickle!" called out Branch just as Pickle was about to release the ball. It scuttered down the alley and knocked down all the pins except for the seven and the ten.

Pickle turned, his face as red as a beet in a beetpress. "Look what you made me do! A split on my first ball!"

"We want to talk to you about an important matter," said Branch, barely modifying his in-your-face tone.

"Well, can't you see I'm trying to relax? Can't it wait until tomorrow, or, better, next week sometime?" At this moment, someone called Pickle's name: it was VP T.P. Sealey, his bowling partner.

"Hey Don, let's see if we can take these guys two out of three," he said, oblivious to

Pickle's reddened face.

"I can't imagine what can be so important that you have to track me down like I was an aardvark or something," complained Pickle, whining. He had tried to intimidate Branch and he realized that Branch was not going to be intimidated.

"Give me five minutes, and then we'll get out of your hair and you can bowl as many splits as you like," said Branch. Circassian was beginning to think that if the conversation got any louder, people would begin to watch, and when people watch something happening in a bowling alley besides the cascading of pins, that means there's going to be trouble.

"Well, for heavens sake, what is it?"

Branch told him. Pickle smirfed and blickered, amused.

"So that's how Jack Swift operates. I thought there was something no-nonsense about him. But I really don't see what we can do; after all, the English department is now the property of Intell-Ex. It's a separate entity, even though it's still housed in the University."

"But what about due process?" asked Circassian, as he saw Branch about to launch another broadside in Pickle's direction. There was no doubt about it; people were beginning to stare. "Unless this is another example of Option Three," Circassian added.

"I guess just about everybody's trying to figure that one out," said Pickle with a little chuckle. "Using Option Three, it's obvious: We can't have a true University without an English department, and we realize that we can't keep the English department at what it's costing us, so we sold it off providing that it stays in the University. All that makes perfectly good sense. But when you bring up due process . . ."

"Due process should come ahead of Option Three. It's somewhere in the Constitution, I think," said Circassian, lying but certain that Pickle wouldn't take him up on it.

"Well, you do have a point there, Yossarian," said Pickle.

"Circassian," corrected Circassian.

"Yes, this merits some thinking. The jurisdictional disputes might get pretty complicated. I'll tell you what: I'll appoint a committee to study the question and have it get back to me in no later than . . . one month. How's that?" Pickle was beginning to look a little impatiently at his ball and the split he would have to try to convert. He hated splits because when he made them he rarely converted them. Whatever else one could say about Pickle, he did not have a split personality.

Branch Stark was not mollified, but Circassian sensed that this was a considerable concession from Pickle, who was known for never meeting anyone halfway.

"Tell you what, Branch: Since your nose is so out of joint over this, why not you be on the committee? You'll get a letter from me next week appointing you," said Pickle.

"Well, I hope you're not pulling my chain, Pickle, because if you are I'll be in your face so fast you won't have time to pee," said Branch, stalking out of Tony's with the same energy that had propelled him into Pickle's office earlier that day.

The next week, as Pickle said, Branch got a letter from him appointing Branch to the committee. But when he had read the whole letter with the list of the other members, he let out a yarp, a few "holy bleepin' shits," and strambled over to Circassian's office.

"Would you believe this?" he said to Circassian, who had been trying to explain to a student the difference in spelling between "woman" and "women," and thrust the note into his hands.

True to form, Pickle had appointed several well-known sycophants to the committee to neutralize Branch, and at the top of the list was the name of the Chair of the Jurisdiction Committee, Jack Swift!

Before Circassian could even think of stopping him, Branch strambled over to the Provost's Office once more. Circassian followed as one about to watch someone fall from a great height or receive a great weight on his head from a short distance. Branch walked past Rachel and into Provost Pickle's office where he was playing a game of mumbly peg with VP T. P. Sealey in a small sandbox that fit in a corner of his office and could be easily and quickly covered by a bookcase.

"What the hell are you doing appointing Swift to investigate himself?" he hurled at Pickle who, taken unawares, jumped from the sandbox onto a couch in one bound and put his hands over his head as if to fend off a swarm of maddened mud wasps.

After he had a chance to recover, he slowly turned to Branch and, with almost withering contempt, shot back: "Who would be a better choice to explain the way Intell-Ex. works — Batman?" This whimsical side of Pickle, rarely seen and even more rarely talked about, took Branch by surprise. For one of the few times in his life, he didn't have a quick come-back. He turned and walked out of the office, whereupon the Provost and VP T.P. Sealey resumed their game as if Branch had never been there.

When Circassian came home that evening and explained to Tina what had happened, she didn't bat an eye. "I could have told you that's what he'd do when he was going to pick the members of the committee. I'm surprised Branch fell for it."

"Well, what else do you think he could have done?"

"Nothing, honey. You guys still don't know when you're being screwed?"

Circassian knew but he hadn't wanted to admit it to himself; unless he and Branch, who seemed to be the only members of the department concerned about her fate, could get the rest of the members to form a united front, Daphne Dart was doomed. And so, he could see, would most of the rest of the department, one by timorous one.

()

Circassian was walking through the campus the following day when he saw Pastor Castor wambling toward him. He was wearing a big yellow button on his coat: "Public Rules — Private Sucks," in big, bright red letters.

"What's that all about, Padre?" asked Circassian.

Pastor Castor stopped and in a whiffling voice explained that it was in support of keeping the University public. "There's a lot of pressure these days to do to some of the other departments what's been done to yours and History," he said.

"But what's happening to us is terrible. Why would anybody else want to do the same thing?" asked Circassian.

"Because it is so terrible, I guess. You know how much the Administration distrusts the faculty. Well, if they can sell off most of the University, the faculty will be off their backs," he said.

"But if there isn't any faculty, what are they going to do?" Circassian was making the big mistake he had often made recently: being logical in an illogical situation. If he had been illogical, he would have had no trouble seeing the true motivation behind Pickle's and Bendminer's plan.

"They haven't worked that out yet, but by the time that happens, they will, or else they figure that they will all be close to retirement anyway," said Pastor Castor.

"By the way: who came up with that button? It doesn't sound like you."

"Mona Pilgrim. She and Tilly Owlglass have been at each other ever since the privatization got started. Mona decided that she was going to try to prevent Tilly from getting the Psychology department contract and wants the Psych students to have a demonstration. Who knows? It just might work. You've got to have faith, Circassian, in something."

Pastor Castor walked away whiffling to himself, and Circassian decided that he would just see what was happening in the Student Union. He knew that if he saw Mona, as long as he was in public, he wouldn't have much to be worried about. Or he hoped he wouldn't have much to worry about.

When he walked into the Student Government office, it seemed that Chaos had pitched its tent in the middle of it. On one side were piles of boxes with sweatshirts — paid for with Student Government funds — emblazoned with the University logo and the words in big black letters, "Don't Be a Public Fool: Private's Cool." On the other side were boxes of buttons like the one worn by Pastor Castor. Mona Pilgrim was distributing buttons to students who were walking in and out, as much amused by the little war as interested in the outcome. Todd Zarathustra was sitting behind the desk with the boxes of sweatshirts on it, giving them out to the Greeks who were dutifully lined up to receive them.

Mona was so busy that she didn't notice Circassian until he came up to her.

"Hello, Mona; I see you've got your hands full of buttons," said Circassian, trying not to startle the now-startled young woman.

"Oh, hi, Doc. I'll be finished here in a minute. Somebody's coming to take over soon.

Want a button?"

Since Circassian was already in the realm of the Private, it struck him as a little odd that he should be wearing a button, but it would have been even odder if he had worn the swearshirt. He took a button and seemed to have decided that he didn't want to wait until Mona had some free time since he didn't know how free Mona would be with it when her replacement came in.

"Give them out to any faculty that might wander in here, too. It counts almost as much when some prof walks around with one of these on as the students. Hey, Doc, wait up."

Circassian had turned the corner of the office and was almost out the door when he felt a hand tug on his arm. He had prepared something to say in case the two of them were alone for a moment. It would be very polite and chillingly correct. But before he could say a word, Mona was walking with him hand on arm.

"Mona, I don't think it's appropriate for us to walk like this," said Circassian.

"I know you have someone else in your life, and I respect that," said Mona, as they winched into an empty room, she leading the way. Circassian had allowed himself to be led because he was afraid of a scene. Scenes depressed him.

"Mona, what happened the other night was a . . . misunderstanding. I really think you are a wonderful young woman but . . ."

"You don't have to say anything more, Doc; I know how you feel for me, but it's just not meant to be, right now. I can wait. I will wait."

She threw herself into his arms as she had done the week before, and he emitted a yarp just as Tilly Owlglass walked into the room, looking for a deserted spot to smoke a reefer Todd had given her.

"Whoops," said Tilly as Circassian almost dropped Mona on the floor.

"Whoops," said Mona, turning and realizing who had said "whoops."

"Whoops," said Circassian, not knowing what else to say.

Before Mona had time to think of an explanation, Tilly had disappeared like a very large sylph.

"Don't worry, Doc. I have plenty on her. She always tries to find a place to smoke some weed. She's been doing it since her freshman year. She won't say anything."

"What would she have had to say?" asked Circassian, frumpling for words.

"Nothing, Doc. There was nothing happening, was there?" Mona tittled.

"Absolutely," said Circassian.

Two days later it was announced in the *University Chatter* that the Psychology department had been sold to Compel-Tex., a rival of Intell-Ex. Their announced goal was to double the number of Psych majors in the next five years at the expense of every other department, including English and History. The Ex-Tex Wars or, as Branch put it, Intell-Compel Hell had begun.

Part IV-i

When Circassian went to bed that night he had a very bizarre dream. He was walking in a train station with Tina and a little boy, about two years old. They were just a few feet behind him, but as he got to the exit, he turned and looked for them and they had disappeared. The rest of the dream was confused, and all he could remember about it is that he never found them. He woke up suddenly and turned to Tina; but there was no Tina. He looked at the alarm clock next to the bed: it was five-thirty.

Frunkishly, Circassian stammered out of bed, his heart beating like a ferret's, and began walking feverishly around the house, somehow afraid that he would never see Tina again. When he got to the study, he saw a dim light under the doorsill, opened the door and there was Tina, staring at the computer, which had now turned off the program she'd been using and was displaying floating clouds and little golden angels.

"Tina. Hey, Tina, it's five-thirty!" he said in a crushed whisper. But Tina remained as she was, staring at the angelic screen. He shook her several times, but to Circassian's amazed and dazed eyes, Tina did not change her position by either a jot or a tittle. Her face remained immobile, her eyes riveted to mindlessness. Circassian clapped his hands, stamped his feet, giggled, snapped his fingers in front of her face, lit a match before her eyes, stood on his head, yodled, gargled, sang off key, farted, prayed, belched, did a mime routine, coughed, flapped his hands, and still Tina stared at the screen.

He decided to try to look her in the eye. Then he realized that her pupils had dilated to the point that they covered her irises: her blue orbs had now become a souless blank black. He finally came to the conclusion that somehow she had hypnotized herself with the images on the screen. Circassian didn't know much about hypnotism; he'd never been hypnotized, as far as he knew, and had never any intention of getting hypnotized. The whole idea appealed to him slightly less than if he were to insert his pinky into an electric pencil sharpner; it just gave him the woolies. But he also believed that unless Tina was snapped out of the state she was in, it might do irreversible brain damage.

Thinking quickly, after a half hour of panic, he decided to call the emergency room at the local hospital. As far as he could tell, Tina was breathing regularly if very slowly, and although her hands and arms were very cold when he touched her, he thought that was better than if they'd been hot. At least she wasn't feverish, just freezerish.

"Hello," he said as soon as he had heard a voice at the other end of the line. "Is this the emergency room?"

"Yes. Is this an emergency? If not, we open at 9:00 A.M." said a very satisfied voice.

"I think it is. My friend has hypnotized herself and I'm afraid I don't know how to wake her," Circassian said in a froozled voice.

"How did she hypnotize herself?" asked Satisfied, calmly.

"I don't know. She was working at a computer and she must have seen something that got her hypnotized. I haven't a clue what it is."

"What have you tried to do to wake her?" asked satisfied, patiently.

Circassian listed everything he had done except for the farting.

"Sounds like you've done everything wrong so far. Bring her down here and we'll see what we can do."

"How do I do that? Carry her?" Circassian fumated.

"Is she a big person?" asked the voice.

"I'm not a big person," said Circassian. "She's just staring at the screen and doesn't look like she's going to budge."

"Well, have you turned it off?"

"Turned what off?" Circassian had begun to panic again.

"THE COMPUTER!" said the voice.

"Oh, no, I didn't think of that," said Circassian, apologetically.

"Well do it. You do know how to turn off a computer, don't you? I'll wait and tell me the results," said the voice exasperadoly.

Circassian dashed into the study and turned off the computer. Tina stared for another moment, then began to blink.

"Huh?" said Tina.'

"Are you okay?" Circassian asked.

"Sure. What time is it?"

He told her.

"My God! What happened?" He told her that too.

"Tina, don't you think you may be working too hard with that computer?" asked Circassian, trying to be reasonable about an unreasonable situation, something that was getting to be very familiar for him.

"Well, if we don't want to lose this house, somebody's got to be making money around here," scotted Tina, and then realized she had made a faux pas.

"Thanks a million, or should I say a billion!" said Circassian, and stalked out of the house. He came back several moments later since he was only wearing his pajamas and it was 10º below zero outside.

After Tina let him back in, she looked contrite.

"I'm sorry. I know it isn't your fault, Circassian," she said.

"You're hootin'-tootin' right it isn't my fault! And I still think you have to get those people who seem to be running your life to ease up. I don't want to find you glued to that thing and discover it's sucked up your brain," said Circassian. It was at this point that he noticed a noise coming from the living room that he hadn't heard before. It sounded like a human voice in distress.

"What the hell is that?" asked Tina. "Sounds like somebody's being stung by mad paper wasps."

The two stealthily shucked into the room and it was then that Circassian remembered he hadn't gotten back to the voice on the phone.

"She's fine," he said and hung up.

"You called up somebody to find out how to get me awake?" Tina asked, in an unusually shy voice.

"I don't know anything about hypnotism, but I love you," admitted Circassian.

His admission had an hypnotic effect on Tina who, tired as she must have been from staring at clouds and angels for four hours, collared him to bed and spent the next two hours in the ecstasies of newly discovered affection. When Circassian finally arose again at 7:30 A.M., he quietly got out of bed, dressed, and left the house, leaving Tina curled in sleep. When he got to his office he realized it was Saturday.

ii

The following Monday was the mid-term period, or, as Jack Swift put it in a memo, "Sweeps Time." It was the time to get the faculty geared up for the push for an increase in volume for the fall season. Students were beginning to make up their minds about what courses they would be taking the next semester, and for Jack Swift, this was his first opportunity to reverse the downward trend in volume in the English department numbers. Profits were up, true, but not volume. A greater challenge was awaiting this dementerated entrepreneur: Compell-Tex was also gearing up. They had contracted one of the biggest advertising firms in the state to get the ball rolling and the wheels spinning, and the mills grinding for Psychology.

That afternoon there was to be another meeting of the English department at the request of Jack Swift. Bendminder wasn't going to be there, but someone from Buchanan, Fitts and Startz, a prestigious if local advertising firm, was going to attend according to the memo.

The Committee on Jurisdiction had already met and it was decided that Daphne Dart would be able to complete the semester but that her continued employment was contingent on her improving her numbers for the coming season. That was considered a fair compromise as far as Pickle and Dean Lean were concerned, but the department and Daphne especially were not satisfied.

"He can pick us all off, one at a time; low man on the totem pole is gone," said Toddy Dance. He was second from the bottom after Daphne and was fretting in the whiney way that many of the faculty were dealing with the new challenges before them. Branch's attempts to get a united front against Swift had been aborted by the decision on Daphne. Nobody wanted to be "next," except for Branch, who didn't seem to care anymore. His face was looking as red as Pickle's had been when he'd made the split.

Circassian had gone into the dining room and decided that he didn't want to sit anywhere near The Table. Ralph Null was trying out some black humor on the rest of them, and Ron Burble was strangely silent. He'd been warned by Swift to get his numbers up. Circassian found himself sitting next to Josh Gutsky and Seth Shotman. Josh was his colleague in the English department and Seth was in History, so the two of them had a lot of miserable things to say to each other, which, Circassian sensed, made them happy.

"Say Circassian," said Josh. "Did you hear the one about the two Jews who were walking down a street? The first said to the second: 'Oy vey,' and the second answered: 'You're telling me?'" Seth laughed, and Josh waited for Circassian's reaction. When there wasn't any, Josh asked: "Would you like to tell us an Armenian joke?"

"I don't know any Armenian jokes," said Circassian. "They didn't travel well to the United States. You see, they're all about Turks."

"What do you think, Circassian: do you suppose Jack Swift might be Jewish?" asked Seth.

"What makes you think that Jack Swift could possibly be Jewish?" brumbled Circassian, trying to eat a jalapeño salad.

"Well, if he is, maybe Seth and I might find an angle. Make him feel guilty about what he's doing," said Josh. "It might work. Guilt's a good thing for most Jews to feel once in a while. He'd thank us for it."

"I never heard of anyone named Swift who was Jewish," said Circassian, making the mistake once more of trying to be logical.

"Well, you never can tell," said Josh. "After all, Harrison Ford is part Jewish and I can't imagine a less Jewish name."

"Besides," added Seth, "we were figuring it was on his mother's side."

"What was on his mother's side?" said Circassian. He was beginning to feel confused again. He thought they were talking about Harrison Ford.

"He could be Jewish on his mother's side. His name wouldn't really tell us anything," said Josh.

"Why would it matter if he was Jewish on his mother's side?" asked Circassian. He knew he shouldn't be asking the Eternal Jews any questions, but some maddening implosive drove him on.

"Because that's the side that counts!" said Seth.

"Why is that the side that counts?" asked Circassian.

"It just does. And we have a reason to think so," one of them said.

"Think what?"

"That he's Jewish."

"Who?" Circassian was beginning to lose track of the conversation.

"Jack Swift," said Seth. "We noticed something about him that could be a give-away."

"And what could that possibly be?" fundled Circassian. He didn't like hot food and certainly not jalapeños. He had thought they were odd-shaped cherry tomatoes and had crunched down two before he realized his mistake.

"The way he crosses his 't's' in his signature. There's a little extra dip in it that could have come from years in Hebrew School. I have it; Josh has it," said Seth. "Look." He was about to show him when Circassian suddenly jumped up as if an ant lion had bit him.

"Yaargh!" graffled Circassian. The jalapeños had finally penetrated through his mouth to his esophagus, lungs, liver, spleen and lower intestine. He streeped through the lunchroom and out the door to the water fountain.

"Well, how do you like that?" asked Josh to Seth.

"Not very much," said Seth to Josh.

"Maybe it's when I asked him to tell us an Armenian joke?" queried Josh.

"Some people just don't have a sense of humor," said Seth.

When Circassian had gotten out of the bathroom, after getting rid of the last of the jalapeño effect on his digestive system, he realized that he was going to be late for the second meeting with Jack Swift. He rushed over to his office and got his folder with all of Swift's memos in it. He noticed, as he was whimfling through the papers, that Swift did have a noticeable dip in the way he crossed his 't's,' but he didn't think that it could possibly mean anything except to a couple of obsessers like Seth Gutsky and Josh Shotman. Or was it Josh Gutsky and Seth Shotman? He was so fuddled that when he got into the conference room, he didn't realize that Jack Swift was in the middle of his introduction of a short, well-tanned, sparse-haired, red-headed, loose-limbed, fast-talking gentleman who was obviously, from his Armani shoes and Gucci ties, very prosperous and full of himself.

"Excuse me. Gastrointestinal emergency," fittered Circassian and sat down.

Swift continued with his introduction after a quick glare at Circassian. "I give you a man who was responsible for the Dura-bind Bunny, the Magi-Blender campaign and several of the local McCarthur Radio commercials. He's going to give the organization a new image and believe me, we need one! I want to introduce you now to Harry Bliss, one of the creative forces behind Buchanan, Fitts and Startz."

There was polite if scattered applause, except for Branch Stark, who sardonically whistled.

"Thanks, everybody. I'm not here to tell you what to do in your profession; that's your thing and I can respect that. What I am here to do is to introduce to you a few of the techniques we are going to use to make what you do more attractive, more dynamic, more accessible. I've brought a video which illustrates some of my ideas. I'd like you to look it over and tell me what clicks for you. That's all I'm asking. . . ."

"For now" added Swift with ominy.

The video began in a similar way to Swift's for Fun-100, only in this case, it was mellower music, with a bassa nova beat. The scenes were of sunsets over tropical islands, attractive people under the age of twenty-five, helicopter pans of forests, lakes and mountains. Circassian, who had not been sleeping very well since the night Tina had hypnotized herself, began to nod off. Then a voice that sounded like vintage Ed McMahon intoned: "Tired of the hype about hot new courses? Relax. We've got tradition on our side: English is where it's at just as it's been for decades. While fads come and go, we're here, we're solid, we're the future."

Suddenly, the sound zoomed up several decibles and a line of bikini-buttomed, tank-topped beauties appeared on screen kicking their legs high and chanting: "E is for ecstasy, N is for New Age, G is for glamor, L is for loot, I is for intellect, S is for super, H is for hot and that's what we've got: ENGLISH! ENGLISH!! ENGLISH!!! RAHH!!!!"

Then a series of images rushed quickly across the screen, including Shakespeare in Love, the Artful Dodger, Huck Finn, Marilyn Monroe, Casey at the Bat, Tim Finnegan, Frank Sinatra, Krazy Kat, the Lone Ranger, Humphrey Bogart, Bill Cosby, Jerry Lewis, Elvis Presley, James Joyce, the Eiffel Tower, Dealey Plaza, the Rockettes, Steven Spielberg, Richard Burton, the Statue of Liberty, Apollo Thirteen, Pope John Paul, Vernon Jordan, Frankie Avalon, Tom Mix, Lucille Ball, George Clooney, and many others too numerous to understand.

Branch raised his hand before Harry Bliss had a chance to ask for a reaction. "What the hell does most of that have to do with English?"

"It doesn't," answered Harry Bliss. "But these are some of the images and personalities we've field tested that create the most interest in the average knowledge-consumer. Then once you get their attention, you can start marketing the product. You've got to break through the resistance, and then you've got them. They'll be willing to learn almost anything, as long as you keep them stimulated. This little demo is just the beginning. Wait until you see the others. And here are a few suggestions for the coming season. You can start with some of them now if you want."

Harry Bliss passed out a single sheet of paper. After a few moments there was a collective gasp from the English faculty. Some of them started laughing, others quietly weeping. Harold Hanes raised his hand.

"You want us to wear sweatshirts with an English department logo on it? Can we wear it under our suits?"

"Suit yourself," crickled Harry Bliss. "The logo is going to be very stylish: something like a coat of arms — a lion reading a book and a unicorn watching a video."

"I thought we weren't supposed to be into reading," quipped Branch. He knew he should have resisted, but there was something irresistible about Harry Bliss that eggled him on.

"Not in Fun-100," said Swift, sternly. "That's to get them hooked on English. Once you have them in the advanced courses, you can introduce them to reading — only you've got to approach it gradually." '

"Well, that's one hell of a relief!" said Branch. A few of the faculty tittered and guffed. The rest were stone-statue silent.

"I gather that these are just suggestions," said Josh Gutsky. "You really don't expect us to wear those green and white shorts to class," he timmered.

"Not in winter, of course, but these are the same kind of suggestions that I gave you last time. Of course, if you have a better suggestion, I'll be glad to consider it," said Swift.

"Why don't you have us show up in front of Main every morning and do a kick line dance, using that catchy cheer from the video?" sardoned Circassian. He was beginning to feel a little reckless.

"I'll look into that one," answered Swift, without blicking a smile. "With a little pressure on Pickle, I think we could swing it."

Daphne Dart darted a look at Circassian that read. "Keep Your Big Mouth Shut," in very large dripping red letters.

"Mr. Swift . . ." — no one wanted to call him Jack; it felt too human — "I was only kidding," said Circassian, sheepishly.

"I'm not," said Swift. "Go on, Harry."

"We're in a war, gang," said Harry Bliss. "Compell-Ex. is a very shrewd company, and we can't afford to give any quarter. Be sure that you don't hand out any low grades to the students; keep them happy. Cut back on the reading assignments. Make sure that the papers you assign them are short and can be done successfully by the dumbest student in the class. Think the unthinkable. Be innovative. Make your lectures more colorful. I've contracted the services of Marilyn Muse, a second runner-up in the Miss Pulchritude Contest in Samoa. I've also signed on Larry Lustig, one of the finalists in the Mr. Gorgeous in California competition. If you feel you need either to pick up student interest in your courses, just give me a week's notice and I'll have them come in to your classes."

"What do they know about literature?" asked Phil Frasier. The rest of the department members gave him a double-take. No one ever remembered him speaking up at a department meeting before.

"Absolutely nothing!" said Harry Bliss. "That's the beauty about the whole thing. They won't make any of the students feel inferior, at least not intellectually, no matter how clueless they might be," he charfled.

"What you want us to do is help you end Western Civilization as we've known it," said Josh Gutsky, again, not raising his hand.

"Exactly!" said Harry Bliss. "I'm glad you understand where I'm coming from . . . what is your name?"

Josh gave his name.

"See me after the meeting. I think a bright young man like you will be able to go as far as you can imagine in this new approach to learning."

"Mr. Bliss," said Josh Gutsky, also sheepishly, "I was only kidding!"

"I'm not," said Harry Bliss. "I hope you aren't going to fall into Folly, Professor Gutsky."

Circassian just realized that Harry Bliss had made a witticism, but he wasn't sure anyone else had realized it, since no one had expected him to.

"Now, Sweeps time is coming up very soon and we have to dazzle the students for next semester. I've made up a couple of posters in very bright colors so the consumers will notice them on the bulletin boards. Make sure you announce the new and upcoming courses in your classes starting next week. Psych is going to do a media blitz the week after so we have a headstart on them. Our media blitz will come just before the consumers begin to make their product-choices for the fall season. If you all take these suggestions to heart, I can guarantee that our student share will go up exponentially, along with the profit margin," fundicated Harry Bliss.

"We're considering going public next month so if anybody wants to get in on the ground floor, I've developed a shareholding plan to supplement your pensions that will be very attractive," puncated Jack Swift. Nobody knew what he was talking about; they couldn't imagine it.

When the meeting was over, Josh Gutsky came over to Circassian and asked that they speak in the privacy of his office.

"Did you catch that pun he made on his name?" asked Josh.

"Yes. I didn't think anyone expected it," Circassian said.

"I think that that was a hint meant for me," Josh thused.

"What kind of a hint?" asked Circassian. He knew what was coming by now, but he wanted to be sure he heard it from Josh Gutsky's very own lips.

"I think that he was trying to tell me that he was Jewish and that we shouldn't be too concerned about his ad campaign," Josh yimped with pride.

"What makes you think he's Jewish?" said Circassian, determined to get to the bottom of Gutsky's obsession as a way of distracting himself from the horrors before him.

"It's the way he looked at me," said Josh Gutsky.

"How would he know you were Jewish?" pursued Circassian.

"Oh come on, how could he miss? My name, my appearance . . ."

"Some people, including you, think I look Jewish," said Circassian.

"And we still think you might be, if you'd bother to find out. But Harry Bliss can tell; one Jew always knows another," spinkled Josh. "And anyway, Bliss: that's a made-up name. It was probably Blitzstein or Blitman or something like that."

"Okay, just suppose he is Jewish; what the hell difference would it make to us if he is?"

Josh was finally silent. He had been so focused on proving to himself that Bliss was Jewish that it hadn't occurred to him why it was so important.

"Well . . . he might take pity on us since we've been a persecuted people, don't you think?" stammled Josh Gutsky.

"Tell that one to Michael Eisner!" shot back Circassian.

When he got home that afternoon, Circassian found Tina sitting in front of the television, but decidedly unmesmerized.

"Putski's done it again!" she creened as he was pulling off his coat. "He's made another budget cut!"

"How much this time?" asked Circassian. He wondered how this would affect his salary again. Although he wouldn't be getting a pay cut directly from the State, he knew by now that Jack Swift targeted his salaries with those at the University, always making them lower, but with a promise of bonuses for productivity.

Putski's face was still on the screen. He was a man who talked like he had just been cheated out of his rich uncle's inheritance; he had the worried look of an embezzler on the lam; his gaze shifted like a cross-eyed snake's; his hands were always busy pressing or pushing or twiddling something; he was a nervous wreck.

" . . . And we can assure you that the tax cut will benefit the entire State once those earning over $250,000 receive their refunds and pump the money back into the economy. Unfortunately, some further savings will have to be made in the State University system . . ." Circassian switched off the television. He didn't want to hear what the damage would be. He had been hoping for a bonus because he had been in the top third of the department faculty in productivity. But he knew that Jack Swift was going to react soon to Putski's cuts. He wasn't called Jack Swift for nothing.

"Let's go out for dinner tonight," said Circassian. "We haven't been out to dinner since the semester started. Let's just kick back and enjoy ourselves."

"I've already put on a bean and rice pot pie," said Tina. "We can't afford to eat out too often, you know; it's not cost-effective."

"Screw cost-effective! Today's Friday: let's have a little fun in our dreary and obsessive lives." Circassian was determined that he and Tina had fun since it was likely that it would be the last time they would have fun for a long time. Tina's hours had been cut at the firm she worked for because of a down-turn in business.

"Today's Thursday, Circassian, but okay; I guess we might as well," traffled Tina. They went to Gatz-B's. It was one of the few decent restaurants in the area and they served a very good slumgullion which wasn't easy to find anywhere. Tina, who was a vegetarian, enjoyed the mulligatawny soup and the Welsh rabbit. The food was not inexpensive, the service was very slow, and the customers noisy. It was the ideal place for the two of them to forget their troubles.

"Hi, Friend Circassian." He heard the unmistakable voice of Frank Short behind him. He turned and there was Frank, walking in with his wife, Kara. They looked like they had just come out of the rain in an MGM musical which was a little odd since it was snowing outside again.

Seeing that Tina and Circassian had been looking at their menus, he asked: "Mind if we join you?"

Tina had only met Frank a few times at faculty functions but she gave Circassian a nod and they shifted their chairs for the other couple. And Circassian suddenly realized that rare as it had been for them to eat out, it was even rarer for them to eat out with anyone else.

"I don't want to spoil the evening before it's started, old man, but did you hear about the new cuts in the Putski budget?" said Frank after they had finished their drinks.

"I turned off the TV before I had a chance to hear it," said Circassian.

"Well, then I won't spoil the evening, especially since these cuts are only affecting the publicly owned departments," said Frank.

"Want to bet?" said Circassian.

Kara Short interrupted. She was an attractive woman, about ten years younger than Frank, with the suave manner of a European who had lived in the States long enough to be accepted but not long enough to blend in. "Why don't we talk about something nice and pleasant?" she said.

There was a long pause; all of them were lost in thought. Then Frank suddenly looked at Circassian and they both started to snicker; then the two women joined and they all erupted together.

It turned into a wonderful evening; everyone was witty and bright; but there was an edge to their enjoyment of each other's company, as if something ominous ahead were looming for all of them and they were all quite aware of it. When Circassian and Tina came home, she turned on the television just in time to get a summary of Putski's budget cuts. It would be another 10% across the board. It was a regrettable but necessary action "for the sake of the State's economy," Putski plauted.

The next morning, there was a notice in everyone's mailbox: "Due to the recent cuts in the State University, we have had to take the following measures beginning in the new season: All level C employees will have their course rate reduced from $1,900 to $1,700. All level B employees will receive a 6% cut in salary. All level A employees will receive a 10% cut in salary. If anyone wishes to discuss this matter, please let the secretaries know and they will make an appointment for you.

"Regrettably,

"Jack Swift"

Circassian was a level C employee. He had already figured that at the rate he was being paid before, if he included all the time he spent in grading papers, attending meetings, and holding office hours, he was making one dollar above the minimum wage. He was certain that the new calculations would be bring him below the minimum wage. Instead of trying to complain to Jack Swift, which he knew would be useless, he decided to see Dabs Budweiser.

When he saw Dabs, she was in the middle of organizing a new campaign on the budget cuts.

"Sorry, Circassian; right now all I have time for is getting the membership out on this gimmick Putski's trying to pull on us." She was busy unpacking a box of bumper stickers: "Putski's Cuts Are Nuts." A second box was of buttons with the same slogan. The phone was ringing constantly and the Union secretary was rapidly losing control of the natural flow of things that every union office should have.

"I just figured out," said Circassian, "that with the latest cut I got from Jack Swift, I'm working for less than the minimum wage," he huffled at Dabs.

"Nothing we can do about that, Circassian," said Dabs. "The word just came down from Central Headquarters: I'm afraid you guys are now on your own. As a separate corporate entity, the Union no longer has any jurisdiction about anything that happens to you."

"Thanks a lot," cargled Circassian. "So I suppose that Daphne Dart's case has been settled against her."

"The report came out yesterday. The University has no jurisdictional rights concerning any Intell-Ex. employee. But I have a suggestion."

"Now what could that possibly be?" asked Circassian, as Dabs pinned a button on his jacket.

"You could start organizing your own union and then reaffiliate with us. I'm sure that many of the faculty in your department are fed up enough to do anything," said Dabs.

"They're scared enough to do nothing," yarkled Circassian, fluming. "You know how much academics are willing to stick their necks out around here," he added somewhat maliciously. Dabs' call to action had not been an overwhelming success.

Circassian looked at the button pinned on his coat and decided to take it off. "Hey, Putski's not my boss," he said, leaving the office in high dragoon.

"Think about organizing, Circassian. It's your only chance at a better life," Dabs called after. Dabs was another one of the faculty who didn't really understand irony. She only thought she did.

iii

Camille Faux had just come from a meeting of the Board of Trustees, who had heard the latest report from Bendminder. Things seemed to be going according to schedule and she was planning to have lunch with Ambler Slaughter at the Sphinx Club, the most exclusive restaurant in the capitol.

Camille thought of herself as a humanist in that she regarded the classics as something no University student should do without, if they deserved to have such an education. But since, in her view, most of the students at the University were wasting their time, it wasn't necessary to have very much of a University. She and Circassian might have seen eye to eye in some respects, but where they differed is that while Circassian felt that every student should be given a chance to show worthiness, Camille believed that that was a waste of money, and the best thing to do was to shut down most of the University and let only those at the top of their class attend. That's why she agreed with each budget cut Governor Putski made: it was moving the University closer and closer to her ideal model.

Camille lived well, was unhappily married to a boorish executive, and had two very fine children who had been given the kind of education she knew they deserved. She thought of herself as something of a scholar, having received the requisite degrees, and was never intimidated by any of the faculty that the Board of Trustees rarely saw. It wasn't a good idea, they felt, to see too many faculty, and certainly no students. To do so would be to put in jeopardy everything they believed in and some of the things they didn't believe in but thought they were supposed to believe in. Camille was their leader and wore her leadership well: She had the courage of the convictions of the rich and powerful, the ones that are hardly ever challenged and always prevail.

When Camille met Ambler Slaughter at *The Phoenix*, she was in a particularly good mood. According to Bendminder's report, the University was being more quickly privatized than he had hoped. Since Bendminder was both an executive with Intell-Ex. and working under the table for Compell-Tex as well, he had been able to anticipate what each corporation would do when the next one made a move. According to the report, it would probably be just a few years before the University was absorbed by both, and the competition between them would be fierce which would drive down the budget much more quickly than Governor Putski could ever do.

At this point, Intell-Ex. seemed to have been outflanked by Compell-Tex. when they bought the Psych department, but Intell-Ex. had plans of their own to outflank their rival. Something was in the works at the corporation's headquarters, and as soon as he got wind of it, Bendminder would let Camille know.

"I think things are just humming," she said to Ambler, a neat man with an unruly head of hair which he had never figured out a way to get to behave. As Jack Swift was particularly proud of his tallness, Ambler Slaughter was particularly ashamed of his hair's unruliness, since he prided himself on being always organized. He had once acted as a comptroller at one of the branches of the University and knew all the ropes and pulleys in the system. That's why his position in Operation Change was so devastating to the University. Between him and Bendminder, they felt that they had the whole operation snafudled.

"What did the Board recommend?" he asked Camille.

"Well, they approved of the Governor's cuts. It's a good way to get those people to really look for places to save. But they're getting used to it by now," she chaggled.

"What I'm really getting optimistic about is the privatization. There are three departments so far; have you any news of more?" Ambler Slaughter relied on Camille for the tidbits he needed to put into the Operation Change newsletter.

"Bendminder told me that there may be more developments. Intell-Ex. is now in a price war with Compell-Tex, so there are probably going to be more buy-outs soon," she said, daddling with her confit of ptarmigan.

"What else happened that's worth my interest?" asked Ambler Slaughter. He was doddling with a duck paté, of which he was unusually fond.

"We talked about some new requirements for all the branches. An idea I came up with: Latin for everyone. It's the one thing every educated person shouldn't do without. Of course, this will probably weed out quite a few of the drones," she excapulated.

"We owe it to the quality students to get rid of the ones who are cluttering up the system. Yes, Latin should be an all-University requirement: *In te speravi*," he toasted her with a Muscatel.

"*Confundum hostem*," responded Camille, returning the toast with a Pinot Noir. "And Bendminder has come up with another idea that we will be putting into effect soon. Intell-Ex. has decided to do an assessment of their employees, and if it works as well as he thinks it will, the University will follow soon. After all, accountability is a good buzz word for the public. They love to think they're saving money somewhere if you throw enough numbers at them," she said.

"Does the idea have a name?" asked Ambler. He was thinking of putting it in as a feature in the next "Operation Change" newsletter.

"Yes," Camille said, a brilliant smile on her face. "It's called 'DICTATE.' It's better than all of those other assessment programs around the country. Believe me, this will get results very quickly!"

()

While Camille Faux and Ambler Slaughter were dining, up on the fourth floor of the Administration Building VP T.P. Sealey was vulterating with Tilly Owlglass. She had made an appointment to see him after she had gotten into a shouting match with Mona Pilgrim over the slogans each was using. Tilly took exception to the word "sucks" in Mona's pin, and Mona did not think that calling someone a "fool" was appropriate for a slogan either. Neither was willing to give on using their slogans, so Tilly had decided to out-maneuver Mona, something she had been doing for years to most other students who had presented an obstacle to her plans.

"I really think that she's gone over the edge," said Tilly. "Supposing someone with a button appears on cable? Or worse, is interviewed when one of the local networks gets on campus?"

"That could be a problem," agreed VP T.P. Sealey, "but there aren't too many things we can do about it. You don't want the ACLU on our backs about a free speech issue." VP T.P. Sealey loathed that organization because once a few years ago he had censored a student for putting a hammer-and-sickle banner in his window, and the student had gotten a retraction with the help of the ACLU. It was in all the local papers, and he'd been so embarrassed that he handed in his resignation, which was — as if he didn't know — refused by Pickle.

"Well, I have an idea," said Tilly. "Why don't you just have Mona dismissed from the University?"

"On what grounds?" asked VP T.P. Sealey. He was almost intrigued by Tilly because she was so perfectly like him. Still, he looked at his watch to see if it was getting on toward two o'clock. During the winter months he was the bowling partner of Provost Pickle and in the spring and summer, the golfing partner of President Fred. It was a very ennervating routine, but VP T.P. Sealey was still in excellent shape.

"I think we can make a case for her fraternizing with one of the faculty," she said. The compromising situation that she had found Mona in with Circassian had not gone unnoticed, and unknown to Mona, the Administration knew that Tilly smoked grass; they just chose to ignore it as long as she wasn't caught by one of the campus police.

"I think you've got it backwards, Tilly," exclumpered VP T.P. Sealey. "The woman is almost always the victim in these cases. It's the man who's in trouble. Who is he?"

Tilly decided that it wasn't the time to reveal Circassian's name. She could hold it over Mona, which would be much more effective than giving it to the VP, since all he would do was to can Circassian.

"Well, I could be mistaken," she said. "I think I'd better check this out before I go any further. But there must be some way to get her to stop handing out those buttons. They're actually getting popular!"

"Well, I'm afraid I have another appointment, Tilly, but we'll think this over and come up with something, I'm sure." VP T.P. Sealey would have felt much better if Tilly came up with nothing. She was valuable in her way, particularly in manipulating and intimidating the Student Government. But she could be a royal pain in the ass when it came to using common sense. She just couldn't take anyone who had the guts to defy her. But Mona was no threat to Option Three; Bendminder would make sure of that.

Now he had to hurry to change his clothes in the executive bathroom and come out ready for bowling. He didn't like to keep Provost Pickle waiting; he knew what side of the butter his bread was on and VP T.P. Sealey always made sure he was on the right side of the butter.

()

While Camille and Ambler Slaughter were finishing their lunch and VP T.P. Sealey was on his way to Tony's Lanes, Circassian received a very strange letter from Marigold Markham. She somehow saw Circassian as an ally in what she regarded as her own guerilla war against Option Three. Of course, since her office was bugged and her e-mail was channelled through the Provost's office, she had to write letters to be sure she wouldn't be detected. The one to Circassian simply read:

6-Mainsteps
MM

He realized it was from Marigold, but he had no idea what she wanted to tell him. He called Tina to let her know that he would be late for dinner.

It was quite dark by 6:00 P.M., and when Circassian got outside of Main, he saw Marigold already there, muffled up in a puffy parka with a thick scarf over her face.

"I have to be careful" she stittered to Circassian. "There are spies everywhere." She slipped a piece of paper into his hand. "I got this from a fax that Jack Swift sent to Bendminder. I think you'll be interested in it." Then, while Circassian began to look at the piece of paper, Marigold disappeared into the darkness.

Circassian went back into Main and immediately began to read what was a memo from Swift to Bendminder.

Dear 'Stats':

Here's the latest sample of what our researchers are doing to make the product more marketable: it's part of a new translation of Shakespeare's *Hamlet* and it even rhymes. I'm sure the students will get a lot more out of this than trying to wade through that old English jargon. Maybe if you had read this when you were in school, you might actually like Shakespeare. It's from the 'To be or not to be' speech, and it's just what we needed to put our best foot forward:

Should I live or should I die?
That's the riddle: tell me why.
Must I live with aggravation,
Or die if that's my inclination.
Yes, die and take an endless snooze,
That's the nobler way to choose.
But in death could I have a dream,
Perhaps that way's a bit extreme.
Still, who'd dare take all the crap,
That bitter life drops in your lap.
Live long enough, you'll get the shaft,
'Til all that's left to do is laugh;
But here's Ophelia, nymph is she,
By her my sins remembered be.

I know the last two lines are a little too artsy fartsy; we're working on that. The first edition of the Revised Shakespeare should be ready to do a test market on before the end of the semester.

See you at the next board meeting.
Keep up the good work.
Jack

Circassian decided that the best thing he could do was snickle. After all, no one in his right mind would swallow this kind of thing. He was certain that the "Revised" Shakespeare would be laughed out of existence.

As he was driving home, however, he began to think about it again. Maybe some of the faculty were so intimidated by Swift that they would play along with anything he did. No, that's not possible, he thought. There are limits to what the English department faculty would be willing to put up with. But what exactly were those limits? Were those limits reached when Daphne Dart was told to pack up her books and computer at the end of the semester and go elsewhere? Were they reached when the English department faculty started wearing those dumb shirts over their other clothes? Were they reached when everyone wore green hats and vests during St. Patrick's Day?

When he got back home, he was in a very low mood.

"What's the matter, lover?" asked Tina. She had prepared a real treat for Circassian: sorrel soup and boiled pig's feet.

Without a word, Circassian showed Tina the note. After reading it and pausing a second she said: "This is a joke, right?"

"Nothing that Jack Swift does is a joke, Tina," Circassian sulted. "That is, it may start out as a joke to us, but if it's not a joke to him, we stop laughing. He doesn't like to be laughed at."

"Well, if he tries to pass this off as Shakespeare, a lot of people will be laughing," said Tina, hopefully.

"Who? Me? No. The rest of the English department faculty? Definitely not. The rest of the non-privatized faculty? Maybe. Only they know that their turn to suffer will be coming soon. Maybe they'll laugh at Harvard, but I'm not sure of anything now." Circassian looked at the sorrel soup as if he could read his fate in its globules of fat.

"Why not show it to Branch? At least somebody will do something besides hide behind their interrogatives," quimpled Tina.

"Branch? Not on your life! He'll storm and rage and do all sorts of very Branch-like things. Besides, if I show it to him and he shows it to anybody else, eventually they'll know it came from Marigold," he said.

"Why not tell him you got it on the net; that way if it gets back to Bendminder and Pickle, it'll make them paranoid," she yibbled.

"Well, why the hell not?" he said.

The next day, before he had time to get to Branch's haven, Circassian's attention was taken by Josh Gutsky, who seemed to be frimulating. He had pulled on Circassian's sleeve, and before Circassian had a chance know what he was doing, he found himself in Josh's office.

"I was right," Josh said, after a moment's pause in which he heaved a great sigh.

"Right about what?" asked Circassian.

"Harry Bliss is Jewish. I sent him an e-mail to his address asking him if he was. It took a lot out of me to do it because I always prefer to ask someone face to face. That way you know when he's hiding something," said Josh.

"And what did he answer?" said Circassian.

"'So what?' That's all: 'So what?' It was humiliating. In all the years that I've asked people if they were Jewish, I've never received a 'So what?' answer before. I don't understand it." Josh looked about as forlorn as a child who had lost his pet hamster.

After leaving Josh in a pile of woe, Circassian knocked on Branch's door. It was always closed now, and he could still hear the sounds of thumping going on inside.

"Who the hell is it now?" said Branch.

"It's me again," said Circassian. "Your partner in crime."

"Well, come the bleep in," said Branch.

The posters on the walls were the same, but all sorts of obscene additions had been made after Branch had exhausted the possibilities on the original images. He had been imaginative in his improvisation: a vulva coming out of Camille's mouth, genitalia spewing from Ambler's ears, Pickle with a large breast coming from each eye, and Bendminder with what looked like testes scattering from his teeth. Most of what else remained of the posters was almost unrecognizable, so covered were they with Silly Putty, Branch Stark's new weapon against the Evil Ones.

"Some hacker picked this up off the net and gave me a copy," Circassian lied. He knew that Branch could not be trusted now to keep any confidence; it would have just flamminated from him in a moment of high dungeon. Branch read the paper, stared at Circassian, then stood upright.

"This is the last hoop I'm jumping through," yarped Branch. He flung open the door and, like Hercules setting forth toward the Augean Stables, clampered down the hallway to Dean Lean's office. Circassian decided that this time, he would let Branch go all on his own. Besides, considering what role Circassian had played the last time Branch went down the hall, he was as superfluous as a dingbat at a rummage sale.

He wondered what Branch could be saying to Dean Lean and Dean Lean saying back to Branch. He wondered if they might have an actual fight, but he knew that the Dean would probably be killed and that wouldn't help Branch at all in his quest for sanity. He wondered if Branch might actually convince the Dean to do something, even if the English department was no longer under his jurisdiction. He wondered for about ten minutes and then he saw Branch slowly gralumphing back down the hall. He looked like a broken man.

Without a word he walked past Circassian, the paper in his hand, and went into his office. He stared at the wall until Circassian finally asked: "Well, what happened?"

Branch paused a moment, the pause having the effect if not the intent of a pause by Hank Schecht. "He liked it!" said Branch, in a vague grawkle.

"He liked what?" asked Circassian, unwilling to accept what the antecedent had to be.

"He liked this piece of shit!" said Branch, rolling the sheet of paper up and tossing it back to Circassian. "He thought it was clever, that the students would 'dig it.'"

"He actually said 'dig it?'" asked Circassian.

"What the bleep's the difference, Circassian? We're at the edge of the precipice, like Butch and Sundance, only there's no river to jump into, just a pile of horse manure!" yammled Branch.

Circassian didn't know what to say. He could have pointed out that Butch and Sundance eventually end up in a shoot-out with some Latino soldiers and get very dead, but he didn't want to point out anything to Branch at the moment. Branch was beginning to build up another head of steam and mayhem.

"Remember what that stupid shit Harry Bliss said when Gutsky told him that he was ending Western Civilization and he agreed? Well, that's what this is all about, Circassian: the Barbituates are at the Gates and we've got to beat 'em back," saddled Branch.

"How do we do that, Branch?" Circassian asked. "The Barbituates have all the weapons and all we have is what's left of our integrity."

"That should be enough, even if it isn't much," said Branch. "Do you think it would help if we took this to President Fred?"

He doesn't like Pickle. Maybe it's worth a try," said Circassian, doubtfully. He wasn't sure that he could rely on any of the Administration to do anything anymore. Dean Lean liked the doggerel "To be or not to be"; Pickle was stonewalling as usual; and it was possible that President Fred would be no more sympathetic than Camille Faux. After all, he could have vetoed the sale of the English department and the History department if had wanted to. At least Circassian thought he could, but then again, Option Three might have made Fred as helpless as they were.

"Do you think it would make more sense if one of us talked to him when he was at some function? Marigold's office is bugged; maybe his is too," said Circassian.

"If it's bugged, he'd be the one to do it. Besides, I think it's better if we were there together. I'll try to get a few more people to come up with us, if they have the guts," Branch brambled.

"What about Josh? It's in his name," quimpled Circassian.

"What the bleep is it with the jokes?" yoiked Branch. "But do you think Gutsky'd be willing to? He seems to be a typical chicken shit as far as I'm concerned."

"Don't underestimate Josh; underneath all of that fright and despair he's a real fighter," insisted Circassian

"Maybe you can convince him that President Fred is really Jewish on his mother's side; that would get him going," squeered Branch.

"Is he?" asked Circassian.

"Who the bleep cares?" trepled Branch.

Circassian was tempted to tell Branch that Harry Bliss was Jewish but he knew he'd get the same reply. Suddenly he realized he was thinking about all the people he knew who might be Jewish and all the ones that couldn't be Jewish. He realized he had to have another talk with Josh Gutsky if he wanted to straighten himself out about Jewish matters.

When Branch sent off a note requesting a meeting with President Fred, he got the following reply. It was clearly the work of Bendminder.

To: Associate Professor and former Chairman Branch Stark
From: President Dick L. Fred
Re: Request for a meeting

Dear Professor Stark:
I would love to have a meeting with you on any matter you choose to bring up, but you must be aware that I no longer have any jurisdiction over the English department. If this matter is substantive, I would suggest that you take it up with your district supervisor, Jack Swift. I am certain that he will be able to address your concerns to your satisfaction.
Cordially,
D. L. Fred

iv

Over the next few weeks the competition between Intell-Ex. and Compell-Tex. heated up. Jack Swift instructed the faculty to note any students who were planning to switch out of English as a major, particularly if they were going to move into Psychology. Swift wanted their names and i.d. numbers. Branch found out through Marigold Markham that these students were being offered special deals on travel and even, in some cases, cash bonuses if they would remain in English. If that didn't work, they were threatened with bodily harm. Most settled for the cash.

The internet was flooded with junk mail from both Intell-Ex. and Compell-Tex. vanulat-ing the advantages of each product and using negative advertising against the other. Intell-Ex., through Harry Bliss's campaign, suggested that Psych majors often fall prey to mental disorders after a few years due to the nature of their subject, and a disproportionate number of elderly people who had been psychologists or psychiatrists were known to contract Alzheimer's. Compell-Tex. fought back with an "English majors are nerds and losers" campaign that had a temporary effect in halting the growth of their numbers.

Both Intell-Ex. and Compell-Tex. bought up most of the advertising on the closed-circuit student station, just in case any of the students turned to that channel. Compell-Tex. had a snappy commercial for Psych with someone doing a Freud imitation and two of the Spice Girls sitting on his knees. Intell-Ex. countered with a campaign featuring John Travolta reading a volume of *Little Dorritt* and Natalie Portman *The Return of the Native*.

Still, the numbers who were majoring in Psych continued to grow, and it seemed that Compell-Tex. was winning out when Intell-Ex. made the coup they had been planning since mid-semester. It came in the form of a memo from Jack Swift, and Circassian, who had gotten in early, was the first to take it out of his mailbox.

NOTICE TO ALL EMPLOYEES: A NEW ACQUISITION FOR INTELL-EX

As of the beginning of the fall season, the Education department will have become the property of our company. All employees should welcome their new colleagues into the Intell-Ex. family. We are proud to have them on board. There will be a get-acquainted party this coming Saturday evening in the ballroom of the Golden Horn Hotel. All employees are strongly advised to be there to meet and mingle.

Sincerely,
Jack Swift

Circassian stared at the notice a moment and then shrugged. He had an idea why Jack Swift had arranged a purchase of Education. It had the largest number of students and the largest student-faculty ratio. But most of the faculty were exhausted and dispirited, the program was in danger of falling into chaos, and Dean Steen was determined to hold onto the tiller of this floundering vessel and land it securely on the rocks. There had to be another reason besides increasing volume behind Swift's plan, and Circassian thought he knew what it was.

Meanwhile, the rivalry between Mona Pilgrim and Tilly Owlglass for the souls of the student body was heating up. Mona had decided to use some of the money from the Wishin Ryu and Tai Chi Clubs, both of which she headed as president, to buy red-and-white uniforms for the "Truth Squad," which she formed out of about a dozen like-minded students. They would walk around campus telling the knowledge-consumers of the as-yet publicly owned departments to be careful that they might be next to get privatized. Meanwhile, Tilly Owlglass had recruited about two dozen pledges for Nu Mu to fulfill most of their pledging obligations by making sure that whenever they saw a "Truth Squad" member haranguing someone, they would harangue him back. They were dressed in blue-and-white uniforms, and they all wore bowties and buzzcut hairdos.

A few fistfights between the two squads broke out, and VP T.P. Sealey called Tilly and Mona into his office to "cool it."

"She's trying to stop people from speaking," said Mona.

"You're right about that," maffled VP T.P. Sealey.

"She's telling lies about privatizing; it's the future, Mona, give up!" said Tilly.

"You're right about that," snaffled VP T. P. Sealey.

"But how can she be right and I be right at the same time?" asked a puzzled and reblitted Mona.

"You're right about that, too," bleagled the VP. "Now, since you're both right, could you just calm down and settle your differences like the mature young women you are?" he smuttered.

They agreed that they would try to act more in the enlightened spirit of the University. The next day, they decided to meet in the main lunchroom of Sprockett Hall. On one side sat Tilly with a dozen of her supporters, and on the other Mona with hers. All of them had filled their trays with the most glutinous food they could find in the cafeteria: chocolate pudding, mashed potatoes with gravy, roll mops, Apple-Brown-Betty, meat balls, thinly-sliced liverwurst, head cheese and other delicacies. The cafeteria tried to cater to a lot of tastes, and it rarely succeeded, but the variety of the foods it offered compared favorably with most of the other University cafeterias.

Mary M. Magdalene intoned a prayer for all those assembled, saying that God was watching over them and would keep them all from extreme forms of harm. At an agreed-upon signal, the two groups began to throw their food at each other, some with practiced aim. Most all of the other students who had been innocently eating their lunch when the mayhem began cleared out, but several were pelted with stray meat balls, beef stroganoff, and strands of fettucine alfredo.

At the end of five minutes, the combat was over. Both sides had run out of food and were besmeared and grimed with an assortment of puddings, pies, cakes, viands, vegetables, fruit and pasta. Mary Magdalene declared the contest a draw and everyone went back to their dorms to wash up. When VP T.P. Sealey heard about it he breathed a sigh of relief: There hadn't been any violence.

Circassian and Tina went to the get-together at the Golden Horn Hotel, an unusually large structure that had been built in the 1890s. It boasted a Vietnamese chef who had been trained as a demolition expert in his home country during the War before he left for the Golden Gates of the States, and the food he served reflected his early training. The service was also very poor, but the ambience was lavish in a turn-of-the-century manner, complete with Tiffany-style lamps and Duncan-Phyfe and Art Deco-style furniture. In fact, almost everything in the place, including the food, was a "style" of something else.

The chef had an elaborate imagination for preparing foods, since he had lived in a country where people had to make do with substitutes for things they wanted but couldn't have. So the menu at the Golden Horn often consisted of shrimp-style bacon or lobster-style cod. One of his favorites was tofu-style sirloin, which was about as close to real sirloin as mince pie is to lemon meringue, but for some reason, as long as they didn't get food poisoning, the customers seemed to tolerate the dishes as "exotic." Besides, the Golden Horn Hotel was about the only place to eat in town that had real silver and china instead of plastic spoons, forks, knives and heavy-duty paper plates.

Before the meal began, cocktails were served, which, as it turned out, were fairly tolerable, since the owner had a special deal with one of the local distilleries. Circassian found himself talking to Camilla Still, one of the veterans of the Education department and someone who was prone to episodes of manic depression. But since the department was a pretty gloomy place anyway, her erratic behavior generally went unnoticed. There was, however, the incident in which she tried to jump off the roof of the Blenheim Science Building and was only saved when a rather courageous Physics professor, Pete Decal, caught her by the wrist as she made the plunge. Of course, the next day she had forgotten the whole thing and everyone thought it would be better not to remind her.

"Hiya, Len," she said to Circassian, since she rarely spoke to him and didn't know he preferred his last name.

"Hi, Camilla, and it's Circassian," he said.

"What's Circassian?"

"My last name."

"Of course it's your last name."

"I like being called Circassian."

"Oh, why?" Camilla asked.

"I don't know. I just like the sound of it," he said, refusing from a waiter some frank-style turnips that were being passed around as hors d'ouevres.

"Well, what do you think of Jack Swift's new acquisition, Circassian?" asked Camilla.

"I don't know what to make of it. How do you like it?"

"Besides being told that I've lost tenure and that my salary is being cut 35%, I think it's a great idea." Heavy irony was Camilla's strong point.

"Do you have any idea why Swift would want to acquire the Education department?" Circassian asked, hoping for a serious answer. He got one.

"I think it's to get everyone in the department to quit or retire early so he can hire adjuncts for everything and really make a killing," said Camilla, looking very serious.

"You may be right. Jack Swift seems to be that sort of person; he'd sell you his grandmother, and he'd deliver." Circassian wanted to keep it light.

"I don't know about that, but he gave us some kind of talk yesterday about how proud he was of our productivity, although he hoped he could get it to increase a little to keep up with the competition. Then he cited the figures from some place in the Upper Peninsula of Michigan — Moosehead State, I think — and showed us that their Education department was even more productive than ours. That got us all in the right mood," said Camilla, by now mumbling into her drink.

"So what are you going to do now?" asked Circassian. He was hoping to see a sign of rebellion in Camilla.

"I think I'll kill myself," said Camilla, still looking very serious. "I'm joking, of course," she added. "I'd never think of doing something like that!" She laughed and excused herself to talk with another group of jolly faculty.

Meanwhile, Tina had gotten into a heated discussion with Bendminder and Daks Rhombus, the one computer fanatic in the Education department. They had been arguing about on-line courses and the new-generation computers, and their technical talk was far too technical to be transcribed here in any intelligible way.

"You'll see," said Tina. "If you don't watch it, they'll really be able to replace you guys."

Bendminder didn't say anything. He was already beginning to calculate the savings to the University if they could just replace one third of the faculty with adjunct teacher-computers that could be rented monthly, since they would probably be too expensive to buy outright in sufficient numbers.

"Nothing will replace the teacher," said Daks. "Well, maybe in fifty years," he added.

"Why fifty? Why not twenty?" asked Tina. "In the last few decades, everything that was predicted to take place far in the future has happened sooner."

"Well, in twenty years, I'll be long retired," said Daks, with a slight sigh of anticipation. Daks loved teaching, he just couldn't stand most of the students and believed that if they'd just go away, teaching could be a very enjoyable experience for him.

"Some of these technologies are developing quicker than even you might think," said Tina. "What about that paper-grading computer they've just developed? Circassian gets nightmares about that one; he thinks he's trapped inside one of those things, pushing all the buttons and levers to make it run."

"We'd have a profit of fourteen million!" exclaimed Bendminder. He had been calculating in his head the savings to the University with the one-third staff cut against the yearly rental costs. Of course, all of this was hypothetical, but Bendminder was very comfortable with the hypothetical.

"That's nice," said Daks. He didn't particularly like Bendminder, but he knew, since he needed his help to support his requests for additional computers and software, that he would have to tolerate his furry-minded slitterings.

"Okay," said Tina. "How do you teach your classes, Daks? Straight lecture or discussion?"

"Lecture, of course. What do you think I want to do, confuse them?" answered Daks. He was a man of medium-height with a young beard and old hair. He liked to wear sportscoats and enjoyed teaching the most advanced students since they could understand what he was saying to them about computers most of the time.

"And what kind of exams do you give: essay or short answer?" asked Tina, who had heard this argument from Circassian many a tiresome time.

"Short answer, of course. Do you think I want to go nuts trying to figure out what those kids are saying?"

"Then why wouldn't it be easy enough to replace you with a machine that could lecture and another that would grade your exams?" she asked.

"We've already got a machine that grades the exams," churpled Daks.

"So you're half-way there already," said Tina.

"They just won't find a machine that will replace the way I lecture," insisted Daks, and he trambled off to another group of happy people.

"Do you know, Tina," thusled Bendminder, "if we could get those kind of machines, this place would be making money hand over fist."

"No shit," said Tina and walked off to join Circassian.

Before dinner was served, Jack Swift made another pep speech. He told everyone that now that Intell-Ex. had acquired the Education department, another piece of the corporate puzzle was being solved. With Education now in their camp — meaning Intell-Ex.'s — the whole Big Picture would be changing soon. He went over the numbers that would be added to the knowledge-consumer yield: another twelve hundred majors. He projected the figures for productivity gain: Since there were only sixteen full-time and eighty-seven adjunct faculty in Education, productivity would be bumped up considerably. Everyone was to applaud, but only Bendminder did until the rest slowly and reluctantly joined in.

"Now enjoy your dinners," said Jack Swift.

Dinner consisted of Mock Turtle Soup, Welsh Rabbit, Swiss Chard, Hungarian-style imitation goulash made with collared greens, and a large helping of ice cream-style frozen yogurt. Several of the guests unexpectedly visited the restroom in the middle of the meal, a line began to form in front of both bathrooms somewhere between the goulash and the yogurt, and there were many embarrassing moments from the diners while waiting their turn.

"Hello, Friend Circassian." It was Frank and Kara Short. They seemed in good shape since they had once dined at the Golden Horn before and knew what to avoid: everything but the yogurt, which was passable. They had wisely had a decent meal before they came to the dinner. The reason Frank had figured that Jack Swift had chosen the Golden Horn instead of any other place (or had some catering service or the University food service to prepare the meal) is that Intell-Ex. had just purchased the Golden Horn with the promise of converting it into classrooms when the Intell-Ex. segment of the University went off-campus. The rental fees for the classrooms were a large part of the outlay out of profits, and getting a place of their own struck them as a sound investment, albeit a temporary solution to a long-range plan.

Frank and Kara were intending to go home, as were most of the invited guests, some holding their sides or stomachs in a gesture of extreme discomfort, but they decided to join Circassian and Tina at one of the local eateries for ice cream. It would expel the pasty taste of the yogurt-style yogurt.

"Now, why do you think Intell-Ex. bought Education, besides what Swift said?" asked Frank, gellatating, as he were about to eat a spoonful of Radical Chocolate Surprise.

"I think they're trying to pull something on Psych," said Circassian, "but I don't think they can get away with it."

"Are you thinking what I'm thinking, old man?" asked Frank Short.

"Yes, I think I'm thinking what I think you're thinking, Frank," said Circassian.

"What the hell do you guys think you're both thinking?" wandled Tina. Kara said nothing; she was used to Frank's elaborate ratiocinations.

"You first, Frank," said Circassian.

"No, friend," alphonsed Frank, "you first."

"Well, I think that the first thing Swift is going to do is bribe a group of willing people to make a few changes in the requirements for the degree in teaching," said Circassian.

"Such as?" eggled Frank.

"The requirements for Psych can be changed so that students don't have to take Psych 100 in order to get Child and Adolescent Psych. I just don't know how he can get away with that," added Circassian.

"By hiring out some of the people in the Psych department to teach those courses in the Education department and then getting them to write up a paper proving that nobody needs Psych 100 to learn the more advanced courses," said Frank, twirling a fudge ball with his spoon.

"Do you think the State Ed. department would fall for that?" wondered Circassian, digging into a soya burger.

"The Education Department writes the rules and then State Ed. approves them. That's how they get all of those requirements written in. Didn't you know that?" Frank wondered. For all his sophistication, sometimes Circassian exhibited lapses of naiveté.

"This sounds a little fantastic, even for a crud sucker like Jack Swift," said Tina.

"I agree," said Kara, finally venturing an opinion after listening to the conversation with amused forebearance. "Once they start monkeying around with the course requirements, those guys will have a surprise for them, I'm sure."

"I think the surprise will be on us, Kara," said Frank. "Never underestimate the depths of your adversary."

"Well, I still think it's out of the question. There's just so much crap the University will tolerate, and if what you say is true, Jack Swift has overreached himself," said Kara, finishing her French vanilla sorbet.

"We shall see," ponted Frank, "we shall see."

V

The following week, there was an announcement in *The University Chatter*:

New Requirements Planned for Education Majors in the fall

The All-University Curriculum Committee has approved a plan by the Education department to become more autonomous. As of the fall, all Education majors will no longer have to take Psych 100 nor Adolescent and Child Psychology within the department. On approval from the State Education Department, Child and Adolescent Psychology will be taught by two newly appointed faculty, Edward Stith and Belle Barr, formerly Adjunct Acting Visiting Assistant Professors in the Psychology department, who will assume their duties the first day of the new term.

In place of Psych 100, all Education majors will take a course in English or American literature, according to Dean Steen. "This change will help students with their language skills and will enable the department to have greater control of the curriculum being used in these important courses." Dean Lean has scheduled a conference with Dean Steen and the chairs to discuss issues that will arise from these changes.

Circassian called Frank Short to tell him about the *Chatter* piece, but when he got him on the phone, Frank was already ahead of him.

"Listen, Old Boy, we got that one right, but don't think that Compell-Tex. will take this lying down. I'll bet you a dinner at any place besides the Golden Horn that there's another move afoot to mess up the curriculum even more," he said, a slight chickling sound in his voice.

Meanwhile, Dean Lean was staring at two very unhappy psychologists: Bop Rogers and Si Abrams, who looked at him as if he had personally been responsible for the change in Education requirements.

"Don't look at me as if I've been personally responsible for the change in the Education requirements," remonstered Dean Lean, who had had a trying day the week before when Dean Steen had found out that he was doing obscene crossword puzzles. This happened when his e-mail and Dean Steen's got mysteriously interchanged and the next time he logged in he discovered that he was getting a message from Maggie Jones inviting him to a luncheon of the AAUW chapter at the University. What Dean Steen received was the latest crossword puzzle from "Jugs, Inc." which was based entirely on words describing the female pudenda in four different languages. Dean Steen was not amused, and Dean Lean was embarrassed. It was this little indiscretion that made it rather difficult for Dean Lean to protest the summary disappearance of five hundred potential students from Arts and Science to Professional Studies.

So in one sense he *was* responsible for the change in the Education requirements. Just how the mix-up in the e-mail occurred — it only happened that one time — was something he could ponder and "Stats" Bendminder would know. However, in exchange, Dean Steen had pointed out to him that with the new English requirement, most of the students would be taking a similar number of courses in Arts and Science; it just wouldn't count for Compell-Tex., that is, for Psychology.

"I want you to know that as much as I would like to do something about this change in requirements, I no longer have any jurisdiction over the English department and Dean Steen no longer has any say in what goes on in Education. We don't own them anymore," said Dean Lean.

Bop Rogers looked at Si Abrams as if the both of them were ready to give the Dean a good thrashing but they thought better of it.

"What we want to know is how the All-College Curriculum Committee could possibly approve of these changes," said Bop Rogers. Bop was mostly interested in animal behavior but had discovered that some of his subjects too closely resembled some of the students he knew to make him entirely comfortable when he "sacrificed" them. Si Abrams taught Child Psychology and often brought his own children in to demonstrate some of his theories.

"Well, the way the committee is constituted now, there is one representative from English, one from History, and three from Education. And the other Professional Studies reps went along, so you lost your courses on a vote of twelve to six. But hell, guys, that's what democracy is all about," chiggled Dean Lean. He had never liked the faculty in the Psych department very much; he thought they were too sure of themselves and they often ignored him.

"You could have gotten Dean Steen to stop it if you'd wanted to," Si Abrams protested.

"Did she make a deal with you?"

"Of course not," Dean Lean lied.

"We're going to see Pickle about this," Bop Rogers said.

"Provost Pickle went to a two-month conference in Tasmania. He'll be back the first day of finals," expoupulated Dean Lean.

"But by then it will be too late to change the schedules!" Si Abrams remonstrated.

"So you can see how this turns out," said Dean Lean. "If it doesn't work, we can always switch back."

"But by then five hundred students will be exposed to learning Child and Adolescent Psych the wrong way," whined Si.

"I thought those two Adjuncts the Ed department hired had taught the course in your department," wandled Dean Lean.

"But there's something about that department that's going to make everything confused. Everyone's confused there," steamed Si.

"Yeah," said Bop. "They'll confuse the students."

"I think the students around here are used enough to being confused that they'll be used to it if they take these courses in Education," Dean Lean pointed out, with rare acutement.

"Well, we'll see President Fred!" wailed Si.

"President Fred is on a good-will trip to Iraq and won't be back until graduation," said Dean Lean.

"Then we'll take it to the Chancellor!" stampered Bop.

"The Chancellor approved these changes by fax, since this was a University-wide change in basic policy," said Dean Lean, showing the two the piece of paper with the Chancellor's signature on it.

"Then we'll take it to the Supreme Court!" throndled Si.

"Lots of luck, gentlemen," said Dean Lean, and the two strambled out of his office like termites fleeing a three-toed sloth, whooching and crimbling to each other as they went.

While all of that was going on, Dabs Budweiser and Hank Schecht were in the process of getting a restraining order against Intell-Ex. for gross interference in faculty governance. They were unsure whether it would work, but the Union felt it had to do Something since up until now it had been doing Nothing.

Circassian had been miffed and snoffed enough by Dabs, so when she called him on the phone a few days after the Ed-Psych switch, he was not in a very congenuous mood.

"I thought you had no jurisdiction over what happened to any of us anymore," he said.

"Well, there's a principle here that we have to try to uphold or else those two corporate jokers are going to walk all over us," Dabs said.

"And what have they been doing until now, waltzing all over you?" said Circassian.

"Look, let's not quibble about this," said Dabs. "You've been a loyal member of the Union ever since you got here. We need you to help us in planning this legal manuever."

"Why me?" asked Circassian.

"Yeah, why him?" asked Tina, listening on the extension. When she had answered the phone and knew it was Dabs, she suspected that they'd try to rope Circassian into doing something self-destructive.

"Because you still believe in ideals," said Dabs.

"I do?" asked Circassian.

"Of course you do! Weren't you the one who went with Branch all over the place to try to help out Daphne Dart, and cornered Pickle in a bowling alley? Everybody knows about it," said Dabs, starkulating.

"Why not ask Branch? He's been here longer," said Circassian.

"We thought of that, but Branch is angry at everybody at the moment, and he's also fed up with trying to unravel the meaning of life. He wouldn't be any use to us right now."

"And I would?" said Circassian.

"Of course. We need you, Circassian. You wouldn't let us down, would you?" Circassian thought of Jack Swift and Bendminder and all of the other people who would be on him if he threw in his lot with Dabs. Then he thought of the Union and what it had done for him in the past. What had it done for him in the past?

"No dice," he said, and hung up.

"I'm proud of you, honey," griggled Tina.

"What did I do?" he asked.

"You said 'no dice' and that's what I hoped you'd say. Besides, we still need every bit of your salary if we're going to keep making the payments on the car. The boss cut my hours again," said Tina.

Two weeks later, Dabs Budweiser and Hank Schecht applied to the Circuit Court for a restraining order on Intell-Ex. and Compell-Tex. to cease and desist any further acquisitions of departments from the University and any further interference in University curricular matters. The request was denied by Judge Franklin Sowerby, a Putski appointee. In his decision, the Judge declared that any interference in the present situation at the University would be a "restraint of trade" and declared any future disputations on this subject null and void. But as Frank Short predicted, Compell-Tex. had a few tricks of its own up its corporate sleeve and would be using them before the semester had come to its fractitious end.

Part V

It was in the middle of the spring semester (called spring because it was the dead of winter at the University until May, but no one wanted the students to think of spring as winter) that Jack Swift scheduled a general meeting of the departments that had been acquired by Intell-Ex. in order to introduce a new program that would "sharpen up" everyone for the future, although most of the faculty by now had been dulled down enough to yearn for the past.

Bendminder, ever mindful of all of the trends in education, had decided to capitalize on the Assessment Movement that was sweeping lower and creeping higher into education. He would do the movement one better than had ever been imagined, even by the minions who ran the assessment organizations around the country. Although the departments in question were no longer publicly funded, Bendminder was aware that Intell-Ex. was the cutting edge on the chopping board of the Future of Education, and knew that if his project succeeded, it would be quickly emulated by the rest of the University system, privatized or not.

His plan was simply a logical extension of all of the assessments that had been inflicted on the University in the past: "DICTATE." It was adapted from a system used to great effect in some of the small Southern colleges with meager budgets and no unions to worry about. This was the concept that Camille Faux had mentioned to Ambler Slaughter at the Phoenix several months before, and now it was ready to take root and branch out.

When Circassian got to the meeting, he noticed that most of the faculty were beginning to show the effects of working for Jack Swift: glazed looks of incredulity were etched on their faces, mingled with grief and a sense of loss. He could see Toddy Dance and Josh

Gutsky visibly shuddering with anticipation at whatever Jack Swift was about to inflict o them. On the other hand, Branch was scowling and werbling to anyone who would listen to him about the State of Things. But no one would.

"Ladies and gentlemen," Swift intoned like a train conductor on the Road to Erewhon, "I would like to introduce you to a new initiative refined by Intell-Ex. that is certain to find favor with our consumers. It is a way of assuring them that quality control is first in our minds and hearts. This program is derived from all of the other assessment programs that you've been visited with in the past few decades: 'Middle States,' 'NCATE' and the like. On this one, 'DICTATE,' we are certain will be the model of the future. And once it is implemented, I can assure you that what remains of the public sector of the University will follow our lead."

"Where?" asked Branch. He wanted to say "into the crapper," but decided against it.

"Wherever," said Jack Swift, snootily. He was trying to find some way to get rid of Branch, whom he regarded as a very large thorn in his side, but he realized that Branch was now near the top in productivity among his colleagues, being a very popular teacher despite his tendencies.

"What does 'DICTATE' stand for?" asked Josh. He was only mildly curious, but he wanted to move the meeting forward as quickly as possible.

"DICTATE: Developing Incisive Computations to Assess Teacher Excellence," Jack Swift said proudly. Camille had realized that the original words for the acronym would not go down very well with either the staff or the public, although Marigold Markham had found out the true intent of DICTATE and sent it on to Circassian: "Demanding Irrelevant Calculations to Atrophy Teacher Endurance."

"Unlike most of the other methods of assessment, which tend to be a little vague and pointless, DICTATE's objectives are very clear. As you can see," said Jack, now using a Power Point, "the requirements for the assessment project are specific. No one will have any doubt, once the numbers are published, that we are doing our job."

A series of directions flashed on the screen:

1. All members of the faculty employed by Intell-Ex. will be divided into groups of ten. Each group will be responsible for producing ten pounds of data beginning in the fall semester, their assignment to be completed by the last day of the following spring semester. The data must be on 60-lb. bond paper, double-spaced and one-sided. It will be weighed at the "Weighing-In Ceremony" on the last day of classes.

2. Each member of the faculty will be assigned to produce one pound of data as a contribution to his or her group. Since all of the members of each group will be responsible for precisely one pound of data, we believe that this will produce the needed ésprit de corpse to enhance the chances of success.

(Circassian wondered if the misspelling of "corps" was deliberate. There were a few snickers, but Jack Swift ignored them.)

3. If any member of a committee is short the pound of data by the deadline, he or she will be subject to severe disciplinary action, which will likely result in a significant pay cut and curtailment of privileges such as access to the company bathroom and dining room.

"Are there any questions?" asked Swift. It seemed to him that there needn't be, since the instructions were clear enough even for a four-year-old to understand.

"What kind of data are you looking for?" asked Toddy Dance, timorously.

"Oh, that's your responsibility," said Jack Swift, smirkling with a twinkle in his eye. "You should know more about those kind of things than I do. But once all of the data are collected and weighed, we can then report to our consumers and the general public that we have done the most thorough assessment that any institution of Higher Learning has ever undergone. If the whole University follows our lead, and I have no doubt that President Fred will do so, we can produce half a ton!"

"Can we assume that the purpose of this assessment is to determine that we are understaffed, underpaid, and overworked so that additional funds could be allocated to run the University," asked someone who was dressed in an oversized raincoat.

"Of course not! Everyone knows that you are understaffed, underpaid, and overworked! That's just in accordance with the new trend in education. Especially in our public university systems. The public isn't interested in rediscovering the obvious."

"Then why are we doing this?" Again, the question came from the foggy-voiced anonymous-looking person in the raincoat.

"To reassure the tax-paying public and our consumers in particular that we are giving them the biggest bang for their bucks, of course!" said Swift with the patronizing tone of a Greek god at a Cub Scout reunion.

"Even if the data are meaningless?"

"Do you think your average taxpayer would be able to understand whether or not data are meaningless? I'm a pretty sharp guy, as you know, and most of the time the data I get are meaningless, unless, of course, we're talking about the Bottom Line. That's the only data that have any meaning around here, and don't you forget it!" And with these dismissive words, Jack Swift terminated the meeting.

In the next few weeks, the faculty of Intell-Ex. was divided into groups of ten. Circassian was delegated to the "Student Responses in Class" Committee. His assigment was to write up an assessment program to determine the nature and extent of student sleeping in lecture classes. The categories were divided into "Sleeping," "Snoozing," and "Dozing," and each had specific parameters.

To determine whether or not a student was sleeping, the lecturer had to go up to the suspect with a book that weighed not less than two pounds and drop it not more than four feet in front of the suspect. If the student awoke, the category he or she would fall into would be "Snoozing." To determine the distinction between "Dozing" and "Snoozing," the requirement was for the lecturer to clap hands vigorously three times, no closer than two feet from the student's face. If he or she awoke abruptly, the appropriate category would be "dozing." Circassian had been toying with a "Dazed" category, but since most of the students in lecture classes usually looked dazed, the category was too broad to be meaningful.

Other factors that were to be considered in this part of the assessment were original size of class, number of students actually attending by the last two weeks, time of class, size of room in proportion to number of students, mean temperature in the lecture hall during the class period, and other stuff that would fill up the one-pound quota. By the middle of the fall semester, Circassian discovered that he had almost three-quarters of a pound of data. This, unfortunately, was not the case with Toddy Dance, who had been assigned to gather data on "Subjects Discussed in Cell Phone Conversations of Students Walking through the Quad." Toddy was slightly hard of hearing, and whenever he got close enough to overhear the students' end of cell phone conversations, he was glared at, especially if the conversation was between girlfriend and girlfriend.

Circassian suggested that Toddy ask Jack Swift for help, since this was a matter of technology, and several days later he saw Toddy with a big smile on his face. Jack Swift had given him a special listening device pioneered by Intell-Ex. for CIA surveillance. It had worked perfectly, since it could be concealed in his ear and had a range of three hundred feet.

"It's terrific, Circassian!" said Toddy. "But some of the things they say to each other on the phone! I had no idea there were so many positions!"

Circassian was tempted to ask Toddy to clarify what he said, but then thought better of it. He also wondered what kind of data Toddy would report, and realied that it wouldn't matter since no one would ever read it.

❀

Several days later, Circassian heard a knock on the door at about midnight, but when he went out to see who it was, all he found was a mysterious-looking envelope at the front door, and he heard the screech of tires as a car tore off down the block. He opened the envelope and read the following: a transcript of a meeting among Ambler Slaughter, Camille Faux, Bendminder, and Jack Swift. There was no date on it, but Circassian could see that it was recent. He had no doubt where it had come from: Marigold Markham. And once he had finished reading it, he knew that his suspicions about the true purpose of "DICTATE," as had been suggested by the real meaning of the acronym, were confirmed.

Bendminder: Well, how are things going, Jack? Any resignations yet?

JS: Only two: one in English and one in History, but both of them were on the low end of the pay scale and were getting jobs elsewhere.

CF: Any chance for more? We still have the whole spring semester ahead of us.

Bendminder: According to the data I have, Jack, you should be doing better. At the other universities that've used "DICTATE," they've averaged five resignations, two early retirements, and three suicides.

JS: Well, these guys are tough. They've already been through ten annual budget cuts with Putsky and the Board. They're used to being put upon. I think some of them actually like it!

AS: Hey, I have an idea! Why don't you increase the poundage from one to two?

JS: It'll make me look bad, Amberler, and I still need the confidence of the staff to get them to bring up their numbers. I'm hopeful that the pressure will get to them and we can realize a net reduction in staffing of about 15%.

Bendminder: And then, of course, the market forces will set in and about 10% of the students will drop out, which will justify the previous reduction in the staff. Then when the two numbers reach an equilibrium between students and faculty . . .

AS: We'll institute a new round of "DICTATE!" Brilliant!

CF: And in a few more years, the University will be down to the size it belongs: at 10% of the student body it has now! Then everybody, especially the students, will be happy.

Bendminder: Not only does it make sense fiscally; it's sound educational policy!

JS: To DICTATE!

All: To DICTATE!

Circassian wondered what he could do with this information, but he realized that even if he could leak it safely, nobody would be a bit surprised.

{}

Because of the role of DICTATE and Option Three in distorting the lives of faculty and students, President Fred quickly adopted the new assessment method, since he didn't want to be thought of as an "old stick-in-the-mud." There was now unusual competition for positions on the Faculty Senate. In former times, as Circassian was well aware, many of the positions went unfilled, especially in Professional Studies, where most of the faculty were besieged enough by students to be becalmed by other faculty. Circassian knew of this because he was offered the chance to be a Senator for the five consecutive years that he'd been at the University.

But this time, there was a fierce fight between Betsy Bowdein and Jackson Pawlick for a position on the All-University Curriculum Committee, and a second between Frank Pissakowski and Manny Sqands for another. The candidates actually hired pollsters and campaign managers, and some faculty wondered where they had gotten the money and what the stakes were. When Pawlick and Sqands won in a cliffhanger, the answers to those questions were evident. With some horse-trading and a few strategic abstentions, the All-University Curriculum Committee recommended that Freshman English be dropped as a required course. Intell-Ex. appealed to Dean Lean and Provost Pickle, but neither wanted to make a ruling, since, according to Option Three, the English department wasn't under their jurisdiction.

Numbers began dropping very rapidly in Freshman comp. until Intell-Ex. was able to offer each student who stayed in the course a refund of half the cost of tuition for that semester. The numbers bumped up again, but the damage had been done. Even with Fun-100 some students hated Freshman comp. so much that they were willing to forego the found money in order to avoid the course. Part of the reason for this was that grades were still relatively low, since the faculty had not yet adjusted to the new philosophy of Intell-Ex. of "give them what they want." What students wanted even more than found money were found grades.

The spring passed quickly for Circassian. Tina's workload had been increased again, and they were almost feeling comfortable. Of course, because of the anticipated shortfall in revenues, Circassian's pay for his summer school teaching was cut from $2,000 to $1,500, but toward the end of the summer he received good news: He had been promoted to Fully Assistant Professor. This did not guarantee him job security, since tenure had been abolished, but he actually received a 20% increase in his salary, which put him back to where he was as an Acting Visiting Assistant Professor before he had been hit with Option Three. Of course, instead of the four-course load he had carried before, it was now increased to five.

But Daphne Dart was gone, as were Toddy Dance and Harold Hanes; so were Ron Burble and Ralph Null. The Table had been decimated. And some of the other formerly tenured faculty could see their time coming, too. The Adjuncts, having been given a taste of "competitive bidding," were far more ingenious in figuring out ways to attract students. One agreed to teach a Shakespeare course using the new "Modern Translation" that had been rendered by the staff at Intell-Ex. Once students got the word that they didn't have to look in a dictionary or glossary to understand Shakespeare, they flocked to the new course instead to the one taught by Bonswell Truman. But Circassian was pleased to note that a lot of students who seemed to want to learn the traditional Shakespeare remained in Bonswell's class. Jack Swift dismissed them as "stick-in-the-muds," but enough stayed to save the Shakespeare scholar's job.

Soon the summer session was over and the new semester was raring to go. Circassian approached it with the tentative feelings of a beginning swimmer jumping into the ocean. He didn't know if he would drown with all those courses to teach — but he wasn't going to let on to anybody about his doubts. Tina gave him a very special lunch of a tofu-style steak sandwich and his favorite desert, marzipan.

When he got to class that morning on a late summer day, Circassian discovered that his roster had been reduced by eight students. Nobody seemed to know where they had gone. Circassian wasn't used to losing this many for any reason, and since he made his first classes pretty stimulating and enjoyable, it was rare that more than one or two students dropped out. He was pretty sure he knew where they'd gone when he looked at the productivity graph that Bendminder had turned out, which adorned the department bulletin board in bright blue and red: Treat Billingham, one of the Adjuncts who had ambitions of some day making a living wage, had gotten an increase of eight students from his previous numbers.

Curious rather than angry, Circassian found Treat in the lunchroom after class, eating his curds and whey. He particularly liked whey since no one knew exactly what it was and it provided him with no end of conversational gambits. Circassian approached Treat casually, which made the adjunct very suspicious. No one was approaching anyone casually anymore in the English department but rather dyspeptically or paranoically.

"Say, Treat, I was wondering about your students' enrollments," said Circassian as Treat spooned a bolus of curd into his mouth. "I lost eight students from my previous numbers. Would you, by any chance, know if you picked up any of them?"

"I'm pretty sure I did, Circassian, and you have only yourself to blame," said Treat, defensively.

"I'm not trying to blame anybody; it's just that I'm curious to know what happened to make them all leave," Circassian said.

"You to find out, me to know," said Treat quislingly, and then left abruptly.

It was a few days later that Circassian saw his amourmesis and main source of student information in the hallway and stopped her. Mona Pilgrim was more on her guard now that she knew that Tilly knew that she knew that Tilly wasn't intimidated by what she knew Mona knew about her marijuana habit. Still, she had a soft heart in her head for Circassian.

"Hey, Mona, how's the new semester?"

Mona hadn't seen Circassian all summer, especially since she had spent it in Sierra Leone, helping children learn to do mime for a project she was working on in the arts and third world cultures. She was almost tongue-tied with pleasure.

"I'm finally, I'm fine," she said. "How is everything with you, Doc?"

He explained the situation with his enrollment. He was feeling a little harried since the lesser number in that class had put him in the lower half of the departmental pecking order in productivity. But now that he had been promoted to a Fully Assistant Professor with the opportunity for a renewal on his contract every five years, he felt he had something to lose again, something he hadn't felt in years of working at the University.

"It's the grades, Doc," explained Mona. "Treat Billingham and a couple more of the Adjuncts are trying to get those positions that all the professors who were let go vacated, and they think that the ones with the highest enrollments will have the best chance, so they're all promising everyone who gets into their classes that they will get an 'A' if they show up at least half the time and hand in a paper, any kind of paper . . . on any subject . . . written by anyone."

"And if I had offered all my students an 'A' they would have stayed in my course?" wondered Circassian.

"The ones who did stay are the ones who really want to learn; they think you're a good teacher or they would have gone for the sure 'A.'"

The next time his class met, Circassian noticed that six more students had apparently dropped out. That left him with sixteen, and perilously close to having the class cancelled, since Bendminder had convinced Swift that fifteen was the minimal size for any class below the graduate level. Circassian felt that kind of quiet desperation that could get very noisy if he let himself go, something Tina had never seen him do.

He decided to go to Dean Lean himself, since Branch would probably stunglamp the whole thing if he had told him. Besides, Branch probably knew this was happening and had already strambled once more over to the Dean's office.

Dean Lean had abandoned his obscene crossword puzzles on the net now that Dean Steen had gotten wind of it, and had decided instead just to read obscene literature, which he always covered with some report in case he was taken unawares. This had been happening infrequently, since Dean Lean was being involved less and less in the workings of Arts and Sciences. Compell-Tex.'s coup had put more pressure on English to increase productivity, and they had also put out a bid to acquire Sociology and Phys Ed., which they were planning to combine in some way in order to cut back on staffing. As he was about to read how Raoul had ravaged Henrietta down to the last shred of clothing, Circassian walked into the office, barely waiting for a secretarial announcement.

"Circassian!" jelted the Dean. "What are you doing here? Aren't you supposed to be teaching?"

"I finished my classes for the day," said Circassian. "I'd like to know if you know about the grade inflation that's going on in our department."

"But I have nothing to do with your department. It falls under Option Three. I thought you'd understood that," cheffled the Dean.

"But what's happening in my department can have an impact on the departments you still have jurisdiction over," explained Circassian. He then told the Dean what had happened.

"That's very interesting, Circassian. I suppose that it's hard to stop people who have some initiative from doing that, but what can I do? It would be restraint of trade. And you know how President Fred feels about restraint of trade," rationalated Dean Lean.

"But doesn't that sort of thing disgust you, Dean Lean?" asked Circassian.

"Circassian: I've been Dean for three years, and I was chair of my department for five, so by this time nothing that can happen around here could disgust me. I am disgust-proof, so if you want someone to be disgusted you've got the wrong man," permodulated Dean Lean.

Circassian walked out of the office as if he were a broken man. He knew now how Branch had felt when he'd gone into Dean Lean's office with his complaint about "To be or not to be." Circassian toyed with the idea of going to Dabs and the Union about this, but he remembered that the Union never involved itself in such matters. He imagined that it would have been restraint of trade to them as well.

The next week, he noticed that there had been another shift in course enrollment; Treat Billingham's figures had gone down and Bob Thong's, another of the up-and-coming Adjuncts, had risen by the same number. Circassian, still curious about all of the latest lunacy, saw Bob Thong in the locker room after they both had had their swim. Circassian swam now to relieve tension, and it was a pleasant enough way to cool off at this time of the year.

"Bob," said Circassian, "sorry to talk shop now, but you've been doing a great job getting your enrollment numbers up."

"Did Treat put you up to asking me?" said Bob, suspiciously. The Adjuncts were very suspicious of the Fullys since the Adjuncts were doing things that would make almost anyone suspicious.

"Nobody put me up to it. I just want to know, without revealing trade secrets, how you did it."

"Well, since it won't be a secret for long, I guess I can tell you. Treat offered his class all 'A's, so I upped the ante," he said, a flantiful smile on his face.

"Now how could you do that? Offer them 'A+'s?" quipped Circassian.

"Fuck the grades! Most of us are guaranteeing 'A's anyway. My angle is that I write their papers for them. That way they can concentrate on whatever it is they can concentrate on," explained Bob Thong.

"But that must take an enormous amount of time!" exclaimed Circassian.

"Nah! I write three standard papers and then I duplicate them and give them out to the students at random. Then they give them back to me and I give them all A's," he raftled.

"But what do they have to do for the 'A's besides hand the papers back to you?"

"You think I just give out the 'A's like that! What do you think I am, Circassian, a shnook? I *insist* that they read the paper at least once before they hand it back to me," he said.

"And how do you know they've read it?" asked Circassian.

"I use the honor system, of course!" said Bob Thong, who, now dressed, made an equilibidous exit.

()

For the next few weeks, things began to boil and bubble in the English department, and simmer in Education. History had managed to keep its profile comfortably low. No one had bothered trying to abolish requirements concerning their courses, and most students who took them seemed happy enough with the door prizes and raffles offered at each class, which included an all-expense trip for two to Latvia. (Since most of the students didn't know where Latvia was, the interest in the raffle was lively.)

Of course, what History faculty had been able to do that was more difficult for English faculty was get dressed up as easily recognizable personalities. Frank Short had agreed to impersonate Joe McCarthy, and Seth Gutman, Moses. Perhaps, though, one of the reasons that Ron Burble was no longer at the University — having taken "compulsory retirement" —was that he had decided that he should get dressed up as historical personality he found most fascinating: Adolph Hitler. His impersonation had been so convincing that he was pelted by assorted Jewish and Gypsy students and had to be rescued from evisceration by the campus police. He had wondered if perhaps, when he had barked out, "All Jews must be liquidated" at the top of his voice, it might have caused the stir that resulted in the bombardicide — especially since, on that fine spring day when he did it, he had taken his students outside onto the quad.

Several of the other faculty in the History department had been satisfactory as Gandhi, George Washington, and Fidel Castro. The English department was not so lucky, since except for Shakespeare, most of the students wouldn't know what one writer looked like from another. So when Josh Gutsky dressed up as Dickens he was taken for Longfellow, and Circassian's impersonation of Ibsen, complete with mutton-chop whiskers, was assumed to be Ralph Waldo Emerson.

Another feature of the History department's success were the many videos they were able to obtain of historical moments. It was far more difficult for the English department to get such videos of dramatized novels and short stories. So the students in History were kept happy if not particularly healthy, with that far-away look in their eyes when they finished the class and stumbled out into the — to them — blinding lights of the corridor.

Education students generally didn't need much inducement to stay in their major, since most of them felt that Education was the only thing they had any clue to doing at all, correctly or otherwise. Still, with Compell-Tex.'s impending purchase of Sociology and Phys. Ed., more curricular mayhem was anticipated. All of this dismayed Circassian, and although he at least had a job with some minimal security, he was working harder than ever.

Circassian had decided that even though he was a non-believer, he once again needed the spiritual advice of Pastor Castor. He had not seen much of the minister since the beginning of the semester and wondered if he was ill. As it turns out, Pastor Castor had felt morally sick from what he was seeing around him, and his soul was afflicted. So when Circassian saw him in his office, the good Pastor was not at all happy about his flock.

"Hello, Pastor Castor. How was your summer?" Circassian asked.

"It was tolerable, Circassian, tolerable. I visited my brother in Wales and my sister in

Pasadena. But whenever I came back here, I saw another abomination imposed on this poor, God-forsaken faculty."

When Castor said "God-forsaken," he meant it in the spiritual sense.

"I'm dismayed by what I see around me, too," said Circassian. "But what can we do about it? Every time I go to the Dean, he washes his hands of the whole business."

"A very appropriate metaphor," said Pastor Castor approvingly. "What of the Provost?"

"He's never around, and when he is . . . he's never around. They seem to think what happens to us won't have any effect on the rest of the campus, whatever is left of it," whimfed Circassian.

"And President Fred?" the minister inquired.

"He seems to get away from campus as much as he can, but he did send me a memo that told us where he stood." Circassian told Pastor Castor about the "restraint of trade" statement.

"Well, then, Circassian, all you can do is your job and hope that's enough to sustain you," said Pastor Castor.

"What sustains you?" asked Circassian. The two of them seemed in a dark mood, and a cloud suddenly blotted out the sun obligingly.

"Once one of the students came to see me. She was very young, even for a freshman, not much more than sixteen, I'd say. And she made a very strange request," he said.

"And what was that?"

"She wanted me to excommunicate her ex-boyfriend because he'd dropped her for some other girl," he said musingly.

"Do you go in for that sort of thing, Pastor Castor?" asked Circassian.

"Not usually. But when I asked her if she knew what ex-communication meant, she really didn't. All she knew was that she was angry at her former boyfriend and wanted to get back at him."

"And what did you tell her?"

"I told her to forgive him, and she laughed. It was a very strange laugh, soulless. I told her I couldn't do an excommunication, from what she had told me, and she left," said Pastor Castor.

"That sounds very sad," said Circassian.

"Believe me, it was. Now, I know better than almost anyone on this campus except maybe for Father Ansell and Rabbi Stillman what a serious thing excommunication is, but if it were any help, I'd excommunicate Jack Swift and the rest of that bunch, including Pickle and Bendminder," said Pastor Castor, speaking with more vehem than Circassian had ever heard from him before.

"Thanks, Padre, but I don't know what good that would do," said Circassian.

"You think it's gone beyond God's help?" asked Pastor Castor.

"I wish I knew," said Circassian.

"Well, don't give up your own faith in what you're doing. God sees," said Pastor Castor.

"I hope so," answered Circassian. He couldn't bring himself to share his thought with Pastor Castor that if there was a God, she must be blind.

Since his talk with Pastor Castor had depressed him even more than he had expected, Circassian began to think about resigning at the end of the semester. There were plenty of other people more than willing to take his Fully Assistant Professor place. But then he thought what Pastor Castor had told him about doing his job. Maybe Pickle and Bendminder and Jack Swift would want him to quit; he knew that if she had known how he felt, Camille Faux would have been thrilled if he had quit. These thoughts made him decide that the last thing he was going to do was quit. If he had thought about it more often, it would have made him so mad he would have stopped functioning and would have had to quit. So he decided that he would just do his job and let come whatever may, although he knew whatever may come would make his job even harder.

()

Tilly Owlglass was in a frumptious mood since the beginning of the fall season. Revenues were coming in from all over and Todd Zarathustra was madly in love with her. Actually, he was madly in love with her power.

At the end of the previous semester, Tilly had appointed herself to head the Student Activities Board, the power behind the President. Now, instead of having to work with someone else to make policy, she could make it on her own. And since Tilly had a Bendminder mind in a younger brain, she could be even more inventive in her flights of entrepreneurial fancy.

The student access channel was now filled with locally made commercials for everything that was being merchandised at the University. This included Revised Shakespeare mugs, decals, pens and pencils of one's favorite major, complete with major logo: for English the lion and unicorn; for history, Washington rampant on a field of CD's; for Education the three R's in red and green with a school house in the background; for psychology Freud with his head split in two and a rat running a maze through the aperture.

Tilly had also run through SAB and had approved by the student Senate and new President Mary M. Magdalene another fee: a user fee for all facilities on campus that excluded classrooms since, true to Circassian's predictions, there was an occupancy fee Intell-Ex. and Compell-Tex. had imposed for all other rooms.

In exchange for the new fee, there was an all-campus block party each weekend, some of which lasted until the middle of the next week, and opportunities to model designer clothes and get a contract from one of the modeling agencies that were now recruiting for University talent thanks to Tilly's efforts.

"You are amazing!" said Todd Zarathustra as he and Tilly lay in bed together one Sunday afternoon in the middle of the semester.

"What amazing are you talking about?" asked Tilly. Tilly considered herself moderately interested in sex, as long as it had a point to it. She found Todd a decent lover but totally clueless when it came to more practical matters. She was somewhat mollified when he answered: "You've got this campus eating out of your hand."

"Well, that's more like it. I thought you were going to talk about sex," said Tilly. As moderate as was her interest in sex, she loathed talking about it, since she regarded it a waste of breath. Besides, anticipating the kind of "this and that" conversation Todd would have come up with about the act of Love, she would have been more interested in a lecture on the merits of aardvark co-habitation in Tasmania.

That very afternoon, several of the more attractive Greek males culled from the local fraternities were going to have tryouts for "Mr. Gorgeous," which could lead to a contract with one of the more exclusive modeling agencies in Spokane or Duluth. Tilly had the tiresome task of being the judge along with Todd and a nonentity named Lydia Languish, the President of the Sororities on campus.

While Todd was getting showered, Tilly checked her e-mail to see how her various enterprises were getting along. The $10 user fee enabled Tilly to invest in a number of cheap and available variety acts that would try out their material in the campus coffee house, but it also gave her the reputation around the College Circuit as an operator whom you shouldn't mess around with. That enabled her to book some of the biggest names on the Circuit when she wanted them. The profits from the draw for most of these big acts gave the Student Activities Board a surplus of over $2 million. In fact, Tilly's methods were so successful that similar organizations at other universities were asking her to come in as a consultant to set up their own programs. She was also going to be honored by the Junior Chamber of Commerce as "Young Entrepreneur of the Year," an event sufficiently prestigious for her father to take a day out of his busy schedule to attend.

What she read on her e-mail was all good news — almost. The shares she had bought in Compell-Tex. had gone up two points; three more universities were asking for her advice; the modelling agency was planning to expand its search for talent on the campus; and Mona Pilgrim had lodged a complaint the previous week with the Attorney General's office that Tilly had been illegally appropriating public funds. How Mona had gotten wind of this, Tilly would hardly know, but since much of what she was doing was passed through Bendminder's office, Marigold Markham had leaked it to Circassian who gave the information to Mona.

When Todd came out of the bathroom, hair slicked down, pectals flexing, he expected Tilly to give him the admiring once-over. But she could scarcely refrain from gasping. Todd looked to her not like the handsome brute he was in his own eyes, and in the eyes of quite a number of pneumatic maidens he had deflowered in his career; to Tilly, he resembled a sleek California seal clambering out of the bathroom with a fish in his mouth rather than a toothbrush. She rushed past Todd into the bathroom and vomited copiously in the toilet. She suddenly felt soiled, violated by an inferior creature who had clambered into her bed — until she remembered that she was in Todd's apartment.

"Let's get dressed and get over to the fashion show," said Tilly, now cleansed of her self-disgust. They dressed quickly and walked out separately from Todd's apartment onto the campus. Under Tilly's supervision, the appearance of the campus had considerably changed since the previous spring. Billboards advertising everything from cough drops to feminine hygiene sprays lined both sides of the walks in the quad. In front of Main was a large neon sign that lit up at night with the words: "Compell-Tex. Education that Add$ Up." Over the side entrance of the building was a similar neon sign: "Intell-Ex. For a Future that Compute$."

Tilly thought that Compell-Tex.'s slogan was catchier, but the special effects on the Intell-Ex. sign were more dramatic.

As they walked to the Pepsi Student Center, past the Vaseline Science Building, they passed by a number of students who were making extra money by wearing sign boards advertising various products for which Tilly had signed contracts in exchange for student discounts. Students could consider this kind of activity as work-study, which would count as credit to reduce their tuition. One of the more imaginative students had decked himself out as an airplane and was pretending to soar, much to the amusement of the many spectators who saw him cavorting.

Students walked around wearing tee shirts advertising more products or else sported the logos for Intell-Ex. and Compell-Tex. When Tilly and Todd finally arrived at the Pepsi Student Center, a group of student reporters and photographers were waiting for her.

"Tilly, is there anything to the rumor that you intend to get the Student Government to invest in Compell-Tex. and Intell-Ex.?" said one plastrated reporter.

"There's absolutely nothing in that," snapped Tilly, lying. She had been planning to invest about $100,000 in the stock of each company on behalf of the Student Government.

"What of your impending merger with Todd Zarathustra?" asked a very enterprising young lady who gave both of them that knowing look that makes people given it want to lynch the lookee.

Todd and Tilly turned the requisite revealing crimson, and then, with presence of mind Tilly replied, "Any talk of mergers is premature. Todd and I have a lot of more important things to worry about." She swept into the auditorium, dutifully and hastily followed by Todd.

()

Circassian came back from Pastor Castor's office with a heavy heart, and looked into his box to discover yet another special bulletin. This one was not from Jack Swift or Bendminder, or Harry Bliss or Pickle or even Dean Lean. It was a bulletin from the *University Chatter*, and was signed by President Fred.

All University Requirements Dropped

As of the beginning of next semester, all University requirements will no longer be in effect. All students need do is take one hundred and twenty credits and they will be given a University diploma. If they wish to major in any subject, that is entirely up to them, but it will no longer be necessary in order to receive a degree. A resolution had been passed by the University Curriculum Committee over the summer abolishing all requirements. It was approved last week by the Board of Trustees and final approval was given yesterday by Chancellor Thwart. All students need no longer go to their advisors as of next semester if they don't want to.

President Fred, in a statement to the Faculty Senate, declared: "This new innovation in our curriculum will free students to choose their own courses. The previous system, although hallowed by tradition, was destructive to the initiative and ingenuity of the student body, and the limitations set by various University requirements were, considering our new situation, in restraint of trade. We welcome the new challenges this dynamic change in the direction of our institution will create, and look forward in this new era to yet another chapter in the University's illustrious history."

"What bullshit!" It was Josh Gutsky, using an unaccustomed expletive, which he usually deleted.

"Do you have any idea why?" asked Circassian. At least he was absolutely certain that Gutsky would not bring anything Jewish into the conversation.

"Why? I'll tell you this, Circassian: If a Jewish provost was running this University instead of a scheisshead like Pickle, this sort of thing would never be tolerated," yoiked Josh.

"How can you know that?" asked Circassian. He was beginning to get peeved at Josh, and he had promised himself that he wouldn't be peeved at anything.

"I just do. It's something I can't explain, Circassian. But of course, if you found out if you really were Jewish, I wouldn't need to explain it to you," said Josh with irritribal logic.

Circassian puzzled the enigma of the conundrum confronting him, and as he went toward the faculty parking lot he almost walked into Mona Pilgrim. Red-faced, she seemed to have been recently crying. Circassian made certain that there were other students around in case his solicitude was misunderstood by the lucretious Mona.

"What happened, Mona?" asked Circassian. "You look like you've lost one of your many best friends," he jastled.

"Oh, it's just so frustrating, Doc!" she looked up at him a half second too long, which made him feel wary about what just was so frustrating for her.

"What's so frustrating, Mona?"

"I just received this letter from the Attorney General's office today, and it stinks!" she statulated.

"May I see it?" Circassian asked sympathetically and considerably relieved that Mona's frustration wasn't the kind he had feared it might be.

"I tore it up and threw it at Tilly Owlglass as she was coming out of that stupid modeling show she was running!" she greared and shod.

"I take it that the Attorney General turned down your request for an investigation of Tilly?" ventured Circassian.

"I should have realized that my request would be given to a Putski appointee," snoffed Mona.

"What was the reason he gave for not conducting the investigation?" asked Circassian.

"Oh, I forgot; something about restraining trade or words like that," marmled Mona, using her handkerchief freely.

"Restraint of trade? That's funny, that's what the President just said in his bulletin about eliminating all University requirements," said Circassian.

"Oh, I know all about that from last week! But you knew that was coming, didn't you, Doc?" Mona yarmed.

"Well, I suppose it's logical; I just don't know why it's logical," he said.

"This frees up Compell-Tex. and Intell-Ex. to go after all the students without their worrying about any restrictions. Students don't even have to major in anything so they can take more courses that have been Privatized. Then, when the public departments have lost most of their students, the corporations can buy them more cheaply, and then they'll have the whole University under their control," said Mona, exhausted.

"That's quite an analysis. Did you come up with that all by yourself?" asked Circassian.

"Not really. Professor Short explained it to us in his Paranoia . . . I mean in his Modern American History class. It makes sense, doesn't it? It's part of Option Three, and we're all doomed!" she croaned.

"Doomed to what?" asked Circassian, beginning to get that paranoid feeling again that he had gotten when he first had received the letter from Pickle telling him that his services were no longer needed.

"Doomed is bad enough, isn't it?" said Mona, and, after giving Circassian a winning smile, she walked off down the quad.

When Circassian returned to his house, he was in a rankish mood and Tina knew that look he gave her. She served him his second favorite meal after sorrell soup and pig's feet: blintzes and baked ham. Circassian could not explain it, but he found himself attracted to the most contradictory foods he could imagine.

"Well, lover boy, what now? You still have your job, don't you? You didn't try to push Pickle out the window?" she asked.

"I'll leave those things to Branch; besides, he'd have a better chance of succeeding than I would. No, it has to do with the University abolishing all requirements," he paggled.

"What's the big deal?" stittled Tina. "A lot of Universities did that years ago."

"But not with two corporations waiting to gobble everything up. The public departments won't have a chance." He was thinking of all the subjects he was particularly fond of like art, music, theater, dance; they'd be blown away into the dust of non-mercantile superfluity.

On the television screen was a thin man with a wide-eyed frightened look on his face. He seemed to be lifting his hands while he spoke in the inappropriate gesture of trying to drive some angry mud wasps from attacking him. It was Governor Putski.

Circassian watched as Putski announced another tax cut and another cut in the University budget. He managed to do it with a straight face, twisted though his mind must have been. This would mean a further cut in Circassian's salary if Intell-Ex. and Jack Swift ran true to form. He told Tina, and she promptly announced that there was a sale on pork and beans at the local supermarket that she should investigate. They both laughed, but there was no joy in it.

While they were joylessly laughing, Bendminder was joyfully adding up in his head the profits that had come from the two corporations' ventures in Higher Ed. The English department, although crippled by the elimination of Freshman comp. as a requirement, was still able to hold most of its market share with special deals and, of course, the success of Fun 100. History was doing a smaller volume but was keeping up their numbers and with the addition of Education, the overall profits were soaring. The public stock in Intell-Higher Ed. had gained 50% since the start of the venture into the University. Since he also had an interest in Compell-Tex., Bendminder was pleased to see that the competition had not hurt them either. Psych was doing well and the newer acquisitions — Economics and Sociology — were holding their own. Where there had been a falling off in student head-count, as the Administration still crudely put it, was in the publicly owned departments. Art, Music and Dance had almost shrivelled up, and Philosophy had completely disappeared.

Though Bendminder wasn't entirely thrilled that there would be less departments — he liked the idea of a lot of departments, the more to attract a larger student share from other Universities — he recognized that a certain amount of sacrifice was necessary for the greater good of the Greater Good. He was going to have a conference with Provost Pickle and was looking forward to giving him the good news.

Pickle was not in the best of humors. Ever since the time Branch Stark and Circassian had startled him and he had made that split, his game had been off. He always seemed to be anticipating someone coming up behind him and calling out his name when he was about to release the ball. This resulted in many unconvertible splits and a marked decline in his average. Some of his bowling partners, out of his hearing — sometimes, he suspected even VP T.P. Sealey — were calling him "Splits," which he regarded as outright insulting. So when Bendminder came into the office, Pickle was distracting himself by trying to solve a Rubik's Cube he had kept as a souvenir of a visit to Bucharest many years before.

"What in hell are you doing here?" asked Pickle, gimbling fiercely when Bendminder entered the office.

"We have a meeting, remember?" asked Bendminder defensively.

"Yeah. Now I do. But wasn't it supposed to be in your office to show me some computer graphics?" Pickle stimmered.

"This is my office," mildly exclaimed Bendminder. He was beginning to think the strain was getting to his boss, although what Pickle could be strained about with all the good news was beyond Bendminder's comprehension.

"Well, you could have told me sooner," said Pickle, finally putting away the Rubik's Cube. "Now what do you have to show me?" he sighed.

Bendminder turned on the computer and demonstrated with a series of graphic illustrations where the University had been before it began to be privatized and where it was now. The figures spoke for themselves: Overall revenue was way up above costs, all the programs in the private sector were expanding, even if correspondingly all the programs in the public sector were contracting, and since the privates charged more and paid the faculty less, they were making up for the loss of revenue in the publics and more.

"But what's happening to the Arts and Philosophy?" asked Pickle, after Bendminder had extolliated him with all the facts and figures.

"Oh, they're on the way out; their figures are negligible, don't really fit into the equation. I put them under 'Miscellaneous.'" He was as full of himself as a tic of blood.

"I wanted the whole University to expand with these programs, you putz! What's a University without the Arts and Philosophy?" This was the first time Pickle realized what was happening. He had kept himself in a stupor of inattentiveness as long as he could, and now he understood that this lack of attention was finally going to cost him. If this trend kept up, he could say goodbye to any plans to become President of Harvard, which had been his childhood ambition.

"I thought you wanted the University to run on a cost-effective basis," whined Bendminder. He was certain he had given Pickle just what Pickle had told him to do. That had been the point of developing Option Three! Now he was getting hell for it. Life just wasn't fair, thought Bendminder.

"I did want the *whole* University to run on a cost-effective basis, not just part of it. What is a University that doesn't support the Arts: a slough of despond and sea of monotony. Look in the catalogues of the Big Ten, the Pac Eight, the Fab Five: you'll see they all have Art and Music and Dance departments."

"Well, we're the wave of the future, Don," declaimed Bendminder. "Whatever happens here is going to happen there soon enough. The two corporations are so pleased with the return on their investment that they're planning to expand into the Big Ten next year. Just wait: they'll be coming to *us* to show them how it's done."

"Well, that's a different story," said Pickle very much relieved. He was ready to usher Bendminder politely out of his office when he realized once more that he was in Bendminder's. He pocketed his Rubik's Cube, eagerly awaiting the next lull in his schedule so he could solve the puzzle, which had been bedeviling him ever since he had completed the Ghost Ship scrimshaw. In fact, he decided to cancel all his appointments until he figured out the little puzzler and could get back his accustomed peace of mind.

Bendminder breathed a sigh of relief. He had no idea what Intell-Ex. or Compell-Tex.'s plans were for expanding, but he had to tell Pickle something, and who knew? If his corporate masters hadn't thought of it yet, maybe he might get a little something extra for his suggestion.

{}

Branch Stark was tired. He had been ranting, raving, and roaring but to no avail. The only one besides him with any guts was Circassian, and Branch was no longer sure of him either.

When Branch had heard about the elimination of all required courses, his first thought had been to see Dean Lean, but he had decided that that was hopeless. The next possibility was Pickle, but he knew that was useless, even if he could find him. Pickle had decided that Tony's Lanes had become too well-known as the bowling alley he frequented, so he had switched somewhere else and could not be found. It seems that Pickle had decided not only to disguise his name at his new haven from the madding crowd, but had disguised his appearance too. He entered the bowling lanes wearing a caftan, a rabbinical hat and a false beard. He would be known as "Yussl Leibschitz," a Hasid from Bayonne, New Jersey. It was a little difficult for Pickle to bowl wearing all of that disguise, but it was worth it for the peace of mind he'd get. No longer would he fear someone coming from behind him calling out "Pickle," a possibility that still came to him in dreams along with the usual fantasies of despoiling his secretary, Rachel Rue, during the sacking of Ancient Rome, a period of which he was quite fond. And though it was particularly difficult for him to execute his follow-through with his caftan flapping around him (so that he looked like a huge mad bat), he noticed that he had improved his game, anyway.

So there was no possibility, even if Branch had chanced to come into these lanes, far from the University, that he would even recognize Pickle if he saw him. He certainly wouldn't recognize Pickle if he heard him because along with the disguise, the Provost had gotten a few rudimentary Yiddish lessons from one of the University's remaining linguists, and if he wasn't conversing in Yiddish to no one in particular when he didn't want to speak to someone, he was still able to fake a tolerable, thick Yiddish accent. It was so good, in fact, that it is doubtful that either Shotman or Gutsky would have detected the imposture.

President Fred was rarely in, and when he was, he wasn't in to Branch. That left him with one wild hope: Chancellor Thwart. Useless as Thwart was for most purposes, Branch had felt that the Chancellor's heart must be really in the right place or why would he have taken the job? He decided to write a letter asking to have an audience with Thwart as soon as possible, expressing the urgency of the situation and that the fate of the University was hanging in the balance — for by this time it was clear that Intell-Ex. would be purchasing Biology and Chemistry while Compell-Tex. was signing contracts to acquire Health Ed., Recreation, and Communications Studies the following year.

To his surprise and near-delight, Branch received a reply from Chancellor Thwart within the week, saying that although he had a tight schedule, he could see Branch and, as he requested, one of his colleagues, the following Tuesday. Branch quickly cornered Circassian into taking advantage of the opportunity.

"Why me?" asked Circassian. "I've only been here five years. Why not pick out a real veteran?"

"I'd think you might notice that I'm one of the few left in the department," said Branch fostulating.

"Can he fire me?" asked Circassian. He remembered what Pastor Castor had told him about doing his job.

"How the bleep can he, Circassian? Anyway, we're only going for a meeting, not a debate," Branch said, although he wanted it to be a debate.

The following week was fall break, and Branch and Circassian drove up to the Chancellor's office in the Capitol. On the way up, Branch rehearsed what he was going to say to the Chancellor: how the University was beginning to disintegrate. He was going to spare him nothing about the changes that had been rendered upon the faculty. He would tear his heart and galvanize him into action. He would get him to save the University. Despite his cynicism, Branch was a naif at heart.

"Do you want to say anything to him, Circassian? I think he's given us half an hour," said Branch.

Circassian was again doubtful. He hadn't wanted to go, but Branch was very persuasive. Branch didn't want to go alone because he had to make sure there would be someone there to restrain him if the meeting got out of hand. But Circassian wasn't in a very restraining mood, especially with Branch, whose temper was known to all at the University as short, fast and ugly. Yet Circassian was fond of Branch; he was the only one who had stood up instead of lying down. And he felt that it was important for his own self-respect to see this thing through. But he told Branch that he had nothing to add that Branch wouldn't cover already.

"You know the score better than I do, Branch, and you can tell it better than I can," added Circassian.

"You mean I can tell it louder than you can," corrected Branch. He was in a pensive mood as he drove along at eighty miles an hour, frightening even the deer deep in the forest with the roar of the motor.

When they arrived at Central Administration and went through a half dozen doors, they were greeted by an elderly secretary who offered them coffee and crullers. They were surprised when it turned out the elderly secretary was none other than Chancellor Thwart, who had dismissed his large collection of assistants for the occasion.

"I don't often see anyone who's actually teaching, so this is an occasion for me, gentlemen. Now what can I do for you?"

Thwart seemed like a kindly man, which he actually tried to be in a weird and twisted way. He had been President of several prestigious institutions in the Far West and when he came to the University as Chancellor, he assumed things would be the same there. When he realized he was mistaken, he knew he had two choices: do the honorable thing and resign, or be an apologist and toady for the Board of Trustees and Ambler Slaughter's crew. After careful consideration, he chose the latter; he had planned to retire in several years and he convinced himself that anyone taking over his job would probably be worse. At least he believed that he was doing his best, in a very small and fairly ineffectual way, of mediating between the University and the Board of Trustees. He was entirely deluded, but he held to his delusions with a fierce pride, somewhat like a confused lion stoutly guarding a herd of antelope or, more likely, a confused antelope guarding a pride of lions.

Branch came right to the point: "The policies of the Board of Trustees and the University Administration are destroying everything that we've worked for, and I think you should realize that," he said, choosing his words very carefully.

"I realize more than you imagine, Professor Stark, but these things will have to take their course. It's part of a new trend in public accountability. It's in the air all over. We're just a small part of the Big Picture," Thwart said, airily.

"Would the Big Picture involve Option Three?" ventured Circassian. He had promised himself he would say very little and decided that this would be the very little he said.

"Ah yes, Option Three. Sort of a carte blanche for privatization, isn't it?" Thwart asked, knowing the answer.

"Almost half of the departments have been taken over by two corporations and now they're fighting for control of the University," said Branch.

"But what can I do about it? Even if I tried to," asked Thwart. He was whittling figures on a wooden cane he had purchased when he became Chancellor. As Circassian noticed, they looked diabolical.

"You mean you think that the University is going in the right direction?" flastered Branch. Cynical as he believed he was, he was naive enough to assume that Thwart shared his humane, liberal arts, sound-mind-in-a-sound-body, well-rounded, open-minded although somewhat parochial values.

"I'm willing to bet, Professor Branch, that you have a fairly low opinion of most of the students that come to you for enlightenment," said Chancellor Thwart, meticulously slicing a tiny sliver from the cane.

"There are some that shouldn't be in any school, yes, but there are many that deserve a sound education," said Branch.

"Many? How many? How many times have you felt that the whole thing is a fraud, a colossal hoax — that most of the really able students will learn no matter what we do to them, and the rest won't no matter what we do for them," he said, a sly smile on his wrinkled, venerable-seeming face.

"I've never thought the whole thing was a hoax," Branch lied. He had felt that way many times after stomping out of a classroom and roaring down the corridors about the "pod people" who were inhabiting the bodies of the students as they had done to the general population in *Invasion of the Body Snatchers*. But he still had some principles, culturally challenged as they were.

"The public sector is becoming a thing of the past," said Thwart. "Option Three is just the first of many strategies to penetrate and destroy it from within. In a generation, everything will be privatized: schools, municipal services, government agencies, the whole enchilada. And I'm glad I'm not going to live to see it," Thwart added with a twist of bitter humor.

"So you don't like what's happening?" said Branch.

"I loathe it, but there's nothing I can do to stop it. I liked Option Three when it first came out, but now I can see it's going too far," Thwart added.

"But you're the Chancellor!" strackled Branch, burbling.

"Who can be replaced in a minute if I try to oppose the Board of Trustees. They're the ones with the power."

"But if we got rid of the Board of Trustees. . ." offered Branch.

"They'd be replaced by another bunch of Putski appointees. And if Putski were no longer in office, whoever was Governor would see things the same way. This is inevitable, gentlemen. You can still fight the good fight in your classrooms, but the way of life we once knew is rapidly disappearing," Thwart sighed a sigh of desterment.

Branch was, as happened so rarely, once again at a loss for words. He shook the Chancellor's proffered hand, but before he left he turned to him for a parting word: "I still think it's all bleeped up and there's some way of making it right again," he concluded in true Branchian fashion.

"Just don't lose your cool, gentlemen," Thwart said as they left his office. "You'll just wear yourselves down before your time.'"

After Branch and Circassian left, the Chancellor sat back at his desk and continued carving the cane. He was quite skilled and it seemed that the horned and cloven-footed figures would spring to life. He didn't mind lying to people like Branch to get them out of his hair. He had heard about Branch from Bendminder and knew the best way to deal with him was to take the bull by the literal horns. In two or three years the entire University system would be privatized and then his work would be done. He had never trusted the public university, it gave too many people a chance to fail. But those days were over. He was proud that he had played a part in the wave of the future. It was fitting that, as old as he was, he could still see far ahead. It was only a pity that these younger, energetic and hopelessly misguided men would cling to the past. With a hint of a smile on his face, he picked up the phone for his secretary: "Get me Ambler Slaughter."

()

"Let's get the hell out of here for a few days!" said Circassian to Tina the day he had returned from his visit to the Chancellor's. He'd noticed that on the ride back to campus, Branch was in a strangely pensive mood. Circassian had expected no more from the Chancellor, so he was relieved that the whole thing was over. Given the tone of the discussion, he believed would even avoid his getting fired by Jack Swift, who would, doubtless, be informed by the Chancellor of everything that had taken place. Circassian hadn't been off campus or out of town since the beginning of the semester, and he was thoroughly fed up with the University. There were four days left to the fall Break. If he and Tina were to take advantage of the season and the changing of the leaves, they would have to do it now.

"But we don't have very much money," protested Tina. She had a little vacation time coming to her, but she had planned to save all of it for the Christmas Season and visit her parents in Green Bay.

"I know someone who has a cabin in the Adirondacks. He's always said that if I needed a place to get away from *it*, I was welcome to his," Circassian said, hopefully. The person he had been thinking of was Frank Short who, he knew, had inherited a small house in the mountains from his parents.

Circassian called up Frank with the hope that the casual remark Frank had made wasn't completely casual.

"Hi, Frank," said Circassian, pretending to Tina that the call was just a formality.

"Well, if it isn't friend Circassian. How're you surviving the improvements in the English department?"

"I was going to ask you the same thing about History," said Circassian. "Are you still wearing the Joe McCarthy outfit to class?" he twitted.

"I've changed it for one of Joe Stalin. A couple of the students thought I was Groucho, but the rest disabused them," Frank said, chuckling. "Who have you been dressing like?"

"I dressed like Ibsen a few times, but nobody knew who I was so I switched to Eugene O'Neill and the first English major I met in my new outfit looked at me and recited: 'Quoth the Raven, Nevermore!' It was a little more humiliating than usual," confessed Circassian.

"Well, what can I do for you, Old Man?" asked Frank.

Circassian told him, following with a few apologies for his presumption.

"You're certainly welcome to use it, Old Boy," said Frank. "It's not doing anybody any good sitting there as it does for all but a couple of weeks in August when I and Kara inhabit it. Come over tonight and I'll give you the key."

Circassian was pleased at the kindness, but he hadn't really been surprised about Frank. He still had that even sense of humor, which kept the rest of the hysteria-driven, panic-laden, paranoia-haunted faculty on a more even keel.

The next morning, Tina and Circassian decided to leave early so that they would get to the cabin by the middle of the day. Tina had packed some sandwiches and a thermos, since the nearest town was about ten miles in the opposite direction from where they were coming. It was a haze-free, sunny day as they drove through the surrounding hills toward the highway. The trees were in full autumn colors, and the vivid reds and golds of the maples, the scarlet of the sumac, and the blue of the heather blended into a palette of pigmentary plenitude.

The trip took about three hours, and they stopped on the way to watch a flock of Canada geese alighting on a pond near the highway. They turned their graceful necks and black-banded heads at the watchers like a crowd of wimpled nuns. Tina was really happy now that they had finally gotten away from everything she disliked about living near the University: living near the University; her job; what his job was doing to Circassian.

They arrived at the cabin just as both were beginning to get hungry. The leaves had fallen thickly on the porch, making a welcome mat for their entrance. After they opened the door, Tina found a broom and immediately began sweeping the porch clean. She dusted away some cobwebs in the corners of the little bedroom and did a quick once-over of the bathroom with some cleanser and a sponge she found there. Circassian watched in awe. She had also done the driving and he was tired. When he awoke from his nap they ate.

The fresh air and change of scene had given Circassian a raging appetite. They each had two sandwiches wrapped in tin foil: albacore tuna on rye with a slice of onion for him; hummus and tomato sandwiches for her. Then they drove over to the nearest town and picked up some supplies: canned soups, some vegetables, chicken breasts, corned beef, tofu for Tina who was a sometime, this time, vegetarian, and breakfast food.

Later in the afternoon, as the sun was setting, they took a walk along a well-worn path that led to a small lake on the side of a mountain. It was getting dark enough that a blue haze was hovering over the lake and a darker blue was settling in the shadows of the trees. They heard the angry laugh of a loon and then saw it lift its head and then quickly dive under the smooth surface of the lake, barely rippling it. When they returned to the cabin, everything was in shadow.

That evening, after a modest dinner of soup and salad, they sat out on the porch and watched the moon come up through the trees. It was a horned moon and Venus was brightly showing its way. And Circassian suddenly felt that vastness of the world around him and the littleness of everything that had concerned so much of the past year of his life.

"We should have done this sooner," he said to Tina. "Then maybe we wouldn't have been so uptight."

"Nah," said Tina. "I don't think we were ready for it."

They heard a sudden crash in the woods around them, a snapping of branches. Then they saw the deer, a white-tailed doe that had been attracted by the light and the smell of food. It nuzzled around the steps of the porch, not more than ten feet from them, and then the wind shifted slightly, and she smelt them, turned at a sharp angle and darted delicately into the wooded darkness. A few minutes later, they smelled a skunk prowling and decided to go in.

Circassian had brought several books to read, and he was in the middle of *Down and Out in Paris and London*, while Tina had decided to catch up on her drawing. She sketched Circassian in the half-light while he read, and when he realized what she was doing, it was finished.

"How do you do it, Circassian?" she asked. "You barely moved a muscle while you read."

He looked at the drawing. It was filled with life even in the quiet of the posture. "How do you do it?" he asked.

They went to sleep in each other's arms after making love. And it was the first time they had been able to sleep in each other's arms in quite some time. The last time, in fact, was the night before Circassian had received Pickle's first letter.

The next morning they woke up early and walked again to the lake. There were some deer drinking water at the margin of the shore; as soon as they spotted Tina and Circassian, they stared at them, unmoving. Then, with a slight bend of their heads, as if signaling to each other, they went off into the woods. Nearby, a family of mallards, a mother and five younger ducks, were paddling near the shore. The ducklings were still not fully grown, but were bobbing their heads down into the water, tail up, searching for fish. Occasionally there was a splash within the shadows where the trees had grown at the edge; Circassian couldn't make out the fish, but a long, silver gleam made it out to be a very big one, possibly a muskie.

They had a breakfast of eggs and corn bread and strawberry jam that Tina had bought the day before, and then decided to take a hike along the trail that wound past the house in the opposite direction from the lake. It was perfect weather for hiking: the sky was clear and sunny and the air had just a hint of chill. They hardly spoke except to tell each other to watch out for some hole in the ground or a particularly muddy patch. It had obviously rained overnight and the air was still fresh with the smell of it, the grass heavy with it.

They came to a clearing in the woods, which opened up on a meadow of timothy and heather. Tina pointed to a monarch butterfly that was lazily gliding over the golden rod growing in yellow abundance at the edge of the road. It looked like the last butterfly from the summer and seemed to be enjoying its solitariness in the middle of the field. On the other side of the meadow they could see yet another group of deer, nibbling on the grasses. There was a buck with a full head of antlers, two does and a spotted fawn, its legs still as delicate as match sticks. Circassian and Tina were downwind of the animals and so they sat still, watching for a full five minutes before the deer went off.

They walked through the field and heard the buzzing of the bees that were still gathering pollen from the autumn flowers. Tina suddenly noticed a shadow dart across their path and looked up. There was a hawk, high above, wheeling and circling in the brightness of the air. Then, as if sensing their presence, it darted down into the treetops at the edge of the field.

The two of them felt that they were the only ones there and the only human beings who had been there in a long while. As they entered the woods at the far side of the meadow, they heard a yapping sound and turned back, expecting to see a dog with someone letting it run free. What they could make out was a large pair of ears that went darting through the thickness of the tall grasses and then disappearing. Tina was sure it was a fox. Circassian said it was a badger with large ears. They laughed and walked about another mile before deciding to turn back.

When they returned to the cabin, they seemed tired and were surprised that when they lay down to nap, they slept for several hours. Both realized that they had been exhausted and their bodies were just beginning to let them understand that.

That afternoon, after lunch, Tina went down to the lake to do some sketching while Circassian resumed his reading. He heard a woodpecker knocking against a tree in the distance, and occasionally heard the snapping of twigs as small creatures skipped along the forest floor. Circassian decided to see what Tina was doing. The weather was still very mild for early autumn, the temperature in the sixties. When he got down to the lake, he didn't at first see Tina and for a moment had a quick plunge of fear. Then he heard her voice: she was swimming about twenty yards from the shore, dog paddling.

"I didn't know you brought a bathing suit," said Circassian.

"I didn't. Come on in; the water's tolerable," shouted Tina.

Circassian noticed Tina's clothes in a neat pile in a crevice of rock, shrugged, and then took off his clothes. When he jumped in he expected the water to be mild: it was cold.

"Youch," he yelped.

Tina laughed. She'd been used to much colder water in Green Bay.

Circassian braved the water and joined her. They swam together for about fifty yards and then returned to shore. They were both shivering by the time they got back to the cabin, laughing at each other's shaking.

The next day went quickly. The sky had turned cloudy and Tina read a book she had brought, *The Autobiography of Benvenuto Cellini*, which she was reading for the third time. Circassian finished his book and took a walk to the lake. It had begun to rain, and he saw the rain coming across the lake in a rush, first tiny drops and then quicker and harder until they were pelting against the trees that were now scattering their leaves in swirls and swoops across the path.

They decided to leave early the following day. They had no idea what the weather would be like, but Monday was coming and he would be back at school and she back at work. As they got into the car the next morning, at about 6:30, Circassian realized that they hadn't said more than several dozen words to each other during the three days. They hadn't had to.

When they got back, Circassian called up Frank to thank him.

"Did you luck out on the weather, Old Man?" asked Frank. "We had a glorious few days around here."

"Even more glorious away from here," said Circassian, "except for the last evening when it rained. But that was fine too."

"Well, you tempt me to bring up Kara for a weekend before it gets too cold," said Frank.

"Did you ever hear of the time Thoreau was still living at Walden Pond and he went to visit his friend, Ralph Waldo Emerson?" asked Circassian.

"Which story is this one?"

"Emerson was getting concerned that Thoreau's health might start breaking down, so he asked him: 'Well, Henry, don't you think it's about time you came back to civilization?' And Thoreau answered: 'I will when there is one, Waldo.'"

Frank laughed. "That sounds familiar. Didn't Gandhi say something like that?"

"Maybe he got it from Thoreau. I think they corresponded, along with Karl and

Groucho Marx," said Circassian.

"Well, welcome back to civilization, Old Friend," said Frank.

"Is that what you call it?" said Circassian.

()

The next day was Monday, and Circassian had his favorite class, Modern Drama. The number of students, lured by offers of greater largesse in other courses, had dwindled from twenty-five to eighteen, but the ones still there seemed interested in the subject. When he entered the room, he was surprised to see one of the Adjuncts sitting in the front row: August Beadsley, a pale, thin young man with a tubercular look on his face.

"What are you doing here, Augie?" asked Circassian.

"I was told by Bendminder to do an observation on you, Circassian. Sorry, but orders are orders," explained Beadsley with a non-explanation.

"But why didn't he choose one of the senior members of the department?" asked Circassian.

"Didn't trust them," was Beadsley's malonic reply.

Circassian began the lesson with the obligatory shill for various Intell-Ex. products, but by this time the class, which was actually interested in what he had to say about Tennessee Williams, didn't take up much time asking questions about the various new software packages and Club Med trips that the corporation was offering.

He then began explaining the motivations of Blanche DuBois in *A Streetcar Named Desire*, and what the only thing seemed to be that kept her going, even in her madness: "Values," said Circassian.

"What's that?" quipped Mona Pilgrim, as if on cue. Some of the class laughed, but most didn't, looking puzzled.

After the class was over, August Beadsley got up, smiled, and left.

Mona stayed after the rest had gone, but Circassian made sure that the classroom door remained open. Although she had kept a respectful distance lately, he was still uncertain of her motives.

"What was that all about, Doc?" she asked.

"Hell if I know," said Circassian. "I'm being observed by one of Bendminder's spies, I guess," he tried to joke, but he was worried.

"You know why the students still look up to you, Doc?" confided Mona. She could see that he was feeling low and thought now was the time to tell him.

"I haven't the foggiest idea," said Circassian, feeling that he was in a fog about what was going to happen to him.

"Because you haven't sold out like most of the rest of them," said Mona, the slightest of smiles playing on her pretty face.

"What do you mean I haven't sold out?" excloffed Circassian. "I'm still teaching here, aren't I?"

"Don't beat yourself up for that, Doc," said Mona. "You probably don't know all the things that some of the English department faculty are doing to keep students in their classes."

Circassian really didn't want to know, but he thought it would be impolite if he didn't let Mona tell him.

"Well, a few are lending their cars on weekends to students who seemed to be wavering about staying in class. Some have taken up housekeeping in the students' dorms and apartments, and they're even getting the freshmen and sophomores phony I.D.'s if they won't drop their courses," said Mona.

The next day Circassian got a note to see Bendminder. Jack Swift was away on business in Hong Kong and had delegated any personnel matters to him. Bendminder was by now a wealthy man, having gotten stock options from Intell-Ex. when the stock on the University venture was first made public. He now was dressed in the latest sartorial finery, including wing-tip shoes and an alligator brief case. When Circassian came into his office, which he hadn't been in since before Option Three had been implemented, he was surprised at the changes. All the furnishings were new and very expensive-looking. On his desk Bendminder had a Tissot clock, a beautiful miniature of the town hall clock at Bern.

"Well, what can I do for you, Stats?" said Circassian. He had had trepidations about what Bendminder had in mind, but Tina suggested that since Bendminder was both a bully and a coward, it wouldn't help if Circassian showed any fear of what was to happen. "After all, the worst that could happen is that you'll lose your job, and that's not too bad an idea," she quillied.

"But I like some of my job," expulled Circassian.

"You can keep the part of the job you like somewhere else, Lover," said Tina. "Not every school in the country has someone like Bendminder."

They will, thought Circassian, but he didn't say anything.

Bendminder looked in a pensive mood, which, given his character, was a rare if not almost impossible thing for him to be in. He was reading some report when Circassian came in and after a few seconds of the most unportentous pause — Hank Schecht and Pickle were good at giving the portentous kind — he handed the report to Circassian. As he had expected, it was the one written by Augustus Beadsley, complete with a caricature of Circassian that was so good it was almost flattering.

"This just won't do, Circassian," said Bendminder. He had underlined in bright red crayon the words, "disproportionate amount of time on task," which had been written at the bottom of the report. "According to Beadsley, and I can imagine it might even be worse when nobody's observing you, you spent about 85% of class time teaching the lesson and about 10% on merchandising the products. The other five per cent was the usual announcements and class attendance. Well, what have you to say for yourself?" asked Bendminder. He was relishing the opportunity to talk down to a faculty member, even one as lowly as Circassian.

"I thought I was supposed to be teaching," he said.

"That comes in it somewhere, but you'd better get your priorities straight pretty soon, Circassian. After all, we're running a business here."

When he got back to his office and checked his mail, Circassian saw a sealed envelope with his name on it. He opened it and the first words he read were: "Don't Read This in Public!" He had the urge to read it in public just because he was tired of listening to arbitrary orders, but when he saw Hank Schecht's and Dabs Budweiser's names at the bottom of the page, he decided he'd go into his office which was where he was planning to go, anyway.

The notice read:

Urgent meeting of faculty who still care.
Meet us at Hank Shecht's house tonight at 8.
It's not too late to still do something.
please burn this in your home; the administration is checking the trash cans for our messages.
In solidarity,
Dabs Budweiser, ULP President
Hank Schecht, ULP Vice President

When Circassian got home, he told Tina about the message and then burned it in the fireplace, even though he didn't think anyone from the administration was checking his trash . . . yet.

"I don't know, Circassian," said Tina. "You can't tell who's going to be there that might be a spy."

"I was thinking of that, but what the hell. You just said yesterday that the worst thing that could happen to me is that I'd lose my job," said Circassian.

"Only I don't want to see you blacklisted," said Tina.

"Hell, I could always teach English in Sweden," said Circassian. He had a friend who had gone to Uppsala University on a Fulbright, married a Swedish woman and stayed. He'd been sending Circassian letters every once in a while inviting him to settle there. "The people are morose but good-natured," he said. There were times in the past few months that Circassian was very much tempted to take him up on his suggestion.

"I don't know if I'd like Sweden, Circassian. I'd get used to it, I guess, being from Green Bay," said Tina. "But it'd be a little more difficult to visit the family all the way over there."

"Maybe it would be an improvement," quipped Circassian. "Weren't you the one who told me that the only way to tell that it was summer in Green Bay is that it got a little harder to ski?"

"Go already!" stritled Tina.

The day of the meeting, he met Josh Gutsky in the lunchroom. There was no longer a Table but just groups of faculty huddling together in various corners, whispering and moaning. It was getting towards "Sweeps Time" again, and students were beginning to look into the catalogue to see what courses they would be taking in the spring.

The regular catalogue had a few glossy pictures in it, but the ones from Intell-Ex. and Compell-Tex. were spectacular. Some of the pictures were in 3-D, others were holographs that zoomed to life in the form of curvaceous young women and muscular young men singing the virtues of their respective majors. One catalogue from Compell-Tex. not only extolled its own but had harsh things to say about Intell-Ex.'s products:

History is History,
It isn't going to last,
It's not such a mystery,
Memory's a thing of the past.

Intell-Ex. had been tempted to fight the negative ads with some of their own about the bipolar psychologist who advertised for a bride so they could swap personalities, but they preferred to take the high road. All they did was leak to the press some sexual hijinks that several of the board of directors were having with some of their advertising models.

"How's it going, Josh?" asked Circassian.

Josh had a smile on his face and, as Circassian had noted, his numbers were up.

"It's going great. I'm getting used to being an intellectual whore; I almost enjoy it now that I haven't a principle left," said Josh with a strange gleam in both of his eyes.

"Have you come up with some new courses?" Circassian was toying with repackaging Modern Drama as "Gays, Guys and Gals" since he'd be teaching Tennessee Williams, Arthur Miller and Lillian Hellman in the coming semester, but decided that he'd rather stick with his original title.

"I've come up with a course that'll knock your kneecaps," said Josh. "It's called 'Jesus, Jews and Jive,' and a whole bunch of the kids from Mary M. Magdalene's club are planning to sign up."

"What's it about?" asked Circassian.

"The hell if I know. Once we start I'll just improvise, maybe show them the connection between the Jewish faith, Jesus Christ and Dizzy Gillespie," Josh chruled.

"Is there?" asked Circassian.

"I guess that's what we'll find out," Josh said. "By the way, Circassian, did you ever try to discover from your parents whether any of your ancestors . . . you know."

"I'll see you later, Josh," said Circassian.

"Because if it turns out to be true, you'll really have a whole different perspective on things, like I do."

"And just what is your perspective on things?" asked Circassian.

"It's like the one about the man walking down the street and talking to himself and laughing, and every once in a while shouting out 'Feh!' So he's doing it all the way down the block so a passerby stops him and asks. 'Why are you talking to yourself and laughing?'

"'I'm telling myself a joke,' said the man.

"'Then why do you say "Feh!" every once in a while?

"'Because that's a joke I've already heard.' Now that's a Jewish perspective," concluded Josh.

"How?" asked Circassian.

"If you were Jewish, you'd know," said Josh and went off to his class, "Psychos, Psychics and Cyborgs in Contemporary Literature."

That evening, Circassian drove over to Hank Schecht's house, which was located in the Heights near the edge of the University. Hank had a big, sprawling Tudor-style house with sliding doors everywhere, even in the bathroom. When Circassian got to the house, he knocked several times before anyone came to the door. Then he realized that Hank must have been looking at him out the window to make sure who it was. No sooner was he in than Hank closed the door quickly behind him.

"Are you sure you weren't followed?" he asked Circassian, a little breathily as if he had raced up a hill backwards.

"I don't think so," said Circassian. "Maybe I should get out and drive around the block a couple of times to throw whoever might be there off?" he whorted.

"We can't be too careful," said Hank. He led Circassian down a flight of stairs in the back of the house into a dimly lit room which was a semi-finished basement.

Seated there, as best as Circassian could make out, was Lee Ann Fitz-Proust, Branch Stark, Trent Butler, Dabs Budweiser and a shadowy figure who wore a ski mask and didn't speak through the entire meeting.

Now that Circassian was here, the meeting could begin. "We're here as the last best hope of mankind at the University," said Dabs. "We've been pushed around long enough by these two corporate blood-suckers and it's time we pushed back."

Everyone grunted or smeagled agreement. "What we need to do is what we did when ULP first came into being: organize."

"What about Option Three?" chruled Circassian.

"There's nothing in Option Three that prevents us from organizing a Union. The only thing we can't do is get you in the private sector to reaffiliate with ULP. So we've given the name of the new organization General United Labor Professions. We think that'd be catchy enough to get members and still keep some of our original identity," she said.

"From ULP to GULP?" wondered Circassian. Some of the people titterlated and one guffawed.

"Whatever it spells out, Circassian," ventured Hank, "it's better than sitting around complaining and letting corporate management pick off the departments one by one without a fight."

"But whom do we organize?" asked Lee Ann. She was very doubtful of the plan, but she didn't want to give up on it before it had a chance to fail. "Most of the faculty are terrified, and the ones that aren't are spies."

"That's why we have to be very careful that we keep this meeting a complete secret from anyone who could report on us," said Hank. "We've got to organize very gradually, perhaps recruiting not more than one or two members at a time."

"And how long will it take before we can demand a vote on representation?" asked Trent Butler.

"At a conservative guess, about seven to nine years, but we might be able to do it more quickly if management really gets tough," said Dabs.

"How much more tough do you think they can get?" asked Branch. "They've got us so bleeped-up now, we've got to follow written instructions to pee."

"Don't worry," said Hank. "We're going to consult some experts who have organized the toughest corporate workers into unions; they've thought of everything."

"I still think this whole thing is screwed up," said Branch.

"Our plans or the University's?" challenged Hank.

"Take your choice," said Branch, and started to humph his way out of the room.

"You'll get another note from us when our organizing consultants come to visit," Hank yelled after him. But the moment for an inspired speech had passed, and the meeting broke up.

When Circassian left the meeting, he felt as if he had lost his life raft on a sinking oil tanker. There was no conceivable way that they could organize a union when everyone seemed to want to get the edge on everyone else. There was even the possibility that Pastor Castor might start advertising, since his sermons were beginning to wear thin on the souls of the hedonists who had sprouted up on campus like mushrooms over a septic tank. And Circassian wondered who the shadowy figure was who had concealed his identity, or was it hers? Maybe it was a spy for Pickle, or Jack Swift? Or Chancellor Thwart? Or Camille Faux? Or Ambler Slaughter?

The next day, even Circassian was not prepared for the bombshell that hit the campus when it was announced in the *University Chatter:*

Systell-Lex. Buys Out Intell-Ex. and Compell-Tex.

Systell-Lex, the multinational corporation that has purchased Nevada and the Rupert Murdoch Empire has just announced its acquisition of Intell-Ex. and Compell-Tex. It is also going to purchase all remaining public departments and amalgamate them into one University system. The new corporate entity that will administer to the needs of the University will be called Ex-Lex-Tex or ELT, a subsidiary of the Privatized University System that Systell-Lex. has been developing over the past few years. The University will join Penn State and the University of Miami as its latest acquisitions. It is expected that as a result of the merger, there will be some necessary reallocation of resources in the coming months. Systell-Lex. began as a law-information system but soon expanded into animation, computer software and pizza parlors. The next edition of the University Chatter *will bring futher details.*

"Well, what do you think about that?" said Circassian to no one in particular. And no one replied.

Part VI

The merger of Compell-Tex. and Intell-Ex. by Systell-Lex. caused a new challenge for the faculty; it was the same sort of challenge that the people in steerage had on the Titanic. The new system categorized departments in, for fiscal purposes, gross volume, net profit, and per pupil cost. In order to balance out departments that were in the red with those that were very successful, most were merged. Education, Art, Music and Dance became the Department of Education in the Arts; Biology and Recreation became the Department of Recreational Biology which made absolutely no sense but was catchy enough to increase biology's share of student consumers. French, Spanish, German and Economics were combined to make the Department of Linguistic Economics, and English was merged with Physical Education to simply become the Department of Physical Education and English. Finally, History and Physics were combined to make the misleadingly titled Department of Physical History.

Naturally, in combining departments, Systell-Lex. took the opportunity to cut back on staffing and retrain some of those who were left in a weak department to help with the work-load in a stronger department. From a business sense this might have been a good idea, but when Sibyl Eaves, Associate Professor of Latin American History, began teaching a class in quantum mechanics, it didn't take the students long to realize that she was out of her depth.

So it went with members of the English department who found themselves teaching several courses in P.E., for as good as the numbers were that English thought it was getting, they were hardly worth noting in comparison with the whopping numbers that P.E. was turning in. Now, with the merger and reorganization, the full-time faculty were reduced from 215 to 140, and the student enrollment, because of the reputation the University was getting for innovation, had gone up 30%, so there was more than enough work for everyone.

Branch Stark and Josh Gutsky had been assigned two courses each in Sports Medicine after having taken several workshops on the subject, and Circassian had been asked to assist in coaching the men's fencing team. Since Branch and Josh still knew nothing about Sports Medicine and perhaps even less after the whirlwind workshops, and Circassian was completely clueless about fencing, the classes they were involved in could get pretty lively.

Circassian offered to help with the bowling team, but that position was already taken by Arlen Bass, who wouldn't know a bowling ball from a matzoh ball.

On paper, the merger seemed quite successful as long as the students were having a good time and didn't care whether or not they learned anything. But a few soreheads like Mona Pilgrim complained to the Deans, and now that they had jurisdiction again of the University, they felt that they could complain to the Vice President for Finance and Corporate Development who had replaced Leon Leone. They were told to "get with the program" and "stop whining" or they'd be replaced, and so once again Mona was turned away from her justifiable rancor with another dose of bureaucratic bullshit.

Dean Lean was planning to resign, although he was only forty-four years old and didn't have much of a pension. He could no longer ignore what was happening to the institution, as Pickle did, by thinking that the University was the "wave of the future"; he was beginning to feel drowned in that wave.

Unfortunately, with the merger and acquisition of the University by Systell-Lex. their reorganizational plans did not include either Dabs Budweiser or Hank Schecht, who were given six months severance pay. Dabs and Hank still tooled around the campus since there was nowhere else they'd rather be, but much of the panache had worn off since they were no longer officially faculty. They intended to file a grievance with someone but realized there was no one left to file a grievance with. ULP no longer represented anyone at the University, and GULP had burst from their feisty imaginations still-born.

One day, about a month after the acquisition and merger — or was it the merger and acquisition? — Circassian walked into Dean Lean's office to find him staring at a report. It was rare that Dean Lean looked at any reports since Pickle had sent him the plan for Option Three, but this report was from the Office of Finance and Development and indicated that Dean Lean's days as Dean might soon be over and he had the option of going back into the classroom. He didn't hate teaching the way so many other former teachers who became administrators did. He was just petrified to think what sort of teaching he would be expected to do. He had heard reports of the weird and depraved versions of teaching that were going on among the faculty, but he had preferred to know as little as possible. Now he was faced with the likelihood that he would be back in the classroom in an environment as alien to him as dandelions are to a manta ray.

He was seriously thinking of taking up the suggestion that his brother had made to join him in Hawaii and become a beachcomber. Good money, he was told, could be made in Hawaii on certain beaches and his brother knew where they all were. He thought about the possibility as a very attractive one: good weather, light work, time to rest and think.

He was startled, as he always was when someone came into his office, when Circassian happened by and watched him staring at the report for a few moments before clearing his throat and his adenoids to let the Dean know he was there.

"What are you doing here, Circassian? Aren't you supposed to be in class?" asked the Dean.

"It's Saturday, Dean Lean," said Circassian.

He hadn't quite realized how addled the Dean was, but he knew that being Dean under normal circumstances must have been enough to addle all but the most already addle-headed people.

"Well, why did you come in on Saturday? It wasn't to see me, I imagine," prosted the Dean, putting the report in a file marked FMEO.

"Actually, I came in on Saturday because it's quiet here and none of the company spies are around, and since I saw that you were in, I thought we might have a nice, relaxed chat." Circassian had not completely lost his optimistic view of mankind. He was just very cynical about it now.

"Well, what would you like to chat about? I'm not too busy at the moment, although I could become busy depending on what you want to say." Dean Lean was convinced that anyone who wanted to talk with him from the faculty would say hurtful, if true, things about him, and he certainly didn't need to hear that on a Saturday.

"I was thinking of resigning, Dean Lean," said Circassian. "I'm teaching six courses now, helping to coach the fencing team, and I still don't know the difference between fencing and roofing."

Here Dean Lean allowed himself a snicker, the first one he had allowed himself in a long time.

"And most of my teaching consists of trying to persuade my students to stay in my course and not drop it so that they can get into 'Football for English majors' or 'Moby Dick for Dick Heads,'" Circassian continued. "I was tired of having to spend the first fifteen minutes of each period trying to sell the students something, and this new crowd wants me to spend at least twenty-five. It's boring, immoral and just not worth the $20,000 I'm getting paid."

"I agree with you that it's boring, immoral and just not worth the money, but don't you see, Circassian: this is a test?" queasled Dean Lean.

"A test of what?" asked Circassian. He was hoping for an answer.

"I don't know of what, but it's a test. You're a decent, honest, conscientious and absolutely superfluous person in this University, and I would like to see you stay. It would make me feel that there is someone who teaches here who still cares."

"Cares about what?" asked Circassian. He was hoping again for an answer.

"I don't know of what, but you do; I know that. There's something about you — from that time you walked into this office and asked me about Option Three, I knew you were the kind of man who believed in something."

"What do I believe in?" asked Circassian. He was no longer hoping for an answer.

"How the hell should I know? But since you're one of the few people left who has some convictions, although I haven't the flimsiest idea what they could possibly be, you're a beacon and model to the students and your colleagues. I think I've made my point."

He ushered Circassian out of the office. Circassian wondered what he had come in for in the first place, then remembered that he had wanted to quit; but there was something in Dean Lean's speech that made him realize he shouldn't, although he hadn't any clue to why that was.

When he got to his office he was amazed to see none other than Mona Pilgrim standing there, crying. She had a bruise on her cheek, her sweater was torn, and she looked in shock.

"What happened?" asked Circassian. He looked her over and except for the bruise, she didn't seem to be hurt. He was about to call security and report an assault when it occurred to him that Mona had stopped crying, although she was still catching her breath, and was giving him The Stare.

"Do you want to press charges against anyone, Mona?" asked Circassian.

"I don't know who it was, but I'm pretty sure I know who is behind it," said Mona between gasps.

"Then give me the name and I'll tell security about it," he said.

"Forget it, Doc. She's too big. Nobody can touch her now," said Mona with the finality of a Sybil.

"Who's too big to be touched?" asked Circassian.

"Tilly Owlglass, of course," said Mona. "She's now a Junior Vice President in Charge of Student Morale and Entertainment for Systell-Lex. She's been keeping this campus in bread and circuses for the last six months, or haven't you noticed?" she asked, an unaccustomed touch of sarcasm in her voice, as well as a literary allusion.

Circassian admitted that he hadn't noticed. He had tried to keep as far away from campus as possible during the times he didn't have to be there, except for Saturdays when it was quiet. "But how do you know she's behind it?"

"Because she's the one who started the Department Hoodlums as an off-hours project. She's got her fingers in everything."

"Department Hoodlums? That's a new one on me," said Circassian.

"Look, Doc, you seem to be able to keep yourself from knowing an awful lot around here, and I don't blame you; that's why the students who care look up to you."

"The students who care about what?"

"Anything. Anyway, the Department Hoodlums are hired by department chairs to try to intimidate students into dropping one course and taking another. Since the payroll of each department now depends on how many students they have, the Corporation is encouraging this competition. It's also a good way to starve out the least successful departments. That's why the Arts part of the Education and the Arts Department is going to be gone soon. Even with the help of Education, the students in the Arts are just too wimpy; they're easily intimidated by the Department Hoodlums and drop courses as fast as they are invented."

"How come I've never heard of the Department Hoodlums?" asked Circassian. He hoped that none of them were working for him or against him.

"You just don't want to know, Doc. One of them tried to get rough with me right now over a course I was taking in French and Economics; she wanted me to transfer into Chemical Anthropology, some course called, 'Know Your Bones from the Molecule Up,' and I wouldn't do it. Then she pushed me down a flight of stairs, but as she tried to finish me off with a karate chop, I kicked her in the groin and ran over here."

"How did you know I'd be here?" asked Circassian, aghast at what Mona had told him.

"Instinct," said Mona and Circassian was afraid he saw her wink. He also was wondering whether or not Mona had fallen by accident and was concocting an elaborate story to make him feel sorry for her and guilty that he had been so out of touch with what was going on.

"Are you trying to make me feel guilty for being so out of touch with what's been going on?" said Circassian.

"What should you feel guilty about, Doc? You're doing your job the best you can. All the students who take a course with you know that. That's why you're one of the hardest people for the Department Hoodlums to convince the students to drop. They really are loyal. One of them has a broken leg because he wouldn't switch to Parliamentary Botany from your Drama Survey. You're loved, Doc," she said, too warmly for comfort.

Circassian decided that he would call up Campus Security; he'd forgotten that it was now privatized along with everything else and was run by Damage Agency, Inc.

"Who are you calling, Doc? Security?" asked Mona.

"Yes. They should know about this," said Circassian.

"Well, they're in on it," said Mona. "They get paid off by Tilly and the Corporate suits at Systell-Lex."

"You make this sound like a conspiracy, Mona. I'm sure they'll be helpful." Circassian dialed the number for Security; there was no one there, but the answering machine provided him with what he needed to know: "Hello, this is Damage Agency, Inc. Your call is important to us so leave your name, the time you called, and your phone number. All complaints about Department Hoodlums are not handled by this office. Please direct any matters concerning them to Provost Pickle."

"They want me to throw this down the Black Hole!" strankered Circassian, looking at Mona with pulverated eyes.

"Forget it, Doc. I'll be more careful next time," said Mona. She seemed to wink again, as if perhaps all of this was just a bad dream or a worse joke. "But thanks for caring," she added, giving him a quick peck on the cheek, and vanishing as quickly as she had appeared.

Circassian went home and told the story to Tina, leaving out the part about the kiss.

"What are you going to do about it, Circassian: find Pickle? He was hard enough to get to when things weren't as wild. Now he's probably going to be more evasive," said Tina. She was getting more work from her firm in the Cayman Islands and was beginning to think that maybe Circassian should look into doing something else. He didn't whine any longer, but he was moaning in his sleep and some of the things he was saying made her doubtful that he could take the strain very much longer.

Circassian had a dream that night. He dreamed he had gone to a ballgame and someone asked him if he'd like to bat. Then Circassian discovered that he was in a baseball uniform. He got out on the field and picked up a bat and strode over to home plate. Then he looked at the pitcher who seemed to be waiting for something to happen.

"We've got no balls," somebody called out. And then everyone on the field was pointing to him and yelling: "We've got no balls! We've got no balls! We've got no balls!"

Circassian woke with a start and a snaff. He looked at Tina, who had been watching him for the past few minutes, uncertain about waking him.

"What happened?" he said to her.

"You were having one of those nightmares you get pretty frequently now. You were even talking in your sleep."

"What was I saying?" asked Circassian. He was afraid she'd tell him what he didn't want to know.

"Something about balls. Somebody doesn't have any balls," said Tina. "Sounds like a pretty sexy dream. Want to let me in on it?"

He told her what he remembered. She laughed, but when she saw that he was upset, she decided to let it go. Circassian was pretty sure what the dream meant, and he was determined that he would find Pickle somehow and let him know what was going on. Maybe then Pickle would pay attention to the University a little more, now that he was an employee of the whole place again.

He was sure Marigold knew where Pickle was and how to find him, but how to contact Marigold? If he used e-mail, it would probably be scanned by Pickle, and if he sent a note, it might be opened by one of the secretaries who was instructed to intercept any of Marigold's correspondance. He decided to call her at home, taking the chance that her home phone might not be bugged.

Circassian heard the following recorded message: "This is Marigold Markham; this phone is bugged. If you wish to speak to me without being recorded by someone else, please meet me at the usual place at the usual time after leaving your name. If you don't want to leave your name, you don't have to, but I don't know how to get ahold of you." Circassian left his name.

Sure enough, Marigold showed up at the same time she had the last time on the steps of Main. Nobody seemed to be following her, but to make certain, she walked around the building once before going up the steps.

"They haven't started following me yet," said Marigold. She believed that was because they were afraid she might call the newpapers, even though she wouldn't.

"Where can I find Pickle?" asked Circassian. He knew the longer they stood together, the more likely it was that one of the corporate spies would report it.

"Three o'clock Wednesdays and Fridays, Bowlarama; he's dressed as a Hasidic Jew. Wear a disguise so he can't recognize you." Then she was gone.

Circassian wondered what possible disguise he might use that wouldn't tip off Pickle. He needed to get the drop on Pickle in order to be able to talk to him, and that might not even work, but he had to try. He knew the Department Hoodlums had to be stopped. He asked Tina what she thought would be a good disguise.

"You can dress like a Wall Street broker; nobody'd recognize you that way," she said.

"But that means I'd have to shave my beard!" Circassian had a thick, dark beard of which he was fond; he had been wearing it for fifteen years and had grown attached to it. "What if I dress like another Hasidic Jew? All I'd need is a big black hat and an oversized black coat; I can get those over at what used to be the Theater department."

The next day Circassian got the key to the wardrobe room of what used to be the Theater department. It hadn't as yet been converted into office space by Systell-Lex. but that would be one of their plans: They were intending to put their regional headquarters right in the middle of the University.

The wardrobe room was already dusty and derelict-looking, but Circassian found the caftan he'd been looking for and even a black homburg for his head. There had been a production of *Fiddler on the Roof* some years before, and they still had the costumes. The hat was complete with false side-locks. He put it on, looked in the mirror and stared for a good five seconds. He certainly looked Jewish now.

Some mad impulse made him decide to see how well the disguise worked on campus, so he began walking from the Systell-Arts Building down the quad to Systell-Main. The billboards that had lined the walks of the quad had been taken down and been replaced with hologrammic images that came from cameras cleverly disguised as bushes. Suddenly, a beckoning young woman in a bikini would wink and nod, promising the delights of a vacation in Java or Micronesia; then a young man in a swim suit with biceps the size of grapefruits would call out for you to sample Stay-Tan lotion for a nice tan on your trip; and as Circassian was about to enter Main, it looked like a large man with a Big Mac blocked his way.

He walked along the halls of Main, fighting the impulse to greet people he knew. But the disguise worked, or so it seemed. Phil Frasier went by him without a word, Trent Butler seemed a bit startled but caught himself before he was tempted to make an irreverant remark. He almost bumped into Mona, who excused herself with a "Pardon me, Father," and walked on by without a glance. When he got to the department office, he was tempted to leave the building, but as he turned the corner, who should walk by but Josh Gutsky.

"Circassian! I can't believe it! You finally are acknowledging your people!" Josh was about to embrace him when Circassian retreated through the back way of Main, took off the disguise and came home. He decided that being a Hasidic Jew wasn't going to work; if Pickle didn't recognize him immediately, he would shy away from someone who looked like him. After all, Pickle knew he wasn't an Hasidic Jew; he had no need to meet one.

Circassian finally decided to sacrifice his beard and wear a pair of dark glasses when he went into the Bowlerama. Perhaps, since no one had seen him without his beard since he had been at the University, taking it off would be disguise enough.

The next day, he waited until Tina had gone into the study to work and stare and then he shaved his beard off. Throughout the day, he was either ignored or mistaken for someone else. Even some of his students would ask, "Where's Professor Circassian?" when he walked into the classroom. Most of them thought he looked better with the beard, but none of them seemed to recognize him until he told them who he was.

That afternoon, when he came home, he momentarily forgot that he had shaved off the beard, and when he walked into the study to see if Tina was still working, he was surprised to see her, a baseball bat in her hand, lifted to conk him.

"Who the hell are you?" threatened Tina. She had seen him walking up the path to the door and at first thought he was some sort of salesman, but when he entered, she decided to hide in the study and then call the police.

"I'm Circassian," he said. "Don't hit me!" "Prove it!" blaricked Tina. "What's my pet name for you?"

"Oh, for heaven's sake, Tina!"

"Tell me my pet name for you or I'll call the police!" she barted.

"Mommy's Little Mou Mou, okay?"

"So that's what you look like without a beard!" said Tina, tittering.

He explained his plan to her. He'd wear a pair of sunglasses, bell bottoms, and a loud shirt, and come into the Bowlerama humming something by the Allman Brothers. She thought this was the best disguise yet and that Pickle would not see him until he had him cornered.

The following Wednesday, his classes were over by two o'clock. Circassian found the Bowlarama and even decided to bowl a few games before Pickle came in. Sure enough, a few minutes after three somebody entered dressed like a Hasidic Jew, complete with the sidelocks which, as Circassian took a second look, were obviously phoney. "Yussl Leibschitz" was polishing his ball, then walking to the alley, turning his head suspiciously from right to left. Although it had been months since the incident at Tony's Lanes, Pickle was still guarding himself against a surprise attack.

He hadn't recognized Circassian. Just as Pickle was about to release the ball, Circassian called out, "Pickle!" Pickle turned as the ball flopped from his fingers. It wambled down the alley and knocked over all the pins, except for the one and the seven: another split.

"That's the first split I've had since the last time I saw you!" graggled Pickle, lying. He looked disheveled and in desperate need of titivation when he wambled over to Circassian.

"Provost Pickle, I need to talk to you!" said Circassian, "and this is the only way I can."

"Well, will you let me see if I can convert this split first!" said Pickle, reasonably.

"I'll pray for you, Provost Pickle," said Circassian insincerely.

Pickle converted the split and was in a decent frame of mind when he turned to Circassian. "I never would have recognized you without your beard. You must really want to see me if you've shaved it off," Pickle said, flattered.

"Where can we talk?" asked Circassian. They were surrounded by bowlers: striking, sparing, splitting, springing, groaning.

"Just talk low and they'll think it's Yiddish. Everyone here thinks I can barely understand English. It has its advantages," nattered Pickle.

"It's about the Department Nazis. . . uh, Hoodlums. You've got to do something about it," Circassian urged.

"What do you think I can do about it?" whined Pickle. He hadn't been a whiner until lately, but now he found himself whining more often than ever.

"You can tell the chairs to stop hiring these goons and let the students alone. Don't you think they'll start leaving when this gets out of hand?" Circassian questioned querulously.

"I think that maybe that's what Systell-Lex. eventually wants," said Pickle plaintively, his caftan drooping dolorously over his hands.

"That doesn't make sense! Why did they buy the University in the first place?"

"Because it was partially owned by their two competitors and they wanted to take advantage of the cheap price for the rest of it. This place was bought at half its assessed value, Circassian," pontrited Pickle.

"So you won't even try to stop the department chairs from this brutality?" angrily asked Circassian.

"Who do you think wants the chairs to hire the Department Hoodlums: Batman?" Pickle seemed stuck on the same sarcasm.

"You mean the faculty wants this to happen, too?"

"Have you taken a close look at the faculty, lately? I haven't, of course, but I get various reports from Marigold Markham and even Bendminder when he's not at his damned computer, and there seems to have been some changes that you might not be comfortable with, Circassian," said Pickle in muted tones.

As if an abyss had yawned and belched its darkness over him, Circassian now understood that he might be more alone than he thought. If the faculty were actually behind the Department Hoodlums, how much further could they sink before they had disappeared into the jetsam? How much further could they fall before they were like a pair of claws galumphing on the floors of silent seas?

"I'll tell you what I'll do," said Pickle. "I'll send out a bulletin halting the use of Department Hoodlums to increase class size. You guys seem to be finally working hard enough for you not to have that worry," he declamerated.

What Pickle had just told him was a shock. It was the first time Circassian remembered him saying anything sympathetic about the faculty. Maybe Pickle was afraid for his own job, but maybe he was beginning to realize what was happening to the University.

"How can you be sure that you can control policy?" asked Circassian. "After all, the executives at Systell-Lex. are pretty much calling the shots."

"The Department Hoodlums was just a bad idea. Tilly came up with it when we weren't making our quota in some departments that I didn't want shut down, and in a moment of weakness I agreed," admitted Pickle. He had that look of contrition that seemed appropriate to his disguise. In fact, Circassian wondered, not without a little of Josh's and Seth's influence, whether or not the outfit made Pickle feel the way he did. Circassian was not acquainted with many Hasidic Jews.

"I know I've tried to distance myself from the problems at the University ever since Option Three was implemented, but I guess I'd finally better face the music. I'd be willing to go back to teaching if that's what they were doing now, but I don't think I would feel comfortable being a salesman for No-doz and Trojenz," said Pickle with a little twinkle in his eyes. He had found out that Circassian had been behind the PUS jape and hadn't done anything about it.

"Well, good luck, Provost Pickle," said Circassian. "I hope you can get away with it."

"Don't worry. The Big Boss at Systell-Lex. is someone I can talk to. We see eye to eye sometimes, when he's not looking," Pickle added. "The only problem we'll have when we get rid of the Department Hoodlums is how they'll make up the deficit for their tuition. They were doing this for work-study."

As Circassian left the bowling alley, he began to regret the harshness with which he had always judged Pickle, and the loss of his beard. Maybe Pickle wasn't really quite that bad. Then Circassian remembered the things Pickle had done to him and felt justified in his original impression. Yet Pickle had said something that stuck in his craw like a raven in the mouth of a salamander: Systell-Lex wanted students to leave. Maybe the corporation realized that the University had too many students for the number of faculty; maybe they wanted students to leave because there'll be a smaller student-faculty ratio when the dust settled. Maybe there was some sense to all the weird and perverted things that had been happening to the University. Maybe the Pope would fly tomorrow. No, there had to be another reason and it had to do with profits. But how could Systell-Lex. make a profit out of a loss?

It is with this question in mind that Circassian returned to school the next day to find in his mailbox, as Pickle had promised, the following note in the *University Chatter*:

NEW COLLEGE PLAN TO CHANGE ENROLLMENT POLICY
Provost Donald Pickle has decided that the measures recently taken to enhance enrollment do not fall within the acceptable bounds of academic decorum and will cease forthwith. The usual modes of persuasion and mild coercion, of course, will remain in place. Will all Department Hoodlums please report to the Financial Aid Office for reassignment?

Circassian had realized that he had not paid much attention to what his colleagues were doing to keep themselves sane. It had been as much as he could handle to keep himself sane. He had done so by ignoring many of the orders being issued by the anonymous Big Boss at Systell-Lex. Whoever he or she was had kept all of the Administrators on edge, particularly Bendminder, who had stopped issuing statistics and figures as abruptly as he had started when the English and History departments were first bought.

Circassian had noticed that some of the people around him were keeping to themselves or even hiding when anyone came. As he walked into his class that day, he was surprised to see the students all standing, and when he sat down in his chair they began to applaud.

"Thanks for getting rid of the Department Hoodlums," called out one student.

"They had to go or we'd go," said another, a young woman who had almost been harrassed into dropping Circassian's course for one in the department of Communicative Geology called "Talk to Your Rocks and They Will Answer."

"You did something around here!" said a third.

Circassian had no idea how the students had been able to connect the end of the Department Hoodlums to him, but then he remembered that Mona would have realized that he had something to do with it and had told everyone within hearing or seeing, once the Provost's statement came out. He felt so good that he hoped the class would be able to go straight to the lesson without the usual sponsorship announcements.

"Aw, come on, Doc." It was Nathan Klotz, one of the better students. The rest took their cue from him and so Circassian had to regale them with the latest offers from spring-Flo bottled water, a subsidiary of Systell-Lex., Perma-Glide skin cream, another subsidiary of Systell-Lex., and In-Tite Exerciser, the "tushy tamer" from Compell-Tex., a subsidiary of Systell-Lex.

Then he began talking about Ibsen's *An Enemy of the People.* Circassian explained that although the play seemed to be about a man who is unafraid of saying what he thinks when he discovers that the spa the townspeople are counting on to bring in the tourist trade is polluted, it's actually about the consequences of idealism. At the end, Dr. Stockman is looked at as a crank because he is unwilling to compromise on any of his principles.

"Well, you could be called a crank, Doc," said Melville Rush, one of the members of the Greek Council who had decided he liked drama despite the fact that there wasn't a theater department at the University.

"You don't think I've compromised on my principles, Mel? Everybody does, and I do it all the time," said Circassian.

"Because you're still teaching here?" the student asked.

"No, in order for me to teach here," explained Circassian. Then he explained how he really didn't want to try to sell the students things and how all the advertising all over campus made him sick.

"But it's so cool, Doc," said Harley Davis, a very bright freshman who had been exempted from Fresh Comp, even if it was Fun-100.

"To me it's not," said Circassian.

The class was surprised. They thought he liked all of those things because he talked them up so enthusiastically.

"I'm just naturally that way, I guess," confessed Circassian, and then plowed back into the trials of Dr. Stockman.

When he returned to his office, he discovered that there had been some kind of altercation going on between Josh Gutsky and Lee Fitz-Proust, who had come over to complain to him about some multi-cultural matter. From what he understood, Josh had insisted that Jews should be considered a "protected class," and he cited a whole raft of facts and figures to prove it, including the number of hate crimes of which Jews were the victims.

Lee was more upset about what had happened to the Multi-Cultural Program, which was now being housed in the Health Department as the Healthy Multi-Cultural Department, and where it was languishing along with a number of other programs that weren't meeting their quotas. When Lee had complained to Pickle that she didn't believe in quotas, Pickle had turned a deaf ear and brain and told her to remember that at least the word "multi-cultural" was still on her stationery and that the Health department had been decent enough to let the title be part of theirs, to Health's detriment.

So when Lee had seen Josh she wasn't in a very receptive mood. Words and small, relatively harmless missiles were exchanged, and then Lee broke down and started crying. Josh joined her, and when the departmental secretaries started bawling themselves, because they were very unhappy about the way Systell-Lex. was treating them, the whole department began to fall into the well of emptiness and rueatude. Even Branch Stark was seen to shed a tear over what he perceived as his wasted life, although he would deny it later. The sobbing was heard all the way down the corridor, and when Dean Lean left his office to see what the noise was about, he realized that there were many reasons why he should feel bad about what was happening to him and so he, too, joined the general dismayment.

As Circassian watched what was happening, he was tempted to begin his own lachrymation, but he decided that he really wasn't feeling that badly after all, considering how badly he could have been feeling. He went into Josh Gutsky's office, where Josh was still wiping away tears from his eyes.

Meanwhile, the crying had now spread to the History department, where undisguised weeping was heard from many and sundry; Frank Short brushed a few tears from his eyes, and some of the others boohoohooed uncontrollably.

"Why are you crying, Josh?" asked Circassian. Josh was now sitting at his desk writing a list.

"I don't know," whimpered Josh. "It's just so sad around here."

"I understand it's sad around here, but we can't let these bastards beat us down. Cheer up. At least Pickle was on our side with the Department Hoodlums. That's something."

"That's one of the reasons I'm crying. I hired one of those little suckers to get more students into my 'Dirty Deeds of Dickens and Dickinson' course and now there's no hope that it will fill next semester," he wussied. He continued to write down a list of names singlemindedly with what was left of his brain, and Circassian, curious, looked at them.

It began with God and Abraham and was now up to Judah Ha-Levi. Circassian was a little puzzled, but then he soon realized that Josh was writing down the names of every Jew in history in chronological order. Or was he? Suddenly there was Henry Kissinger, Allen Greenspan and Fran Drescher on the list. Circassian looked at it and then he looked at Josh. He was writing faster and more frantically, and when Circassian glanced at Josh again, he realized that Josh's eyes were looking very much like Tina's when she had become mesmerized by the computer. Only Josh had climbed inside himself without the aid of any artificial intelligence.

Circassian tried to snap Josh out of it, but there was no computer screen to turn off. He thought if he could argue with him, he might stop his frantic writing. "What are you writing, Josh?" said Circassian.

"The names of my friends," said Josh. "And they're all Jewish too!" He was speaking in the voice of a cultivated eight-year-old.

"Is God your friend?" asked Circassian.

"My very best. He talks to me every night before I go sleep-sleep," whiffled Josh in what was getting to be a higher voice.

"But God isn't Jewish: is he or she or it?" said Circassian. He thought if he could appeal to Josh's logic, he might snap out of the spell he was in.

"Is too is too is too is too istoo istoo 'stoo 'stoo 'stoo!" said Josh.

"Okay, God is Jewish," agreed Circassian.

At this point Lee had come back to Josh's office to apologize for making him cry and heard Circassian say what he said.

"How parochial can you get, Circassian? You, of all people, who come from a persecuted group! That is, unless you think God is Jewish because you're Jewish too," she belted.

"All right, Lee. God is not Jewish, okay?"

But now Josh heard him above his own ululating voice and repeated his insistence louder.

Lee, feeling challenged to the very chitterlings of her being, responded. "God is not God is not God is not God is not God'snot 'snot 'snot!" Thusly, when Circassian walked out of Josh's room, he had left the two of them pointing their fingers at each other and yelling in high and incomprehensible tones something about "stoo" and "snot."

Branch stopped Circassian as he was about to leave his office to ask what the caterwauling was about, and when Circassian told him, Branch asked: "What does it matter if God's Jewish or not?"

"It does to them," said Circassian. And then Branch laughed, but it was not a contagious laugh. It was a laugh of someone who has been there, done that, and come back to do it again. It was a laugh of a man who knew he was near to brain-dead mumblings. It was a laugh of Branch Agonistes.

Suddenly, an unfamiliar figure began striding down the corridor to see what all the noise was about. He had journeyed from the Administration Building, now the Systell-Regional Building, because he had heard from the secretaries what was happening in Main. It seems that the crying fit had taken hold of all of the departments in Main and was quickly spreading to some of the other buildings. There was wailing and moaning in the Systell Science and Spanish Building, gnashing of teeth and rending of garments in the Systell Math and German Building and the tearing of hair and woing at will in the

Systellology Building.

The only ones who, it seemed, were not crying, were some heartless administrators and the students who had never seen anyone over the age of ten cry, and wondered if it was something they could cry about too. But when they found out, they began to laugh. So the tears and mirth mixed on campus and spilled over toward the town.

"Stop your crying at once!" shouted Pickle, but no one listened to him. "All right, what are you crying about?" he finally asked.

"If you have to ask, there's no point in telling you," said one of the secretaries, pushing back a bitter tear.

Circassian went up to Pickle, but before he could utter a word, Pickle was all over him. "Is this what happens when I call off the Department Hoodlums? Maybe they should have stayed for all that's happening now," he nuttered.

"I think that Josh Gutsky's gone a little funny in the head," said Circassian.

"Haven't we all?" barked Pickle over the moans and groans of all that surrounded him.

"But he *really* is nuts. He's writing a list and he can't stop," said Circassian. He had gone back into Josh's office after Lee had left and found that Josh was now writing the list on the blotter of his desk.

"That doesn't sound crazy to me. What kind of list?" said Pickle.

"A list of Jews," said Circassian.

"I see," said Pickle. "You'll have to do better than that to get him put away."

"But he really is crazy," said Circassian.

"Then one of his pupils should complain about it, not you," Pickle said.

"Since when is that a rule?" asked Circassian.

"Company policy. All faculty are unreliable in these matters but students are."

"Why is that?" asked Circassian, with curiosity, horror and disgust mingling in equal portions.

"Because they're the consumers and you're not," blatted Pickle.

"Is this part of Option Three?" asked Circassian.

"It came out of Option Three," said Pickle, "so you might say that."

Circassian went back into Josh's office one more time followed by a curious Pickle. He found Josh sitting on his desk, counting on his fingers, and whistling "Getting to Know You" off-key.

"Josh, do you know what you're doing?" asked Circassian.

"Of course I know what I'm doing!" snapped Josh. "What do you think I am: crazy?"

"You see?" said Pickle.

"So if he says he knows what he's doing he's not crazy even if what he's doing is crazy?" asked Circassian.

"Isn't that proof enough for you?" diddled Pickle.

"Not really. But if he does these sorts of things in class, and the students begin to complain, then he is crazy?"

"Of course, that would be an entirely different story. We are here to give the students what they want. That's the purpose of this University, and if they are happy with a professor who cuts out paper dolls and throws them in the air in little pieces while humming the 'Marseillaise,' then that's okay with us." Then Pickle turned to the office full of crying faculty. "If you don't stop this crying, you'll get no ice cream for dessert!" he shouted, as a last resort.

The sobbing subsided and the wailing wound down. It was silent. Then slowly, all faculty walked back to their offices and resumed their shattered lives.

Pickle used similar tactics in the other buildings and it seemed to work; the last thing the faculty wanted was to lose their dessert privileges.

The next day Circassian heard that Josh Gutsky had walked into class, performed an Irish jig for two minutes, and then jumped out the window. Fortunately, his classroom was on the ground floor, but since the window was closed when he jumped, he had to get some first aid from the Emergency Squad and some of the students complained that he didn't come back to finish whatever the jig was supposed to start. That was enough for Pickle; he put Josh on compulsory leave and replaced him with three Adjuncts who would do twice as much work for the same total salary.

Lee was also not unmarked by the incident. When she went into her class, she was dressed in a nightgown with a pair of bunny slippers, and began babbling about Barry Goldwater. Pickle suspended her from her courses as well and found four Adjuncts who would do thrice the work for half the pay.

The next day, Circassian found that the entrance that he normally took to get into Main was now adorned with a time clock. A sign read: "All Employees Are Now Required to Punch In: This Means You!" Circassian thought that this was another one of Bendminder's cruel jokes, but when he saw several of his colleagues dutifully find their time cards and put them in the clock slot, he thought it might be more prudent if he did the same. It was, in fact, Bendminder's idea, since the Boss at Systell wanted to make sure that his stockholders were getting the most bang for the bucks and that slackards would not be tolerated.

When he got home that evening, he told Tina what had happened. "Well, do they at least pay you by the hour?" she asked. She had pointed out to Circassian that if he'd been paid by the hour at the minimum wage with all the work he had, he would be making about $5000 more than he was now.

"I don't know, but I think they've put those things in as a matter of principle — they don't have any," said Circassian, illogically. He told her about Josh and Lee.

"It's a wonder that you haven't cracked up too, Circassian," she mused. "Are you sure you're perfectly sane?"

"Imperfectly sane, maybe," said Circassian.

There was a letter waiting for him without a return address. It was a local postmark, but it looked very suspicious. Sure enough, when Circassian opened it, it seemed to be written in a strange language with an alphabet he could not even decipher, possibly Sanskit or Urdu. Just then, the phone rang. It was Hank Schecht.

"Circassian, this phone is being tapped so all I can tell you is: 'Hold it up to the light,'" said Hank, and hung up.

At first Circassian wondered whether or not Hank Schecht too had gone, as they said in the area, "a few quarts low," but then he thought that the cryptic message over the phone might have something to do with the cryptic message he had received in the mail. Sure enough, in holding the letter up to the light, there were suddenly decipherable words:

SECOND MEETING OF FACULTY WHO STILL CARE

MEET US AT HANK SCHECHT'S HOUSE TONIGHT AT 8.

EVEN THOUGH HANK AND I ARE GOING SOON, IT'S NOT TOO LATE TO DO SOMETHING.

YOU DON'T HAVE TO BURN THIS IN YOUR HOME BECAUSE IT WILL SELF-DESTRUCT TEN SECONDS AFTER YOU READ IT.

IN SOLIDARITY,

DABS BUDWEISER, FORMER PRESIDENT OF ULP

HANK SCHECHT, FORMER VICE-PRESIDENT OF ULP

And just as the note said, no sooner had Circassian read it than it shriveled up like a spider fallen in a fireplace.

This time, when Circassian went to the meeting, he noticed that the numbers of the conspirators had dwindled. Branch was there and so was the shadowy figure in the ski mask, but Lee Fitz-Proust was no longer able to come — she was being treated for depression in one of the local hospitals' psychiatric ward — and Trent Butler had decided that he was being followed too closely by some shadowy figure in a ski mask. (It turned out that it was some older student's irate husband, who finally caught up with Trent and gave him a sound thrashing.)

"What we do now is begin to organize," said Dabs, as soon as Circassian was seated.

"How do we do that?" asked Branch. "Overwhelm them with our numbers?"

"Irony will not help, Branch," said Hank, jelankly.

"That was not meant as irony, Hank," corrected Circassian. "It was sarcasm."

Hank looked confused, which prompted Circassian to explain the distinction between irony and sarcasm, words that many unwary people interchange in the most mindless fashion.

"What we need to do is have a plan," said Dabs. "We're bringing someone here who can give us one," she said, defiantly.

"Who the bleep could that be?" inquired Branch.

"You'll, see," said Hank. "This man knows what he's doing."

"By the way, who is the shadowy figure sitting next to you with the ski mask on? I'm curious about him," said Circassian.

"Him? I thought he was with you, Dabs," said Hank.

"I thought he was with you, Hank," said Dabs.

Then Dabs looked at Hank and Hank looked at Dabs.

"SPY!" they both shouted, and began to vacate the room, Branch lumbering behind them.

This was the moment that the labor specialist they had been waiting for was just about to ring the doorbell after having nervously looked behind his shoulder several times to make sure he wasn't being followed.

"Spy!" shrieked Dabs, making a quick exit around the startled man.

"Spy!" said Hank and made a whooshing motion with his hands at the beflooded labor specialist.

"Spy!" he echoed, and rushed down the steps, into his car and the awaiting night before him.

As he drove off, Circassian had discovered who the masked figure was. He had gone up the stairs to tell everyone not to worry, but it was too late. Dabs was gone, Hank was donfalooned, and Branch was trying to catch his breath on the living room sofa.

"If you'd only given him a chance, he would have told you himself!" said Circassian.

They went downstairs and sure enough, sitting in his chair, looking as abashed as a leg of mutton in an ashram, was Dean Lean, the mask of his disguise lying on his lap.

"My heart's always been in the right place, guys," he stuffled. "It's just that my head has been somewhere else."

"But now that you've scared away the expert, we'll have to have another meeting to call him back," said Hank. He was bitterly disappointed. He didn't think there was a way in hell that they could organize the faculty against Systell-Lex., but at least with Dean Lean on their side, he felt he could be a tiny bit more optimistic.

"What you can do, Dean Lean," said Circassian, "is give us any information that comes your way about the sneaky, nasty and underhanded plans Systell-Lex. has in store for us. Maybe we can prepare for them then."

"But wouldn't that be unethical?" asked the Dean.

Circassian, Branch and Hank were able, after a few minutes, to persuade Dean Lean that doing something unethical to unethical people was really ethical in a convoluted sort of way.

"Well, there's one thing I can tell you already," said Dean Lean. "Systell is beginning to hologram the faculty. It might take a while, but they intend to get a whole set of holograms from each course, and then they will start testing them on various student populations to see if it has the same impact on learning as the original course does."

"When will all of this start?" asked Circassian.

"For all I know, it might have started already. As we speak there may very well be a concealed camera somewhere in your classrooms taking three-dimensional videos of unsuspecting faculty," he said.

"Then why didn't you warn us sooner?" asked Circassian.

"Because I was afraid I would lose my job, of course," said Dean Lean.

"And you're not afraid now?" said Branch. He was astonied at what he saw as Dean Lean's virtuous and courageous decision to tell all.

"I've gotten notice. My services will no longer be needed next semester. I'm being replaced by an Adjunct Dean who will be so adept, I am told, at getting things done, that she'll only need half the time I need to do what I do, whatever that might happen to be," sorrowed Dean Lean.

"How did you find out we were meeting, anyway?" asked Circassian. After all the trouble Hank had gone to in keeping these meetings secret, it was a little surprising that one of "them" had been able to find out about it.

"Marigold let me know; she got one of your messages about the meeting the first time but decided she'd be more effective in keeping her usual low profile," the Dean explained.

"But how did she know you were on our side?" asked Hank, frizzled.

"She knows a lot more than anyone else around here. Like where all the skeletons are buried. Anyway, she figured that when she sent out the memo that I was going to be no longer needed, I'd be in the right frame of mind to listen to what you have to say. And I agree with you. But I don't think there's a damn thing you can do about it."

"Well, at least we can tell the faculty about these holograms they're taking," said Circassian.

"But will they believe you?" asked Dean Lean.

"They'll believe you, Dean Lean," said Hank. "You need to do this one courageous act and we will all remember you fondly instead of with disdain and hate."

"You mean most of the faculty disdain and hate me now?" wandled the Dean. He had always assumed people knew he was doing whatever he was doing for the best.

"Well, maybe 'hate' is too strong a word," qualified Hank. "But certainly disdain. I would say very strongly disdain."

"Well, that's a little better," whiffled Dean Lean. "I can deal with disdain; I've been doing it for years; it's hate I can't stand. I've been told it's something you have to be carefully taught to do."

The meeting broke up when Dabs phoned Hank and had been filled in on who the mysterious figure was. She was also bitter that the labor expert would have to be called back for another meeting, but she was mollified that Dean Lean was on their side and would actually do something, and besides, Dabs Budweiser loved meetings.

That night Circassian had another strange dream. He dreamed he was in Israel with his mother and that they had just decided to take a trip to find out what things were like there. They were separated from their touring group in some kind of casbah and wandered around the streets for hours. Circassian had taken the precaution of buying an Arabic newspaper and showing it prominently as he wandered the streets. Then an Orthodox Jew wearing the outfit similar to the one he and Pickle had worn came up to him and shook his finger at him, pointing at the Arabic newspaper. When he awoke, Circassian decided it was time to ask his mother about his background. He was sure there was some secret he needed to know; it might even help him decide what he was going to do about his career, such as it was, such as it might have been.

That day, Dean Lean sent out an announcement that was to issue shock waves and mild amusement among the faculty:

NOTICE TO ALL FACULTY:

Systell-Lex. is now or may soon be taking three-dimensional videos of you during teaching. The video cameras can be concealed in a very small space so it is possible that a student might have been hired to take the video. In any case, I would suggest you attempt to take evasive action if you cannot locate the video camera that may be in your classroom. Remember: Once your course is copied on tape, you may never be called on to teach again.

That afternoon, Circassian read a second bulletin that was distributed to the faculty even more suddenly than the first:

NOTICE TO ALL FACULTY:

Dean Dean Lean has been relieved of his duties as Dean of this School. A search committee for his replacement will be convened as soon as the Corporate Directors of Systell-Lex. meet to discuss this development. It is very strongly advised that employees disregard the bulletin Dean Lean issued this morning. It is the product of a deluded and severely overactive imagination of a man who has been disdained by his staff for quite some time, and even hated by a few. Please conduct your courses as you are accustomed to. In the interval, Provost Pickle will act as acting, emergency Dean.

Later that afternoon, after reading the bulletin, Circassian asked if any student knew of any hologramming of faculty that was going on. Several students violated the "don't tell" code and pointed their finger at Denholm Hulk, one of the fraternity bullies and someone for whom most of those students who knew him had disdain. He was found with a camera in the fly zipper of his pants, which explained why he was sitting in the front row and always seemed to have his pelvis thrust in Circassian's direction. The camera was of a square shape, a quarter of an inch on a side, and looked like a smiley face, an appropriate emblem for someone like Denholm to put on that part of his anatomy.

The notice that Dean Lean had put out had its effect. Mini-video cameras were found in students' ears, noses, hair, on earrings, the pads of fingers, belt buckles and contact lenses. One was even found in the pubic hairs of one of the figure models in a drawing class. But many, it was thought, went undetected.

Seth Shotman suggested, to no one in particular, that the faculty take "evasive action," and either teach their classes so badly that the videos would be useless, or do bizarre things that would be unacceptable in any class. This idea did not work very well, since a number of the faculty did not know the difference between teaching well and badly and others acted in such a bizarre way that some students boycotted class and caused a general disruption. This is what Seth and some of the others wanted, but it also resulted in faculty being summarily dismissed from their jobs.

()

About a week after having the dream, Circassian decided to give his mother a call. He talked to her about once a week, but it was generally a liturgy of his complaints about school and hers about his father who had been dead for ten years but still visited her in dreams. The Circassians seemed to be adepts at dreaming, Circassian being only one of many in his family to come up with stunning revelations in sleep.

"Mom, I have a question I want to ask you," said Circassian after his mother had lodged the usual complaints about his father's obtrusive visitations.

"So ask the question, already," asked Mrs. Circassian.

"What is our family background?" Circassian queried. He didn't want to be too direct and hoped his mother would say something first.

"Your father's family came from Armenia; about them, who knows? Mine came Birobidjan, but already you know that," said his mother.

"But what I want to know is if there are any Jewish ancestors in the family. You've never really said much about it."

"You should only ask such a question. Bite your tongue and hope the Evil Eye doesn't get you, Circassian." Even Circassian's mother knew that he preferred that name to his given one.

"You mean we are?" asked Circassian.

"Your grandmother, should rest in peace, was born a Jew but converted when she married your grandfather. Nothing of all that mishegos came down to my generation. So that's the story: you happy?"

"But that means I have Jewish genes, Mom," churkled Circassian.

"Jeans, shmeans, as long as you love your mother!" said his loving mother.

Circassian was excited. It was the first piece of news in a long time that he could really get excited about without getting mad. He told Tina about it and although she wasn't excited, she was pleased that he seemed to have satisfied his curiousity.

"So Gutsky and Shotman were right all the time, sort of," said Tina, amused and droll.

"I'm tempted never to tell them. Of course, poor Josh is now institutionalized and I don't want to set him off. But this probably explains a lot of things about me," said Circassian.

"Like what?" asked Tina.

"I'll figure that out as I go along. But knowing about it makes me feel, well, different."

"How different?"

"I don't know, just different!" yented Circassian. He had no idea what he was talking about, but now that he had gotten to the bottom of this matter, he was determined not to let it disturb him again. His dreams of being Jewish would now melt into his regular and accustomary dreams of being thrown naked in front of a laughing audience at a school play or being pursued by a many-headed giant through the rush-hour crowds of Times Square.

Once the warning from the now former Dean Lean had its intended impact and faculty were certain that they were being videotaped, some perfected methods of teaching that would both amuse the students and have its sabotaging effect on the plans of Systell-Lex. Branch Stark sang his lectures and conducted his discussions in rhyming couplets; Trent Butler did his in mime; Frank Short delivered his classes in French, of which he knew very little and the students less. And Circassian decided that he would do his in the most unique way of all: by giving imaginary information.

Circassian would come into the room and begin his discussion by asking the class what contribution Beethoven made to modern drama. "He invented the well-made play," said one witty student.

"He was deaf, so he discovered the theater for the deaf," said another.

"You're both right. Now tell me, what plays Beethoven didn't write," asked Circassian, not trying to keep a straight face. He knew that someone else in the class had been bought off to bring a concealed camera to his lectures. He could sense the tiny whirring sound of the video as it tried to steal his image from him, something, he had learned, that his mother's mother's people had regarded as an abomination.

"Beethoven didn't write Ibsen's *A Doll House*," said a dull and prosaic student.

"Beethoven was famous for not writing Shakespeare," said a more sympathetic learner.

"Beethoven's Fifth was not a play called *Death of a Salesman* by Arthur Miller," said his class favorite, Ivan Ivanovich.

After about a twenty-minute lecture on Beethoven as one of the greatest non-playwrights that ever lived, Circassian filled up the rest of the class time with the advertisement copy he'd been given that morning by the Systell-Lex Marketing Assistant, one of many assigned to make sure that the routine of the University would remain uninterrupted.

That afternoon, Circassian got a note from Provost Pickle. It was about his teaching. He decided that it was important enough not to ignore, tempted as much as he was.

When he was ushered into Pickle's office, he narrowly missed getting hit with the backswing of the stroke that the Provost was practicing. As Associate of Operations at the University, a promotion that had doubled his salary, Pickle had decided that bowling was too plebian a recreation for him. Besides, he would have a lot of notice before someone could sneak up behind him and spoil his golf game, and there were no splits in golf.

"Circassian," grundled Pickle; "good to see you!" He put the golf club down and offered Circassian his hand. Since this was the first time Circassian could remember Pickle offering his hand to anyone, he looked doubtful but finally, reluctantly, shook it.

"To what do I owe this pleasure, Provost Pickle?" asked Circassian. He was trying to be polite, although he wasn't certain that Pickle would pick up on it, being used to impoliteness most of the time.

"It's about your teaching, Circassian," said Pickle. Circassian immediately assumed that he was going to be given the ax, the old heave ho, the hook, but it turned out quite the contrary.

"I want you to know that of all the faculty who have taken evasive action to avoid the holograms, you have been voted by the students to be the best. Mona Pilgrim took a poll last week and it was no contest. Congratulations!" Provost Pickle looked as pleased as a puppeteer in a shooting gallery.

"They like me?" asked Circassian. He had been certain that the games he had been playing in class for the past few weeks had been mildly tolerated by the students, but that they actually liked what he was doing was considerably beyond his ken.

"And to show you how much we appreciate your efforts, Systell-Lex. has authorized me to give you a promotion to Practically and Almost Associate Professor with a salary increase of one dollar an hour!" Pickle pronounced proudly.

Circassian felt overwhelmed. In the five and a half years he had been at the University, this was really the first time he could remember not getting screwed by someone. With the extra dollar an hour, he and Tina could afford to take a trip to Atlantic City and halfway back. Except that he hated Atlantic City and knew that the raise wouldn't be enough to let him afford a night at a hotel.

On his return to his office, he felt buoyant. The sun was shining and, despite the holograms that were now everywhere, he felt like humming a tune. As he walked down the quad, smiling at everyone, he heard someone else whistling the tune with him. Since it was "Some Enchanted Evening," he wondered who it could be, and guessed correctly: Mona Pilgrim had been walking behind him since he had left the Systell-Lex. Building.

"Hey, Prof., how's it going?" she asked, innocent as Lucretia Borgia on an Easter Egg hunt.

He told Mona about getting the raise from Pickle and thanked her for conducting a poll.

"I fudged it a little, Doc. You actually came in second to Frank Short, who kept everybody going with his Nixon imitations, but since everyone thinks he'll be gone by the end of the semester, I figured that somebody should benefit from the poll, so why not you?"

She walked along with him, turning her blue eyes toward him whenever he glanced in her direction. They went into the English wing of the building, which was sequestered between the hockey rink and the swimming pool, when Mona grabbed Circassian's hand.

Uh oh, I'm in for it now. Especially since she did do me a favor, thought Circassian, wambling.

"Can I talk to you in your office for a minute, please," asked Mona, a seductive smile masking a no-nonsense voice.

"Oh boy, I'm *really* in for it now," said Circassian trying to mask panic with nonchalance and ending up with panchalance. He made sure his door was open when the two of them sat down across from each other on two non-swivel chairs. Circassian had made sure that he always sat on a non-swivel chair.

"I wanted to talk about that wonderful night we spent together," began Mona, whereupon Circassian stood up and closed the door, "but I decided it wasn't something we needed to discuss," she continued, whereupon Circassian stood up and opened the door.

"I want you to know Mona, that whatever we can discuss should always be discussable," nuttered Circassian, now totally flummoxed and becalmed in confusion.

"I agree, so I just want you to know that I've had a change of heart recently, or should I say, my heart has been changed," she explained, incoherently.

"I'm glad to hear it, I hope," stottled Circassian.

"I have finally fallen in love with someone who can reciprocate, and although I shouldn't tell you who it is, I will." Circassian stood up and closed the door.

"Please don't tell me who it is. I don't want to know who it is. I'll be your best friend if you don't tell me who it is. I'm going to sing and shout until you promise not to tell me who it is." But despite this irresistible offer, he distinctly heard the name Trent Butler come from Mona's lascivious lips. Then Circassian opened the door and in medium dudgeon — since he was still grateful for all the young woman had done for him — ushered her out of the room.

When he came home that evening, he told Tina that he'd been praised by Pickle and almost forgot mentioning the raise.

"Your career is beginning to take off," said Tina. "Pretty soon they might promote you again and give you another dollar raise."

"It's better than nothing," said Circassian. "Besides, it probably means that I won't be let go when they've gotten all the holograms they need."

"You want to keep this job that bad?" asked Tina. She was whipping up a peach cobbler while Circassian was cutting some onions and seemed to her in a lachrymal mood.

"Yes, I want to keep this job that bad. Besides, I want to show the sons of bitches that they can't scare me off by ruining what is left of higher education at the University. They should let *me* determine how to ruin higher education at the University."

"I don't think they're doing this just to try to run you off, Circassian," said Tina.

"Well, they won't. But why do you think they're trying to ruin the University?"

"Business," said Tina, as if that would explain everything, and Circassian finally understood: it did. He wasn't sure why, but if he were to ask anyone at Systell-Lex. he was sure that would be the answer. Exactly what the reason behind the "business" might be lost forever in the niceties of high and not-so-high finance, but it was *the* answer.

Despite the high with which he had walked into the room, Circassian was back into gloom when supper came: cabbage and collard green beans. Even with his impending raise, the Circassian household was feeling the pinch. Tina's work had been cut back again.

"I have some other good news for you, Tina," Circassian rackled.

"Fine. Pass the collards," said Tina.

"Mona Pilgrim has found a new love," he said, eagerly passing the bowl of collards to Tina. He loathed them, but he felt obliged to pretend otherwise.

"Oh? Why should that be something I'd find interesting? Don't all of your sweet young things find new loves periodically? Isn't that what they're supposed to do?" said Tina. She was furrowing her brow in a large question mark and Circassian suddenly realized that he hadn't been keeping Tina abreast of the amouronic forays that Mona had been engaged in lately.

"Forget it," ruffled Circassian. He realized that pursuing the subject would be either damaging or deflating.

"I will, and so will you, Circassian," said Tina, humphing. Circassian realized that he was slipping; he was losing track of what he was supposed to tell people and not tell them, and if he weren't more careful, he would be known as a gossip and a snitch, not to mention a very confused person.

That evening, the news brought another bulletin from the Capitol. Governor Putski was calling a state of fiscal crisis for the University, which meant that any contracts about to be issued or recently issued were dull and void.

Circassian was sure that Putski meant "null and void," but perhaps he was hearing things. He was sure it meant that he would not be getting his dollar-an-hour raise until he realized that his part of the University was no longer part of the University and almost felt thankful that Systell-Lex. had bought everything out. At least he wouldn't have to deal with Governor Putski.

But the Governor was actually looking worried. He was planning to run for President and his job rating that had been soaring was beginning to plummet. This meant that some of the people that you could fool all of the time were not as numerous in the recent poll as those of most of the people you could fool some of the time, and even a smidgeon of the people you couldn't fool all of the time were being heard from, too. Perhaps a fiscal emergency would convince them that cuts in the University budget were a Public Good, but it was still remotely possible, Circassian thought, that the people would regard it as a Public Bad, and some might go so far as to think of it as a Public Nuisance.

()

Circassian felt overall well-being when he found out that the class holograms were no longer being run by Systell-Lex and he could go back to his normal teaching. The only problem was that he'd almost forgotten what normal teaching was. He had carefully planned a lesson showing why Franz Schubert was one of the great non-short story writers, and also among the most prolific unessayists in the *Vienna of My Dreams* when he suddenly realized that he would have to go back to teaching "The Merry Wives of Brooklyn" and "Death of a Commercial Traveler," except that this, too, had been part of his evasive plan. He actually had to look at his old notes to bring him back to what he was supposed to be doing, and he was no longer sure that he knew if he should do it. The students were getting some kind of education, he was certain, if for no other reason than they were coming to class and discussing something. He began to realize it didn't really matter what they were discussing, since most of them forgot it all within a few weeks anyway, but that they were involved in thinking about something. They were using their verbal skills, occasional writing skills, and their imaginative faculties, long dormant from their earliest childhood. That was the key to the whole thing, he realized, and that was the great secret that most professors guarded jealously on pain of unemployment.

As he once more walked into the office, however, he began to see a great change in his colleagues. Now used to the kind of teaching they had never done before, returning to their actual tasks depressed many of them and drove several to despair. In fact, it seems that whatever fragile facade of sanity had been maintained through the last few months was beginning to disintegrate before the ingenious machinations of the Big Boss of Systell-Lex. Or, at least, that was what Circassian began to realize.

Seth Shotman was doing backflips down the middle of the corridor leading to his office, and since he had never done backflips before, he did something atrocious to his back halfway to his office and had to be removed on a stretcher. Several of the faculty in the English department were speaking in tongues. Branch Stark had brought his dart board into the classroom and was teaching the students the fine points of aiming correctly at a photo of whomever he had chosen to receive his venom for that day. Looking for cooler heads, or at least one cooler head, Circassian wallached upstairs to see if he could find Frank Short. Frank was sitting at his desk, unmoving, and looking out the window.

It was a particularly sunny day, and Frank's window looked out at the rear of the building where there was nothing but woods and the far sight of the majestic Mount Mountains. Circassian walked in softly but then made a few polite noises. At first he thought that Frank was sleeping, but then he noticed that his eyes were open. He then feared that Frank was dead, but once he touched him, Frank turned to him with a strangely beautiful smile on his face. Circassian then realized that Frank was wearing a very small pair of headphones.

"Sorry, Friend Circassian. I was listening to 'Tosca.' I was thinking how it might feel if I were to shout to the gathered minions who were watching, 'Pickle, we will meet again before God,' but I'm not sure they'd get the reference."

Circassian didn't either. He wasn't much of an opera fan, leaving that to Tina. He did like Gilbert and Sullivan, but he was told by a number of people who should know that Gilbert and Sullivan was not heavy enough for most people who liked opera. He wasn't sure what made Light Opera light but he hadn't checked with someone who would tell him.

"Why are you listening to 'Tosca' and staring out the window, Frank, when people are cracking up all over the place?" Circassian realized that he was expecting an answer from Frank, but Frank gave him that blissful smile that was completely out of character with his normally sardonic expression and simply said, "It's over, Circassian. It's over."

"What's 'over,' Frank?" asked Circassian. He wanted to be sure he understood what Frank, whom he trusted like the wind and sky, was telling him.

"'It': the whole enchilada, the big lobanza, everything in the garden, the works!"

"Could you be a little more specific?" Circassian asked. He was worried about Frank, who, although he had taken the headphones off, still had that far-away look.

"You'll find out very soon, Old Man; sooner than you realize. I just want you to know it's been a very long, strange journey, but now it's near the end."

"You're not retiring, Frank? You're not throwing in the towel yet?" asked Circassian in hushed and sacramental tones.

"It's been done for me, Circassian," said Frank. "It's already over with." He gave a slight shrug of dismissal, put his ear phones back on and turned away to the window. He could see the peaks of the two mountains that guarded the valley in which the University nestled like a broken thumb in a splint.

Everything out there seemed so disarmingly peaceful, and whatever was in Frank's mind would find a more inviting vista than the neonic and hologramming world that faced the two of them whenever they left the building. In fact, Circassian had noticed that some holograms were beginning to invade the hollowed halls of Main. They began to dribble out of the broom closets, seep underneath some of the classroom doors, and drift along the corridors like friendly spirits at a seance. Some even resembled the faculty, waving their hands at an empty space. And then Circassian realized that they *were* the faculty, at least that part of the faculty that hadn't shown any concern about being hologrammed. There was Linda Larsen from Physics, explaining a theorum to the floors and walls; Dan Antler, shown sideways, pontificating on Burke and Bentham to the ceiling. The figures met and merged with each other, talking softly but incessantly, the hands of Bert Beemer, the body of Lou Tannenbaum, the face of Eudora Clay, in one physical and verbal cacophony, with Eudora's nose protruding from Bert's left index finger, and her chin piercing through Lou's shoulder blades.

Suddenly, there was a great yawp from the environs of Branch Stark's office. Branch had been going swimming daily for years in the University pool and had acquired a great deal of souvenirs, most of which he had stacked neatly —for him — in one of the office closets. As Circassian approached Branch's door, he saw a literal storm of towels erupting from the office onto the hall. There were towels in every state of wear and period from the sedate Fifties and the roaring Sixties all the way to the decadent 2000's. It was as if a mad goose had decided to shed its feathers in a moment of goose-stress. There were yawps coming from Branch, somewhere behind the terry-cloth trantrum which Circassian soon realized would only subside when Branch ran out of towels.

"Hey Branch," Circassian said, picking his way carefully from among the mess. He was knee-deep in the pile before he could clear a way into Branch's inner domain. But what he saw Branch staring at was almost as astonishing as Branch's reaction had been. Standing on Branch's table was a life-sized hologram of Branch doing the Can-Can and singing "Side by Side." The hologram was so realistic that Circassian thought Branch would get knocked down by the leg kicks.

"Branch, this is really weird. How did they . . . ?" Circassian began but Branch hushed him.

"Wait, I think the good part is coming up again." He spoke in a dry, flat, un-Branch-like voice.

The hologram spoke in Branch's voice: "We can see in 'Mending Wall' the implicit irony of Frost's voice. . . ." After a few more moments of the lecture, the image again returned to dancing and cavorting on the table.

"How did they . . . ?" Circassian began again.

"Hell if I know," said Branch. "I never let those suckers take videos when I knew about it," he daffled.

"Unless they took these before you knew about it," said Circassian.

"What the hell, Circassian. What the hell," maundered Branch, taking what was the last towel in the room and tossing it through the door. "But if they have me recorded on that shit, it's over. It's over anyway." The hologram suddenly shrank and Branch recited to Circassian in a very distinctive voice: "You shoulda taken care of me, Circassian. I coulda been a contender." Then Branch did another un-Branch thing: he started to laugh. It sounded at first like short, angry barks, but then spilled through his guts like a jellied cranberry factory during an earthquake.

Dean Lean — temporarily rehired since no sane person had applied for the job — had seen the whitening mound from far down the hallway, and walked up to try to understand what was happening. Most of the faculty had stopped showing up regularly to their classes, Circassian being one of the exceptions, and there were tons of student complaints that were pouring into Lean's office with the ferocity of a tribe of angry llamas.

"What is he doing? What is he doing?" shouted Dean Lean. By this time quite a crowd of students had gathered around Branch's office.

"He quit," said Circassian. "It's a metaphor, only when he makes one, he makes it big," he said.

"But he's throwing out the towels," said Dean Lean, trying to extract some humor from a somber situation.

"Depends on your point of view," said Circassian.

The hologram of Branch was life-size again, sitting in his chair in front of the desk while Branch was miming a lecture, wordlessly gesturing to the apparently enthused twin. It was then that Circassian realized that these holograms could be controlled as easily as a puppet. Where they were coming from he hadn't figured out, but that they could be anywhere and appear at any time was becoming obvious.

Dean Lean peered in and began to wring his hands. Since this was a gesture unfamiliar to Circassian in the years he'd known the Dean, he was beginning to wonder if what he'd been watching was actually a hologram of Dean Lean. He decided to take a few tentative jabs at the Dean and felt flesh and bone about rib-high.

"What are you doing, Circassian? Are you going crazy, too?" he fluttered with unnerved despair.

"Why not?" Circassian asked, looking back into Branch's office, where he saw the Branch hologram soundlessly applaud a point Branch was making about what might have been "Mending Wall" or possibly "Two Tramps in Mud Time," since Branch began to mime someone walking heavily across a muddy field.

"Dean Lean!" someone called out in a voice of pity and terror. It was Lavendar Walker, his assistant secretary, who was now doing double duty since the old secretary had left several days before.

"What is it now?" wailed Dean Lean.

Lavendar Walker had been one of the truly unflappable members of his staff, and she was looking completely flapped. "There are people doing very strange things all over the building, Dean Lean," she whimpered. "Leticia Fry was having a trantrum in her Ed. Psych class, and the students think she's just giving them a demonstration."

"Well, maybe she is," said Dean Lean.

"For the last twenty-five minutes?" asked Lavendar, hoping that there would be an answer to that question. "And Clarence Robinson III is reciting the Declaration of Independence to his Organic Chemistry class and Seth Shotman said he was doing it inHebrew."

"I didn't know Clarence knew Hebrew," said Dean Lean, trying to put an edge of levity in the gathering darkness of Despond.

"He doesn't," she said. "At least no one who knows him seems to think he does."

"Well, I suppose I could start talking in Swedish," chuffled Dean Lean. "Jag kan inte tele Svenska," he added, suddenly astounded at himself. "I think I'd better call a meeting of all the sane faculty right away," he decided, hurrying back down the hall.

He thought of calling Pickle, but he decided that Pickle wouldn't be any help, not since he had been promoted to Associate of Operations. He decided to call Pastor Castor, since he had been one of the few calm heads left on campus. He found out, after failing to get him in his office, that Pastor Castor was now in jail, having been arrested for getting into a fight with two of the town bullies at one of the local bars. Since Pastor Castor was a pacifist, this showed how far the faculty had come and gone since Option Three had been introduced. Dean Lean thought he should bail him out, since he felt that some responsible person should be in charge of things. Only a few moments later he realized that there were too many things for a responsible person to be in charge of.

Meanwhile, Circassian had begun noticing as he went by the classrooms that there were very few students in class. What was happening did not seem to bode well for the future of the University. In fact, nothing seemed to be boding well for the future of the University. Although he had come from Pickle's office the previous day with such high hopes, Circassian decided to call on the new Associate of Operations, since he had a little more faith in him than Dean Lean had. He decided to walk into Pickle's office unannounced in hopes that he might find him in.

When he got there, he found Pickle in his office with the secretary, doing a few George Bush imitations with the appropriate gestures. "Circassian! What in Totty Donkins are you doing here?" asked Pickle, using a quaint phrase he'd picked up on his visit to Tonga.

"The faculty are acting very strangely, Provost Pickle," said Circassian.

"I know that!" said Pickle, his voice as smooth as butter on the bottom of an infant.

"Many of them seem to have lost their minds," Circassian added.

"I know that too. Especially now that the hologram system has been perfected," Pickle said, nodding for the secretary to go.

"Branch Stark has . . ."

"I was certain of that too."

"And Frank Short . . ."

"I know, I know."

"Then what . . . ?"

"By Monday, everything will be perfectly clear, Circassian. Just say that we're going to be using Option Three," Provost Pickle opined.

"You mean. since they're crazy and don't know they're crazy . . ."

"Precisely, Circassian. But I can assure you you have nothing to worry about. Why, I'd say that you were the sanest person on campus," said Pickle.

He winked and offered Circassian a cigar, rather absent-mindedly. Circassian, even more absentmindedly, took the cigar, lit up and began to puff until he remembered that he didn't smoke. It was that kind of state of mind he came back with when he entered the house.

"You were right, Tina," he said. "This is business."

"You didn't have to ask me," said Tina.

"What I can't understand is why I still have a job," wondered Circassian.

"I guess you're just lucky that way," twinkled Tina.

"Pickle said everything will be clear to me on Monday."

"Wonderful: you only have three days to wait."

"I'm not going insane, am I, Tina?"

"If you were going insane, you wouldn't be aware you were going insane, so since you are, you're not," she said not slowly enough for Circassian to pick up the logic.

"The Dean has called a meeting of all sane faculty tomorrow: does that mean that some of the crazy ones are going to be there too?" he asked ruefully.

Tina gave him a dazzling smile. "Probably all of them; it ought to be quite a show," she said mischievously.

"Why don't you take this as seriously as I do?" Circassian snapped.

"I can't afford to, darlin'. One of us has to stay sane in this household," she added.

"If I stay sane, would you like to get pregnant? We might even get married," Circassian blurted.

"If you're proposing to me now, I'd suggest you think it over until next Monday; find out what Pickle has in mind."

Circassian was shocked. He was certain that after ten years together, Tina was hoping that they could make it "official," although Circassian had never been sure how official "official" was. He had been a little shy about getting married because he never remembered his parents ever speaking to each other except in shouts and grunts, but he and Tina had seen a lot of things happen to them and each other, and that had almost convinced him that if they got married, it wouldn't ruin the relationship. At least he was almost certain it wouldn't ruin the relationship. The fact that she'd stayed with him through all this turmoil at the University and given up her art gallery without a fight was a good sign. That she hadn't lost her sense of humor was another good sign. That she hadn't jumped at the chance to get married as soon as he had suggested it was a third good sign. As he was trying to remember a few other good signs, Tina indicated that she wanted to make love with him, which he also took to be a good sign.

That night they made passionate love. Actually, it wasn't quite passionate but could be considered good sex. And since they hadn't had good sex since the whole mess with the University had begun, Tina saw it as a good sign. Circassian even called her by her pet name, "Delores," which he'd picked up obscurely from something by Dylan Thomas but he'd long forgotten where. It was a good night for both of them until they ended up getting some Chinese food delivered to them and had very bad indigestion the rest of the night. They had forgotten that they were allergic to Chinese food.

The next afternoon, Circassian went to the auditorium in Main trying not to remember the dream he had had when he finally was able to fall asleep the night before: He was in a parking lot and he couldn't remember where he had parked his car. He walked along a narrow street and discovered that he was in his old neighborhood in the Bronx, where he'd always gotten beaten up as a boy because the other kids in the neighborhood thought he was Jewish. He couldn't find his car there and turned the corner and discovered that he was in London because he recognized the gigantic black cabs speeding about. He searched along the street and still didn't see his car. When he woke up, he first looked out the window to make sure his car was still there. Tina tried to convince him that his dream meant nothing except anxiety, but Circassian was certain that he would be going on a long trip and get lost trying to come back.

As he walked into the auditorium he was a little surprised to see it packed with faculty. He had expected, from what he had heard around campus, that only a handful of the sane would show up. But here was Frank Short, and Trent Butler, and Branch Stark, and Seth Shotman, and even Josh Gutsky, who had been released from the asylum and was seated next to Seth, as always, counting who was Jewish among the assembled. Daphne Dart and Ron Burble also made an appearance. So when Dean Lean showed up, he was hornswoggled. He couldn't help note the rather weird demeanor of many of the audience. A good few were talking to some imaginary person, while others were shaking uncontrollably, laughing, crying or calling out obscenities. A handful were deliberately farting, which gave a certain urgency to Dean Lean's message, that it had better come quickly or not at all.

"Ladies and gentlemen. Please, a little order here."

Those were about the last words Dean Lean uttered before the catastrophe ensued. As if as one, or, at the most, several, the crowd began to shout, scream and yowl at Dean Lean, some throwing things, including bottles, cans, Mah Jong rules, a dead cat, spider webs, and one angry little turd someone had made in the excitement. The few sane faculty that had showed up beat a hasty retreat while the rest began to do weird dances and hop around the auditorium. Circassian, in what was an unexpected show of bravery, rushed up to the stage and rescued Dean Lean from an angry mob who were pummeling him with their fists, false teeth and invectives too terrible to repeat.

As Circassian got him through the crowd of loonies, the Dean was clearly dumbstruck, from the look of sheer disbelief that was frozen on his face.

The riot of the faculty still in the auditorium began to spill out into the corridors. Shocked students saw their favorite teachers doing the jitterbug on their knees, singing loudly and off-key, "We Are the World," and disrobing with gleeful expressions on their faces. Circassian managed to get the Dean behind the auditorium stage where he sat staring out of blindstruck eyes.

It seemed like a longer time than he could imagine, but finally security was informed and came, accompanied by several dozen orderlies from the local asylum. In less than an hour after the meeting had begun, most of the looniest faculty had been carted away to be evaluated by a battery of psychologists, psychiatrists, psychiatric social workers, psychotherapists, and research assistants brought in for the occasion.

The only members of the faculty Circassian realized that hadn't been carted away were two who had simply not moved from their seats: Seth Shotman and Frank Short. And despite some signs of sanity in his demeanor, Frank had that far-away look that Circassian had seen before.

"What are we going to do?" asked Circassian of the two, who had the appearance of being in possession of their wits.

"Go home, Circassian. There is nothing we can do now," said Frank. He walked out the door of Main and did not return to campus again.

Seth and Circassian looked in on the Dean, who hadn't moved from where he had been placed. They alerted one of the orderlies who had been brought in to control the fracas, and Dean Lean was quietly led away, a straitjacket not even being necessary, into a waiting ambulance.

"Cheer up," said Circassian to Seth, masonicly. "I spoke to Pickle yesterday and he said that everything would be clear on Monday."

"You still believe anything Pickle says?" asked Seth.

"Given the alternative, yes," said Circassian, pointing at the procession of the insane academics still being esorted out of the building.

All weekend, loads of students began to vacate the campus. Mona Pilgrim called Circassian to ask him what she should do.

"It's safe now," he said. "All the people who cracked up have been put away. In fact, some of the faculty who were put away are probably sane but can't prove it yet."

"But except for you, that's all of my professors. I can't graduate with only one course!" She sounded peeved, even at him.

"Well, what is Tilly Owlglass doing, for instance?" asked Circassian.

"She's got a good job. She doesn't have to graduate," pouted Mona.

Circassian was about to make a flippant remark when he remembered that Trent Butler, Mona's new true love, had been packed away with the others and was now probably trying to seduce one of the nurses in the psychiatric ward.

"I'll see what I can do, Mona. I'm sure Pickle realizes that a lot of students are in your situation and will make some kind of dispensation so you can graduate," he said.

"This sucks," said Mona, and hung up.

When Circassian returned to the University on Monday, he noticed a change in the atmosphere. Instead of loonies, there was an eery silence along the corridors, the silence that precedes some cataclysmic event. But Circassian knew that the only thing he could do now was go into his classrom and do his job. That's what they were paying him the ridiculously low salary he was making for.

As he passed by the room in which Branch Stark customarily gave forth his views on Frost and other poets of recent memory, at least Branch's recent memory, he heard a Branch-like voice coming from the room. He peered in and sure enough, that life-size hologram he had seen the day before was now holding forth to a small but rapt group of students.

He stared for a few moments. The image looked exactly like Branch except that it was a pale green and the eyes had the hallowed-out look of the Living Dead.

He walked by a number of other classrooms and he could see the same thing: images of faculty who had been teaching but were no longer employed or sane or willing to come back. And the students were staring at these images and writing notes with the rapt attention they had rarely showed to the living, breathing originals.

As he entered the department office, he expected to see a hologram of the secretaries magically typing away at memos and letters, but there they were, living flesh and blood, bent over their computers. Then he noticed the note in his mailbox. He was one of the few in the department that could still look in the mailbox, so Pickle's memo had been sent to only the select few, that doughty breed of men and women, the few who were supposed to do so much for so many.

To: All Functioning Faculty
From: Associate of Operations Pickle
Re: The New Era
As of this day, the University is going to be operating on a 95% automated program. All of you who read this are the 5% that remain, by good luck and the process of elimination, to teach those students who elect to have "live" instructors. We are certain that the program will be the Waive of the Future and will be imitated by countless other institutions of higher learning. You have been privileged to be a part of it. Stay sane!
D. Pickle,
A.O.

Circassian noticed that "wave" had been incorrectly spelled and wondered if this was deliberate, a speck of humor in a humorless memo. He doubted it.

When he got to his classroom, he was surprised to see all of his students there and about a dozen others from other courses. "Hey, Doc, we wanted to see if you were coming," said Horst Fitzsimmons, a lanky lad who played center on the basketball team.

"Well, here I am. And what are the rest of you doing here?" he asked of the students who had interloped.

"We're scared," said one of them. "These things they're doing are weird."

"I think they're neat," said Norm Maclean. He was the captain of the fly fishing team and knew all of the trout rivers in a fifty-mile radius from the campus.

"How many of you like the new 'teachers?'" asked Circassian. He was hoping to get a negative reaction, but most of the students eagerly raised their hands.

"As long as you are around to keep a balance," added Delia Storch.

Circassian gave his first real lesson in more than half a semester and he felt exhilarated that he was actually teaching again. So did some of the students, though most of them doubtlessly missed the fun that had been an inspired substitute for teaching and learning in the last two months. But when Circassian left at the end of the period and walked through the halls, he was surprised to notice that except for a few straggling students, the corridors were empty. Then, at the ring of a bell which he had never remembered hearing before, the students began pouring out of the classrooms. He realized that his watch had been two minutes fast, and that the holograms had been triggered to stop by the bell.

The enthusiasm that he heard around him was something he hadn't ever heard before. He wondered if the teaching had been changed in some way by the holograms, but at the beginning of the next period, when the classes were back in session, he peeked again at a lesson and it seemed to him that the quality of the teaching was no better nor worse than it had been before, except it was virtual reality, whatever that was supposed to mean in the real world. Then Circassian realized that this *was* the real world: bizarre, weird and perverse as it seemed to him.

Tina had needed the car to get her computer repaired and she picked up Circassian in the parking lot. Students were milling around, talking to each other in excited voices about their lessons.

Circassian was flummeted; he barely knew how to speak or what to say when Tina asked him how the "Big Day" had gone. When he explained it to her she said: "No shit. This sounds like the real thing."

"But it's not the 'real thing,' or anyway, not a real real thing, or something that I would call real," said Circassian, trying to seem logical.

"I mean," explained Tina, "that this is where higher education is going."

"Then why am I around if the students will be happy with some three-dimensional imitation of their professors?" he Burbled. He was so upset he could barely make himself clear.

"To have a model of how things used to be? Maybe for the students who still like to go to an old-fashioned class? I dunno." Tina was not going to get herself upset about something that she didn't think it would help to get upset about, even if Circassian was upset.

As they drove through the tiny town, Circassian began to wonder again what he was staying at the University for. It seemed to him that he was in the middle of some sick farce and hadn't the brains or the courage to get out of it yet. But he wasn't really sure if he could get a job elsewhere.

When they got home Tina decided to perk Circassian up with a good roast chicken dinner, the first time they'd had something besides vegetables in weeks. Besides, her boss had told her that they were expecting a big influx of business and she would be very busy for the next few months, at least.

"I think you've got to find out what's really behind all of this," said Tina, as she gave Circassian a second helping of apple pie. "Maybe if you could talk to somebody who knew, you'd feel a little better."

"I don't feel anything at all right now, Tina," Circassian said. He wasn't sure if he meant that, but he knew he meant to mean it as if saying it would make it true. He didn't want to feel anything right then; it would be too confusing.

The next day as he walked along the hologram-ridden quad, he saw VP T.P. Sealy striding toward him. VP T. P. had always been a strider. He decided that this was the man who might know what was "behind" it all.

"T.P.," chuddled Circassian, "do you know what's behind it all?"

"Beats the hell out of me," answered VP T.P. Sealy as if he knew what Circassian was talking about, which it was remotely possible he might have. The Vice President for students was now Associate Director of Instruction and Entertainment, and since much of what he was doing was hardly different from what he had been doing before, he felt comfortable in his new job.

"Well, do you know somebody who might know?" Circassian asked.

"Check with Marigold Markham; she's now Associate Director of Communications. She knows just about everything there is to know around here," said VP T.P. Sealy, and walked swiftly by. He was afraid to be late for a golf date he had with Pickle, and knew how upset Pickle was with anyone who was late for something as significant as that.

As Circassian walked into Main, he saw a number of students leaving their classrooms in what was obviously the middle of the period. He was hoping it was some sort of protest demonstration, that some of the students had finally realized that the wool had been pulled over their eyes and that a number was being done on them, but when he looked into the classroom which they had just vacated, he was mildly disappointed. Mildly because what he saw was a form of protest, but not the kind he'd hoped for.

There were about half a dozen students taking notes as they watched the hologram give forth on the major issues of the "gold standard," but among them were about a dozen camcorders focused on the image in the front of the room. In other rooms, as Circassian peered along, he saw no students at all but the camcorders, each propped on a desk on their little tripods, whirring away. He wondered if the students would actually come back to pick them up, or they would just stay there until they ran out of juice? And what were the students doing when they might have otherwise been in class? Getting drunk, writing home, planning to take over the Administration? Or more accurately, Corporate Headquarters? Wherever they went, they seemed to reappear just as the hour ended and took their machines to the next class.

Circassian supposed that this was their way of protesting the disappearance of most of their professors. He even saw a bumper sticker on one of the student cars: "Fight holograms! Hug a Professor!"

Yes, maybe there was hope after all. Circassian wondered, however, whether this wasn't really that wave of the future that Jack Swift had predicted would be coming to engulf anyone who didn't think the way he did. After class, which was now attended by more students than he had ever seen attend one of his classes — either as a protest or because they really wanted to be there — he decided to see if Marigold Markham was in.

The Systell-Lex. Building was strangely silent and Circassian wondered if holograms were now being used to substitute for the staff, but then he saw a few people working at their computers, and realized that holograms couldn't type, at least not yet. He had a feeling that someone would come up with a way for them to type, and perfectly.

When he walked into Marigold's office, he noticed that the secretary was no longer there and in her place, a hologram was seated, if holograms could be seated, reading a magazine. It looked up at him and he seemed to recognize the face: it was Pickle's only with the hairdo and body of a woman. "What can I do for you?" it asked.

"Can I see Ms. Markham, please?"

"Associate for Communications Markham is not available at this time. Please come back at another time," said the hologram.

Circassian wondered if the hologram took off for lunch, and if so, what kind of virtual reality sandwich it might eat, but as he was musing, he felt a slight nudge on his shoulder and turned to see Marigold put a piece of paper that had been in her tightly closed fist into his hand. As unobtrusively as his astonishment could permit, he put the paper into his pocket and walked out the door, almost forgetting to say, "Have a nice day" to Marigold.

When he got into his office, he read the paper: *My office is still bugged and now there are observation cameras all over the building. I think yours is still pretty clean, but don't show this message to anyone. I'll see you at the usual time in the usual place.*

The following evening, Circassian left the house about 7:30 to meet Marigold on the steps of Main. When he got there, the deserted quad looked eerily silent. The holograms had been turned off for the night, the students were all in their dorm rooms or in the bars, and the campus looked at peace. Then he heard muffled footsteps and saw Marigold's form coming through the darkness into the light. But he also saw a man dressed in black following close behind her.

"Save yourself, Circassian; don't worry about me; I'm a goner," shrilled Marigold, the first time he heard her speak above a loud whisper. He didn't know what to expect and turned to leave when suddenly a sack was put over his head, he felt arms pinioning his behind him, and he was led away into what must have been a waiting car. He wanted to ask someone what was happening but he felt something like a gun against his ribs and thought better of it.

It seemed as if the ride went on for hours, but it was only Circassian's fear and loathing of what was going to happen to him that made the trip feel longer than it was. He thought that if he were able to get out of this situation alive, he would stop trying to find out things; he would do what he was told; he would love Big Brother.

The car finally stopped in front of a large building in the middle of a city. Circassian had his sack removed and was relieved to see that what he had thought were guns were only hollow metal tubes which seemed to be made of aluminum. He finally recognized them: vacuum cleaner tubes. He began to recognize his surroundings as he was led, wordlessly, into the building: this was the Central Administration Building for the entire University system, the headquarters of Chancellor Thaddeus Thwart.

He walked down a corridor, led by the two men who had accompanied him on the ride. They took the elevator to the basement and into an elegantly appointed waiting room that seemed a bright contrast from the Chancellor's slightly shabby surroundings when he had visited him with Branch Stark. He noted the antique furniture in what must have been a waiting room: Chippendale chairs, Tiffany lamps, Louis XVI tables. The two men silently left while Circassian gingerly sat down on one of the chairs. It seemed to hold his weight comfortably.

"You may enter now," said a voice that came from a speaker in the ceiling. Circassian wasn't sure what to expect until he entered through an ornately decorated door and saw, behind a massive desk, a pale little man who wore a bowtie and a checkered jacket as if they were meant for him. The man looked familiar, but Circassian wasn't certain where he had seen him. And then he remembered: those posters that Stark Branch had used as dart targets.

"Well, Circassian, we finally meet. I'm Ambler Slaughter."

Circassian was fandoodled into silence for the moment. Here before him was the man who had guided "Operation Change" for the past three years, and in that time, taxes had been slashed by Governor Putski, but so had services and support for the State University. Circassian couldn't put the blame for all those things squarely on Ambler Slaughter, but he thought him responsible for a whole lot of the mess that the University was in. Circassian would listen, but with a jaundiced ear.

"What am I doing here?" he asked. "Am I that important?"

"Why don't you take a seat? I'll answer your questions when I get around to them; right now, just listen," said Ambler. He was obviously the kind of man whom people listened to, even if they didn't want to, and Circassian felt the authority spew forth from this otherwise pallid nonetity.

"I assume you know most of what's going on, but I think you need a few of the missing pieces to get the whole picture," said Ambler. "It has a lot to do with Option Three, which as you will see, has been perfected, or is, at least, approaching perfection."

Circassian wondered what the hell this man was talking about. He had a lot to say about Option Three, but approaching perfection was not one of them.

"We feel that 5% of the faculty is about optimal for our purposes. The rest are just as communicative as holograms as they are in real life, and much less cost-effective. You're one of the few that we feel would be a loss to the students if your lessons had been made into virtual reality. But now, with 95% of the faculty gone, we will have the savings we know were needed to help improve the economic health of the State and still run the University in the most efficient way."

"If you think the students are going to be satisfied with holograms instead of teachers, you're just fooling yourself," said Circassian, struck with that irresistible urge to interrupt this pompous, self-righteous, powerful person. "Once the novelty wears off, they're not going to be coming to class. I've seen a lot of them use camcorders instead of being . . ."

"Don't you think we know that?" said Ambler. He looked annoyed, obviously not used to having people interrupt him. "We counted on just that happening. The drones, the excess population, the ones who should never have gone to the University in the first place, will get tired of the novelty of the holograms soon enough. The ones who decide to stay because they have live teachers, those are the ones we're interested in keeping. We'll let the rest come in and out of the revolving door." Ambler Slaughter pressed a button on his desk. A screen lit up behind him, and soon a series of graphics was shown on it. Circassian particularly liked the blue ones.

"This chart shows the predicted shrinkage in the University system over the next ten years. By that time, there will be about 5% of the current student population with a savings of . . . it's a lot of money," he added cagily and figuratively. "Option Three was intended to address the problem of saving. It enabled us to cut the salaries and other costs of the faculty without violating the Union contract until the Union lost all credibility and the faculty lost the will to teach. That part wasn't easy, but people like Bendminder and Pickle were very helpful."

"I'll bet," said Circassian with biting sarcasm that Ambler Slaughter easily ignored. He was schooled in biting sarcasm.

"Now the next part will be easier: waiting for the student population to decline so that only the best and brightest are left," he said.

"What makes you think the best and brightest will stay once the rest begin to leave?" asked Circassian. He was hoping that his adversary hadn't thought of that.

"We've already thought of that. That's why we're offering each of them a full scholarship for tuition, room, board, books and an incidentals allowance of $100 a week. They also will be told that they will be taking their courses with the best teachers in the institution. Of course, we won't tell them that they are the *only* teachers, but once they find out, they will already have committed themselves to staying."

"What makes you so sure of that?" asked Circassian.

"Because we will guarantee that if they graduate from the University they will have a job waiting for them at Systell-Lex or one of its many subsidiaries. That's an offer not many schools can match."

"You're willing to go that far to make sure you get these students?" asked Circassian, incredulously.

"Yes. Because we know that they will make excellent workers once they get their degrees. And we can afford to get rid of the ones that don't pan out. After all, that's what a University education should do."

"Of course, you know that what you're planning is elitist," said Circassian, without the slightest conviction that what he was saying would have any effect on Ambler Slaughter.

"Precisely! The biggest mistake any politician could make when the University was being built up forty years ago was to assume that the majority of people are capable of really getting a college education."

"Well, plenty do," said Circassian, defensively.

"Not enough to justify the expense. That's why I founded this organization and financed Putsky's nomination. It was really a fluke that he got in, but I was willing to take the chance because I was sick and tired of business as usual," said Slaughter.

"I'm sick and tired of it too, but the business you're tired of isn't the same that I am," said Circassian, embarrassed that anything he said could agree with the man before him who was now smoking what must have been a very expensive cigar.

"That doesn't matter. What matters to me is the future of this state, and the way I see it, the University has been a big drag on it. That's why I got Bendminder to come up with 'Option Three.' So I could save the University."

"You think you're saving the University? By trying to cut its student population by 95%?" Circassian tried to be incredulous but he knew that Ambler Slaughter had a point.

"With most of the students enrolled, it was beginning to become a joke. Almost anyone who wanted to could get in, and it was pretty hard to get them out. Now the only ones left will be the ones who want to be there. You should be overjoyed that I've done for you what most any of the faculty wished would happen anyway, but were afraid of losing their jobs if it happened. Now admit that I'm right, Circassian, unless you want to go on lying to yourself."

Circassian began to feel his grip on his convictions loosening with every word that Ambler Slaughter said. "What about opportunity?" Circassian asked. "What about fairness? What about democracy?"

"No one should have the opportunity to screw up serious and qualified students' education by behaving like jerks; life isn't fair, anyway, Circassian; and as far as I'm concerned democracy sucks."

"It's not the sort of thing you could afford to say publicly," said Circassian.

"Not yet," responded Slaughter, with cryptic conviction. "The great secret of the people who run things, Circassian, if you haven't figured it out already, is to make it seem to the majority that they're running things. That's what we've been doing for over two hundred years and that's what's made this country what it is today."

"I'll say. Half the eligible voters don't vote because they don't see any choices," said Circassian. He wasn't going to let this rich twerp have the last word.

"That's okay, since only 10% have the votes that count. Why do you think there's an electoral college? Because the people who founded this country didn't trust the rabble. And that's what you've had at the University, Circassian, mostly rabble." Ambler Slaughter puffed slowly and luxuriously on his cigar, as if he were about to participate in the act of love.

"All of this, this Option Three, was really just to save money, whatever else you might say to excuse it," said Circassian.

"That's the excuse I gave to people like Bendminder and Putsky, because that's all they can think about, that and cutting taxes. I was looking at the big picture: saving the future for the people who deserve to have one. And don't kid yourself, Circassian, many of them don't come from rich families. I'm the real egalitarian; within the decade a degree from this University will mean as much as one from the Ivy League, and I'm willing to get the legislature to put the money into it that we'll save by not having to put up with the unstudents."

"Well, I teach all the students," said Circassian.

"That won't be happening much longer," said Ambler Slaughter, flicking the ash from his cigar into an elegant silver ashtray on his desk. "Just wait and see. Now I have other things to do. Good bye."

Circassian was going to reply when he felt the arms of his two escorts on his shoulders. He was led back into the car, and since he had seen where he was by now, the sack was dispensed with. He realized that it had been put over his head just to give him a thorough dose of terror.

Two hours later, he was dropped off at the University parking lot, right beside his car. In the whole trip back, no one — not the two men beside him, not the driver — had uttered a word.

When he got back home, Tina looked relieved. He had been gone for more than four hours.

"Where were you?" she asked, straffled.

"You wouldn't believe it if I told you," said Circassian. He told her and she didn't believe it at first.

"Why would he have singled you out?" she finally asked after overcoming her wonder and astonishment. "What makes you that important?

"I guess because I'm a five percenter."

That night, Circassian had the first dreamless sleep he had had in a long while. He woke the next morning surprisingly refreshed. He was looking forward to his day at the

University, although why he should feel this way confused him.

As he walked down the hall toward his classroom, he saw a crowd of students milling around the door. When they saw him, a dozen came up to him with the same question: could they sit in on his class? It was apparent after a few moments that the medium-sized room in which his class was held couldn't accomodate the hundred-plus students who wanted to be there. Circassian, light of heart and swift of limb for the first time in quite a while, excused himself, went to his office and called the registrar to see if there were now any vacant lecture halls in the Systell-Lex Lecture Hall Building.

"Almost all of them are free now," was the reply.

He went back to the classroom where even more students had collected, and announced that they would be meeting in lecture hall B for the rest of the semester, if the numbers held. As he walked down the quad, the holograms' ghostly presence seemed to be almost ignored by the students in the bright sunshine. Soon he heard some of them calling out to their friends to join them. He knew Mona Pilgrim was there, and thought he had even glimpsed Tilly Owlglass. When he turned around before he entered the building, there was a crowd of students gathered behind him. Was it his imagination, or did they stretch for miles? He walked in. They all followed.